TASTEMAKERS
and
TASTEMAKING

SUNY series in Latin American Cinema

Ignacio M. Sánchez Prado and Leslie L. Marsh, editors

TASTEMAKERS and TASTEMAKING

Mexico and Curated Screen Violence

Niamh Thornton

Published by State University of New York Press, Albany

© 2020 State University of New York

All rights reserved

No part of this book may be used or reproduced in any manner whatsoever without written permission. No part of this book may be stored in a retrieval system or transmitted in any form or by any means including electronic, electrostatic, magnetic tape, mechanical, photocopying, recording, or otherwise without the prior permission in writing of the publisher.

For information, contact State University of New York Press, Albany, NY
www.sunypress.edu

Library of Congress Cataloging-in-Publication Data

Names: Thornton, Niamh, 1972– author.
Title: Tastemakers and tastemaking : Mexico and curated screen violence / Niamh Thornton.
Description: Albany : State University of New York, 2020. | Series: SUNY series in Latin American cinema | Includes bibliographical references and index. | Identifiers: LCCN 2020023295 (print) | LCCN 2020023296 (ebook) | ISBN 9781438481135 (hardcover : alk. paper) | ISBN 9781438481128 (pbk. : alk. paper) | ISBN 9781438481142 (ebook)
Subjects: LCSH: Motion pictures—Mexico—History and criticism. | Motion pictures—Aesthetics. | Television—Aesthetics. | Curatorship—Philosophy. | Television programs—Mexico—History. | Violence in motion pictures. | Violence on television.
Classification: LCC PN1993.5.M4 T463 2020 (print) | LCC PN1993.5.M4 (ebook) | DDC 791.430972—dc25
LC record available at https://lccn.loc.gov/2020023295
LC ebook record available at https://lccn.loc.gov/2020023296

10 9 8 7 6 5 4 3 2 1

Contents

LIST OF ILLUSTRATIONS …………………………………………………………… vii

ACKNOWLEDGMENTS ……………………………………………………………… ix

INTRODUCTION
Tastemakers and Tastemaking: Questions of Taste,
Violence, and Gender …………………………………………………………………… 1

CHAPTER ONE
Cultural Institutions and Gendered Taste Formation:
Nelson Carro and the Cineteca Nacional in 2010 ……………………………… 27

CHAPTER TWO
Commonplace and Routine: Amat Escalante's Extreme Realism
in *Los bastardos* (2008) and *Heli* (2013) ………………………………………… 59

CHAPTER THREE
Reversioning and Thick Contexts: The Cinematic Adaptations
of *Los de abajo* …………………………………………………………………………… 87

CHAPTER FOUR
Bodily Excess and Containment: *Bordertown* (Gregory Nava,
2006) and *The Virgin of Juarez* (Kevin James Dobson, 2006) ……………… 115

CHAPTER FIVE
Curating Cruelty and Criminality: The Radical Mediation of
Kate del Castillo ………………………………………………………………………… 149

CONCLUSION
Ethical Reflections on Legitimation and Taste   183

FILMOGRAPHY   193

REFERENCES   199

INDEX   217

Illustrations

Figure 1   Slow cinema inspired by James Benning in *Los bastardos*   63

Figure 2   Opening credits (1939, left, and 1976, right)   98

Figure 3   The wife (1939, left, and 1976, right)   101

Figure 4   Macías in death (1939, left, and 1976, right)   108

Figure 5   Macías's wife after his death (1939, left) and Macías in death (1976, right)   109

Figure 6   Lauren/Lopez as reporter   131

Figure 7   Lauren/Lopez as worker   132

Figure 8   Teresa/del Castillo finding her way   166

Acknowledgments

To get from concept to manuscript takes much energy, time, thinking, and most of all support, encouragement, and nurturing. This is done with the help of many individuals too numerous to mention. These include colleagues and peers, friends and families. I am indebted to them all, but am responsible for the final version.

Thank you to the University of Liverpool for giving me research leave in 2011 to carry out interviews and research in Mexico City and for the award of a Santander Grant in 2015 to complete my research in Mexico. To the staff at the libraries at the University of Liverpool for their support in sourcing material and those at Liverpool John Moores University at IM Marsh for the space to complete the writing and editing.

Thank you to Ana García Bergua for her support and sharing her contacts with me so that I could interview individuals who otherwise were unavailable. Thank you to Nelson Carro of Cineteca Nacional de México in Mexico City for being generous with his time, insights, and expertise. To Elides Pérez Bistrain, Genoveva García Rojas, and the rest of the staff at the Centro de documentación at the Cineteca Nacional de México in Mexico City for finding what I needed and directing me to materials that only the archivists know connect to each other.

As a work in progress over years of thinking, presenting, writing, and conversations this has been the product of many conference papers, blog posts, and the insights and questions of others. Sometimes they've been the result of me trying out my ideas in the world and realizing where they don't always make sense to others. I appreciated all of those responses because they helped make this better. Thanks to those who have read and given considered feedback on drafts including Victoria McCollum. Any mistakes are mine, but the feedback has made it better. Thank you to the two anonymous readers who were brilliant critical friends. Their insights helped me to refine this manuscript.

Thank you to the supportive series editors, Ignacio Sánchez-Prado and Lesley Marsh, and to the editorial staff at State University of New York Press including John Raymond for his attention to detail, Ryan Morris and Fran Keneston for their support, and to Rebecca Colesworthy for her positive, careful, and always cheerful guidance throughout the process, but, particularly, as the manuscript was being shepherded through its final stages.

Thanks a million times over to Liz Greene, for her attentive and patient reading of multiple versions and revisions, and always being a supportive editor and critical friend, when it was much needed, and for nurturing me and giving me much love. All this and more made conceptualizing, writing, and finishing this project possible. Without that unstinting, unwavering, and unassailable support, work, and patience, none of this would have been possible.

To Marmaduke and Rua, because distraction is needed to keep me sane. To Dario, just because.

Introduction

Tastemakers and Tastemaking

Questions of Taste, Violence, and Gender

Taste is a nebulous word. Without a qualifier it is meaningless, and with the standard qualifiers of good or bad, it is an unstable and shifting signifier. Premised on its instability through looking at those who make film and television and create value and the systems in which they operate, *Tastemakers and Tastemaking: Mexico and Curated Screen Violence* examines how taste retains its potency. Tastemakers and tastemaking are terms that draw on a long theoretical trajectory on taste, and simultaneously signal toward a curatorial agency and the cultural context within which tastemakers and tastemaking operate. Professional curatorial practices are not a precondition of tastemaking. Instead, I use the term *tastemakers* to encompass a wide range of influential or indicative individuals who are both determining and reflective of wider patterns and trends.

Questions of taste and value are attached to works determining their inclusion on syllabi, their success in the marketplace, and their duration through critical reflection. Within this framing, a high/low dyad persists, setting one against the other as if they lie in stark contrast rather than recognizing a slippage between them and ignoring the power structures that uphold both the object and those who decide its value. To forgo the persistent oppositional binary and signal its failings, *Tastemakers and Tastemaking: Mexico and Curated Screen Violence* considers tastemaking and tastemakers. That is, who decides what is of value and how creatives in film and television produce work that intervenes in questions of taste.

The tastemakers being examined in this book are individuals involved in the creation or selection of film and television works in which gender and violence intersect. Violence has particular salience because it falls outside of the usual considerations of taste as a consequence of being inherently aberrant. To enact violence is to break with social or legal codes, which has to be justified through specific framing. There are parameters and guidelines to these that fit within national or international codes, but none are concerned with taste. Violence is innately excessive because it exceeds normative behavior and its screening is about provoking an affective response, all of which often indicate bad taste. Nonetheless, screen cultures have participated in the validation of violence, often ascribing it high value, but also interrogating its meanings. This leads to slippages that are not easily mapped and require mixed methodologies to unpack. Violence is enacted upon and by gendered bodies; therefore, to comprehend violence it is important to reflect on the ways the gender of the agent or victim can modify or amplify the violent act and how it is read. I propose tastemaking and tastemakers as a productive way of looking at gender and violence, by looking at who and what informs taste through the patterns and anomalies that are evidenced through the case studies.

Tastemakers are not merely gatekeepers, they are also engaging with and building upon ideas, histories, and traditions established by others. To operate in such a contested and complex field is to be bound by preceding norms and expectations of what should be valued and how particular media and forms can be appropriately deployed. Tastemaking as a verb encompasses the action of a tastemaker and the consequences of these actions. The case studies in this book reveal the outcome of the tastemakers' decisions and the cultural context they inhabit. *Tastemakers and Tastemaking: Mexico and Curated Screen Violence* explores how curation, prestige cinema, adaptation, and star and celebrity performances are all acts of tastemaking.

Screen Violence:
Reimagining the Past, Understanding the Present

Violence is a centrifugal theme in Mexican cinema and television whose recurrence allows for significant patterns and themes to emerge. Audiovisual violence is not indelibly attached to specific genres or styles, and yet it both disturbs and is an indicator of a rupture with normative behaviors. Tastemaking such disruptive events requires careful selection and an applied knowledge of prior patterns of creativity and an understanding of the signification of the violence within and beyond Mexico. The focus of *Tastemakers and Tastemaking: Mexico and Curated Screen Violence* is on three key moments that foreground the intersection of violence and its representation: the decadelong commemoration of the Mexican Revolution (1910–20) launched in 2010; the gendered violence that has taken place in northern Mexico since the late 1990s, specifically, the assaults on and murders of women; and the separate, but contiguous, violence linked to the illegal drug trade that escalated in the early 2000s and continues up to the time of writing.

The Mexican Revolution is the foundational narrative of the contemporary state reimagined according to the vagaries of the political period (see O'Malley 1986 and Benjamin 2000). The Revolution as political project originally functioned as a means of uniting a nation traumatized by violent combat and loss. Written using uppercase and imagined through multiple cultural texts including film and television, the Revolution has become more myth than reality, monumentalized, and, repeatedly, commemorated. The multiple versions of the Revolution have been ever evolving, navigating national and cultural shifts, and reimagined in tandem with political changes as oppositional or harmonizing articulations.

While the Revolution continues to inspire creative responses, reflections on the significance of past violence on the present take on different meanings when considered in the light of the more recent violence against women and those living with the consequences of the illegal drug trade. These bring the national and the transnational into question. Such violence is not unique to Mexico, although it has been heightened because of how the transnational illegal drug trade has dominated economic and political life in the late twentieth and the early twenty-first centuries. Therefore, to portray Mexico's problems requires a transnational perspective and involves transnational interests. To tell these stories of violence requires ethical tastemakers aware of the cultural landscape at a national and transnational level. But it often involves tastemakers who draw on a long history of missteps and false moves.

Irrespective of where it takes place, violence brings into relief how aesthetics can be a weak measure of value. Violence is a serious subject that presupposes clear demarcations of what is tolerable. Yet what is acceptable and deemed significant in its representation is ever evolving. Assessing violence as aesthetically pleasing is always difficult as it sits uncomfortably within questions of taste. The challenge in representing violence is that it can still fall at the edge of what is "good" taste, and yet representations that fall short of prestige productions can be deemed as diminishing to the experience of violence. "Quality" productions centered on violence can prove divisive because they can be hyperrealist and deemed excessive; generic representations can fall short of critical approval because they fail to convey realist violence, but they can prove popular. Violence is a useful way into thinking about tastemaking because despite its often high-value seriousness its appeal is situated and culturally determined.

Choosing to look at screened violence is to consider the spectacle of death and what it says about life. Violence proves a useful tool in considering tastemaking because it is the spectacle of humanity engaged in brutal behavior through inflicting pain or death on another. These are not acts where taste should figure, nonetheless taste predominates because inherent to tastemaking are ethical concerns. When lives are devalued in the representation of pain or death it diminishes life itself. Examining tastemakers and tastemaking violence is to consider who chooses to legitimate that which is often uncomfortable to legitimate and sits at the edges of taste.

Audiovisual Violence, Death, and the Value of Life

The focus on violence in this book allows for the uncomfortable intersection of personal, political, and social concerns that require thoughtful, careful, and ethical considerations that already come heavily mediated because of the prevalence of the representation of violence on film and television. The consideration of violence through the perspective of tastemaking provides a new way into understanding cultural production and those who create and curate it.

Tastemaking violence supposes a series of choices that merit interrogation. This is particularly the case when the violence represented is of national and transnational salience that renders its audio-visualization and circulation potent and resonant for other national contexts. Violence comes with a complex intersection of the trauma of embodied experiences when these are events that are marked by questions of value and taste. Violence is associated with the worst impulses of humanity, yet it can be represented in a multitude of modes, genres, styles, and intentions. From early periods to the present day, there is a long history of audio-visual violence and an ever-expanding catalogue to be found in Mexican film and television that encompasses a wide gamut of genres, styles, and significant events.

While concurrent with the conflict, the earliest inceptions of audiovisual violence, such as *El automóvil gris/The Gray Car* (Enrique Rosas, 1919), drew on nonrealist genre cinema. This continued with few exceptions through to the Golden Age from the 1930s through the 1950s, with melodrama and romances as the most popular choices for films of the Revolution. Although they are numerous, few of these films have been deemed high value. As scholarly writing on film has developed and films have been included in a canon, violence and its representation on-screen attracts most critical attention when real or realist violence erupts in lived or mediated experience. One of these moments occurred in the late 1960s and into the 1970s when at several locations around the world the violent suppression of student protests, worker unrest, and civil rights marches resulted in citizens taking up arms. As a consequence, revolutionary, insurgent, paramilitary, and military incursions led to key conflicts that impacted within and across national boundaries. Firsthand and mediated experiences of violence and its aftermath put into relief the question of how to consider its representation. Violence in the cinema of filmmakers, such as the Westerns of Sam Peckinpah in the US or the documentaries of the Third Cinema filmmakers, brought the question to the fore for scholars and filmmakers of how and why violence should be screened (see, for example, Prince 1998 and 2003 and Chanan 2009). Of concern to many theorists are two separate and interrelated issues: how mediated violence can capture the actuality of violence and the subjectivity of those experiencing and inflicting the violence. Underpinning these reflections are the ethics of filming violence.

Filming violence approximates what it means to experience pain and death, both of which defy representation. Writing on death as a contemporary taboo, Vivian Sobchack (1984, 286) describes it as "a sign that ends all signs . . . always original, unconventional, and shocking, its event always simultaneously representing both the process of sign production and the end of representation." Sobchack's article is about documentary films, but her reflections are a fitting measure of ethical approaches to fiction film, in particular when based on real events. Integral to her approach is an ethical engagement with death on-screen, centered on issues related to the inscription of the body experiencing death, the slippery cultural codes attached to its meaning, the impossibility of its representation, and the act of seeing and looking at death as viewer and filmmaker.

There are equivalences in the dilemmas and questions that documentary and fiction film confront when screening violence. Unlike other aspects of life experiences, there is always value attached to the ethical representation of death because we are confronting our own mortality by observing death made "often excessively visible" (and audible) (Sobchack 1984, 287). Therefore, to represent violence is to attempt to represent that which "is experienced as confounding representation, as exceeding visibility" (Sobchack 1984, 287). Death is both impossible to represent and is inherently excessive, which has proven compelling for filmmakers, in part because of its elemental nature and, also, because it provides ample opportunity to dramatize excess and to experience living more intensely through confronting our own or others' obliteration. Tastemaking violence and death, because of its excessive qualities, throws into relief questions of taste and foregrounds how life itself is valued.

Clearly, then, evaluating violence defies clear and objective thought. Slavoj Žižek (2008, 3) suggests that "the overpowering horror of violent acts and empathy with the victims inexorably function as a lure which prevents us from thinking" and leads to an affective response clouding judgment because violence is "inherently mystifying." The challenge of understanding violence carries with it the vulnerability of life itself because we are confronted with death or its possibility through focusing on the body in pain.

The excess associated with violent death pushes it into the realm of bad taste. A recurrent motif in scholarly work on the representation of violence is the impossibility of conveying its signification because death is unknowable and inspires an affective response. These scholars touch on questions of taste related to violence and draw on our discomfort at witnessing death. Susan Sontag (2003) argues that carefully contextualized images can convince, change minds, and have a propagandistic role, but by themselves change nothing. What they have is a moral value that can be found in the excess and beauty of the image, which should focus and give subjectivity to the bodies in pain and suffering. As a theorist who grappled with the meaning of the surface and where to find its depths, Sontag (2003) considers the long tradition of war artists and photographers and their attempts to convey the horrors of war made more acute at a media-saturated moment when reality for those experiencing conflict or violence can feel already mediated. The morality or ethics lies in that violence is itself spectacular, as elucidated by Paul Virilio (1989 and 2005), that through mediation becomes spectacular. This doubling of the spectacular that becomes more spectacular makes violence difficult to apprehend and often excessive. As a way of understanding taste and violence, I consider how excess is integral to tastemaking violence in both prestige and genre films. Tastemaking violence means to intervene in a visual frame that has a long history and in an audiovisual field that is about creating an unsettling and uncomfortable spectacle of the experiences of pain and suffering.

Although not addressing Sobchack's (1984) or Sontag's (2003) approaches, Judith Butler (2009) has similar ethical concerns around death, life, and its representation. Butler considers the differential value given to individual lives in the way their deaths are understood as meaningful. She explores how lives are given value through being "apprehended" and "recognized" (Butler 2009, 1–6). Apprehension makes cognition and affect possible and determines why we grieve certain lives or ignore others. Recognition is determined by " 'frames' that work to differentiate the lives we can apprehend from those we cannot" and, as a consequence, "subjects are constituted through norms which, in their reiteration, produce and shift the terms through which subjects are 'recognized' " (Butler 2009, 3). She draws on Walter Benjamin's use of the term *framing* to constitute what she calls a grievable life—that is, those lives that sit within the frame. Butler's use of frames builds on how the framing of an image is both a physical and visual delimiter and an allusion to the context in which it is consumed or reproduced. A frame contains both its limit and bears the potential to be undone (Butler 2009, 10). The metaphorical frame is allusive and becomes a specter that "figures the collapsibility of the norm" (Butler 2009, 12).

Butler (2009) plays with and explores the usage of frame to suggest how picture frames can be read as editorial decisions, whereby the frame focuses attention and should be interrogated because this focus provides meaning through selectivity. Framing is like curation. It decontextualizes until the frame becomes visible through stepping back and considering the structures that determine what we are seeing and, in an audiovisual field, hearing. Framing gives lives meanings by choosing whose story matters, which invites "reciprocity" and thereby can "constitute obligations towards others," which leads to grievability and a "presupposition for the life that matters" (Butler 2009, 14). Where Sobchack (1984, 288) writes about the dead as "other" having lost subjectivity, saying that "it confronts us and reminds us of subjectivity and its objective limits," Butler suggests that a figure who is still living also "falls outside the frame furnished by the norm" (2009, 8). Framing is editing, focus, attention, and narrative that can be invisible until you step back to pay attention to the choices made. Tastemaking is involved in this framing. The living and dead others become objects that exist as "a relentless double whose ontology cannot be secured" (Butler 2009, 8). Their lives cannot be apprehended because they fall beyond a recognizable frame. Framing is tied to tastemaking because it is the result of a series of decisions that draw from preexisting practices as well as proposing original approaches. For an ethical approach to tastemaking, the tastemaker must consider all lives as grievable, or at least those included in the frame. So, too, should any ethical analysis.

Life is made precarious when it is not apprehended and, consequently, does not matter. Combining these insights, a frame is a form of selection, curation, and tastemaking. For a death to matter it must be more than mere spectacle. The living and the dead must have subjectivity and be represented with an ethical approach in the full awareness that death has an affective force and is beyond comprehension. A frame helps to go beyond good/bad evaluations regarding aesthetic approaches and considers the subjectivity afforded those who experience violence in film and television. Butler's (2009) conceptualization of the frame informs how I am using tastemaking as a way of apprehending how life, violence, and death are given meaning on-screen.

Gore Capitalism and Framing Grievable Mexican Lives

Value is placed on lives through how they are represented on-screen. To apprehend grievable lives, bodies in pain, and screened violence requires an understanding of the context in which they are produced. While there is a long history of the representation of violence in Mexico since the Revolution, the more than twenty years of violence in twenty-first century Mexico has led to an upsurge in commentary on mediatized violence that articulates the specificities of the local. Sayak Valencia's *Gore Capitalism* (2018) shares some common ground with Sobchack (1984), Sontag (2003), Žižek (2008), and Butler (2009) in her analysis of whose lives are valued. It is Valencia's contention that the macroeconomics of global capitalism, which privileges capital over people, collides with the particularities of the Mexican state, which has seen the dominance of the drug trade and resulted in a business that is transnational with experiences of violence that are highly localized.

Valencia finds the recent violence in Mexico to be integral to the current stage of neoliberal capitalism, which she calls "gore capitalism" (2018). She describes gore capitalism as "the price the Third World pays for adhering to the increasingly demanding logic of capitalism" (2018, 19) that is played out in brutal and violent fashion because "the destruction of the body becomes in itself the product or commodity" (2018, 20). For her, the use of the term *Third World* is intentional and alludes to a South-South shared experience and conveys the continuing North-South (neo) colonial thinking that underpins the lack of subjectivity ascribed to those being tortured and killed. As with other terms she employs throughout the text, it is a deliberate rhetorical conceit to provoke the reader to challenge their own preconceived assumptions and discursive habits.

To convey how central extreme violence is to the late twentieth and early twenty-first century iteration of capitalism, Valencia (2018) takes the word *gore* from the term given to the low-value exploitation movies of the 1960s and 1970s that deploy a form of spectacularized violence as the core element of the narrative. By correlating the spectacle of violence with the current economic system, Valencia (2018) rethinks how the state, precarious labor, and exploitative work practices, alongside a dominant and lucrative drug trade, has led to a population vulnerable to violence either because of their involvement in the trade or as collateral damage. Like Butler (2009), Valencia's (2018) work demands that we reevaluate whose lives are valued as grievable, whether living or dead.

Valencia is positing that there is something integral to the lived experience under this form of capitalism with its precarious labor conditions, exploitative work practices, and mobile capital that facilitates extreme forms of violence and "extends from the peripheries of the planet to the center and vice versa" (2018, 35). She describes Mexico as a "Narco-state" and traces this back to the 1970s whereby "organized crime was born out of a corrupt, dismantled state that led the population into chaos" (2018, 47–48). This account is not unique to Valencia (2018), but her reading of what is taking place in Mexico is that it is an extreme example of gore capitalism. At the same time, she proposes a reframing of the structural and glocal (global-local) roots of the violence in Mexico that shifts it from a state of exceptionalism and highlights its reticular and interconnected nature.

Integral to how violence is performed is a key figure she calls the *endriago*, an individual who has emerged from the particularities of Mexican masculinity as they intersect with gore capitalism (Valencia 2018, 63–65). Gore capitalism has led to the "transformation of the cartel into multilevel corporation" (Valencia 2018, 146), and the *endriago* serves as a highly skilled employee in a complex chain whose methods "create a reticular and managed terror, transferred from the bodies of the injured and murdered into the bodies of those who have not yet suffered such violence" (Valencia 2018, 154). Valencia states that gore capitalism means that "violence is converted into a resource for the gangster to manage, produce, and sell; it has become the tool *sine qua non* to carve out a space in the capitalist ladder" (Valencia 2018, 197). Under this model, violence is not an aberration, it is part of a business model and its specularization is integral to that. Bodies are mutilated, tortured, and put on display so that they will be seen and form part of a terrifying spectacle that is a performance of power.

The Symbolic Power of Language: Cartels, Narcos, and Feminicide/Femicide

Language matters when discussing violence. Valencia (2018) is not the only critic to find fault with representations of the illegal drug trade nor to foreground discursive practices. Oswaldo Zavala (2018) puts forward a challenge to academics, journalists, writers, and those involved in the creative industries (such as film and television) to rethink the language used to describe violence and deaths in the first decades of the twenty-first century. He asserts that the language used, such as "cartels" and "narcos," have their origin in militarized corrupt government activities and that "los 'cárteles' son un dispositivo simbólico cuya función principal consiste en ocultar las verdaderas redes del poder oficial" (the "cartels" are a symbolic mechanism whose primary function consists of hiding the true structures of official power) (Zavala 2018, loc 87).* The language used and the representation of those involved in the drug trade and its control reinforce whose lives are valued and grievable. While not explicitly concerned with taste, over the course of his book he unpacks the popular representation of the figure of the drug trafficker with a particular focus on physical tropes and motifs that signal issues of taste. He describes gendered and status-related wardrobes and self-presentation that indicate whose lives are valued. Drug traffickers and cartel leaders are associated with specific musical choices (*narcocorridos*) and a consistent wardrobe of the *charro* (Mexican cowboy), pointed toe boots and broad-brimmed, high-crown cowboy hat, and are thereby marked as belonging to the rural

---

*Unless otherwise stated, all translations are my own.

working class with its concomitant denigrated taste (Zavala 2018, loc 11 and loc 375). Zavala ascribes blame for this characterization to novels, films, and television, which draw on the Mexican military's presentation of their imagined "narco" who they project as "todo lo opuesto del soldado: indisciplinado, vulgar, ignorante, violento" (the complete opposite of the soldier: undisciplined, vulgar, ignorant, violent) (Zavala 2018, loc 35). In its audiovisual representation, he has identified a differentiated, performative, and highly stylized presentation of taste in the soldier and drug trafficker's aesthetic, positing that the language used underpins suppositions about whose lives are grievable.

Like Valencia's (2018) assertion of subjectivity and agency when analyzing the specificity of the violence in Mexico, the power in interrogating "narco" for Zavala (2018) is to challenge the rhetoric from above whose discursive strategies condition ways of assessing the causes of, reasons for, and legacy of the violence while apportioning blame for what has happened. As has been asserted about the war on terror instigated under George W. Bush (Hables Gray 1997), the "war on drugs" and the control of the cartels is a war without an actual enemy or possible end: "El Estado fue a detener una Guerra de cartels inexistente porque los cartels no existen" (The State tried to stop an inexistent cartel War because cartels do not exist) (Zavala 2018, loc 178). His critique demands that responsibility be placed on the state for its complicity in the violence and on the creative community (he includes artists, writers, and film and television makers in this) for not taking responsible and ethical approaches to the representation of violence. Similar demands for care in representation can be found in Jean Franco's (2013, 15) analysis of the book-reading criminals who claim to be inspired by the heroic protagonists and the violence they inflict on others, suggesting that there are ethical requirements in language, aesthetics, and storytelling. Franco (2013) and Zavala (2018) are calling for an interrogation of the discursive field and, like Valencia (2018), for an ethical approach to the representation of the recent violence in Mexico so that screen violence does not merely reproduce myths or promulgate official versions that serve the interests of the few.

Another area where language is highly contested is the murder of women in Mexico. In the border town of Juarez, the growth of manufacturing jobs since the 1990s led to a large influx of young women. At about the same time there was an upsurge in the assault and murder of women. Few have been arrested for these crimes and, in the absence of justice, there has yet to be consensus about how to name the deaths of these women. While some use the term *femicide*, others use the term *feminicide*. While both terms mean the killing of women, feminicide is more politically inflected with a more inclusive understanding of gendered identities and self-presentation (Fregoso and Bejarano 2010, 3–8, and Driver 2015, 9–11). Rosa-Linda Fregoso and Cynthia Bejarano (2010) and Alice Driver (2015) make a strong case for the use of feminicide when discussing cultural production and representations of this gender-based violence. I have chosen to do the same as the journalist Ed Vulliamy, who uses femicide/feminicide interchangeably to mean "the mass slaughter of women" (2011, 160). In following his lead, I am trying to be as inclusive as possible and to account both for the different views on and uses of these terms, not only by scholars but also by activists and families of the victims, and for the broad spectrum of individuals who identify and read as women.

Valencia's (2018) and Zavala's (2018) contention that structural violence is at the root of the recent violence in Mexico is consistent with that of Tamar Diana Wilson's analysis of the working conditions for women and their experiences of "prevailing gender regimes" (2003, 56). Wilson marks out the gendered dynamics of women's experiences in *maquiladoras*, the large assembly-line factories making tariff-free goods for export that are the most significant employers in the border cities. Wilson finds that women who work in *maquiladoras* have economic independence, which is curtailed by a paternalistic "gender subordination on the shop floor" (2003, 64) that is systemic and foments "a machismo that works in the interests of the class that owns and controls the means of production" (Wilson 2003, 66). Wilson does not discuss femicide/feminicide but does unpack how gendered relations are embedded in the ways women's labor is integral to the current model of capitalism that "is predicated on exploiting cheap wage labor" with women as "the cheap labor force par excellence" (2003, 56). She concludes that there is a gendered dimension to the lived experiences of women in areas where the prevailing culture is the exploitation of cheap labor. These women are already devalued in their everyday lives and the manner in which they are killed is an extension of that. As Ed Vulliamy notes, their bodies are left "in public places, not even like animals, more like trash" (2011, 160). They are assaulted, murdered, and disposed of as if they and their families did not deserve human dignity.

The women's devaluation and treatment as if they were disposable further extends to their treatment by the elite and officials after their death. In the absence of justice for the victims, there is a continued sense that proper investigations are not being carried out and the perpetrators are not being prosecuted. This leads to suspicion of the justice system by the families and locals. As Vulliamy states, there are "either outright denials or silence from the authorities over their [the women's remains] existence—as if there was something to hide; something worse than ineptitude" (2011, 161). Horrific violence has been committed on men and women in the last twenty years in Mexico, but there is a particularity to the gendered violence that has to do with power and the economic shifts in Juarez that has led to much media and activist attention.

The important work carried out by relatives of murdered women, activists, and their allies draws attention to the specificity of the murders, the impunity with which murderers have operated, and the considerable flaws in the Mexican justice system. Wilson (2003), like Fregoso and Bejarano (2010), Driver (2015), Zavala (2018), and Valencia (2018), signals that these systems are not particular to Mexico, they are just heightened there because of the numbers of *maquiladoras* and the practices inherent to them. Wilson (2003) draws on research carried out in other locations across the Global South where similar patterns are in evidence. The murderers have been able to act with impunity because of the particularities of systemic issues within Mexican justice and policing that have been subject to investigation and political debate in recent decades. What is evident from work by Wilson (2003), Fregoso and Bejarano (2010), Driver (2015), Zavala (2018), and Valencia (2018), and the sometimes highly contestatory discussions surrounding the recent violence—whether drug-related, resource-related, or gendered—is that language should be interrogated for its potential to conceal structural problems and to justify and commit further violence. At the same time, the shorthand that certain language allows facilitates discussion and analysis of the broader ramifications of audiovisual representations of this violence. Where I use such contested language as femicide/feminicide, cartel, and narco-violence, in my own analysis of these representations it is with the caveat that I mean to challenge the power dynamics and structures that enable such violence in the first place.

Reflexive and Relational: On Good and Bad Taste

Violence sits within and beyond taste because of its power as spectacle. This allows for reflections on the nature of taste. To ascribe violence a value in relation to taste troubles categories that are already fluid. "Good" and "bad" persist as qualifiers of taste despite their subjectivity and indeterminacy. Both will appear throughout this book to indicate preconceptions of how certain texts are valued. However, prestige, distinction, and value are more useful key words in the analysis of taste. These have emerged from the writings of the French philosopher Pierre Bourdieu (1993 and 2010). Writing about taste and distinction Bourdieu explores how class determines what he calls "cultural competence" because (in France as it is in Mexico) value is linked to access to educational attainment that unlocks the "code, into which it is encoded" (Bourdieu 2010, xxv). The work of art cannot be fully understood without understanding these codes, whereby "the beholder cannot move from primary to secondary meaning" (Bourdieu 2010, xxvi). His is a landmark work that considers how taste is reflexive, because it "classifies, and it classifies the classifier," and relational, because as social subjects, distinction emerges from understanding the codes and knowing what works are imbued with high-value prestige and merit approval or have low value and, therefore, are dismissed (Bourdieu 2010, xxx). It is clear from Bourdieu's work that taste is not fixed; instead, it is the product of evolving interpretations by social actors. To remain hidebound by taste is to attach decisions based on indeterminacy.

Although Bourdieu's work has proven invaluable in exploring taste as a site of privilege that is legitimated by institutions and individuals interested in exclusion and gatekeeping it still has not succeeded in upending rigid ideas about good and bad taste or the ways high and low value are attached to work. Taste—good and bad—is highly situated and historically determined. Good taste is repeatedly validated through cultural institutions, awards and prizes, funding bodies, curricula, and other canonical means. All the shifts, debates, and challenges to what should attain legitimation does not mean that there is consensus about what good taste is, nor, indeed, what taste is. Good taste does not assert itself as such, often validating itself against that which it is not. More illuminating work on bad taste and its links to popular or mass appeal helps to track the shifts in the conceptualizations and challenges to the idea of taste.

To find fuller explorations of the value and significance of how bad taste is attached to work that falls beyond the parameters set out by arbiters of high-value work, it is useful to consider the work being carried out on the concept of kitsch. Upending the idea that kitsch is the "Esperanto of awfulness," Ruth Holliday and Tracey Potts (2012, 120–27) suggest that kitsch, allied with camp as its cheerleader, is a direct challenge to fixed boundaries between "good/bad" taste. As defined by Sontag (1967), camp has been aligned with gay (and more latterly queer) culture as outsider alternative aesthetics that embrace 'bad' taste deliberately and, frequently, ironically. Recognizing this self-awareness and extending Sontag (1967), Holliday and Potts (2012, 141) suggest that camp and kitsch aesthetics show that "one must have good taste in order to know what bad taste is." That is, bad taste has a rich encoding that is often unrecognized and can be a form of "good" taste. Their argument further illustrates how low, popular, and vulgar (pace Bourdieu) taste is merely about the classifier rather than the work itself. What such in-depth explorations of "bad" taste tell us is that taste itself as a pervasive concept persists because it validates insider and outside status while, simultaneously, as a fixed concept or classificatory system it does not exist. To dismiss work and who consumes it as lacking the capacity to understand its codes reflects back on the classifier, who I refer to as a tastemaker. *Tastemakers and Tastemaking: Mexico and Curated Screen Violence* repositions the argument by looking more closely at these classifiers.

Despite the widespread adoption of Bourdieu's scholarship, and further work carried out by others, such as Sontag (1967) and Holliday and Potts (2012), and the shift toward the celebration of trash in film studies led by Jeffrey Sconce (1995), there is still resistance to breaking with binary thinking around taste. *Tastemakers and Tastemaking: Mexico and Curated Screen Violence* proposes that individuals and institutions can be tastemakers engaging in the act of tastemaking. By foregrounding tastemakers I highlight the provisional nature of taste and consider tastemaking as an act that is relational, dynamic, and subject to multiple influences.

The Culture of the National and Public Institutions

Discussions related to value and taste are not new to Mexican cultural scholarship. Jesús Martín-Barbero (1987), Edmundo Paz-Soldan and Debra A. Castillo (2001), Franco (2002), and Paul Julian Smith (2014) have argued for the need for television studies because of television's vitality, circulation, distribution, and significance. Nonetheless, it has yet to take root. While hampered by questions of class, race, and gender, as elaborated by Bourdieu (2010), this lack of wholescale ease with low/bad taste is the result of gatekeeping. In their assessment of the gaps in current scholarship when analyzing Latin American exploitation (Latsploitation) film, Victoria Ruétalo and Dolores Tierney recognize this tendency: "For a critical elite (those who historically define the parameters of national culture) anxious to emphasize the prestige of their own national cinema, those often badly made, 'low'-culture genre films (fantasy, horror, wrestling, sexploitation, gore) provide little cultural capital" (2011, 1). Recognizing the connections between national culture and value and building on Sconce (1995), Ruétalo and Tierney's (2011) work has broken some ground by challenging prior assessments and asserting the value of such films. But a more widespread adoption of a critical position toward gatekeeping is still tentative and slow in Mexican and Latin American scholarship.

Ruétalo and Tierney (2011) are not the first to argue for the need to examine taste, prestige, and value. The work of a number of noteworthy proponents of the importance of understanding noncanonical, populist, low-value work and of examining its cultural significance will inform discussions in this book. A noteworthy figure in Mexico, the journalist, author, and chronicler Carlos Monsiváis (2000, 2004, and 2009), championed popular culture, its consumption, and the representation of gender and class in literature and film. He suggests that kitsch is a Latin American vernacular (Monsiváis 2000, 47). This tells of his nuanced understanding of work that has mass appeal and to which he ascribes encoded depth and richness.

Mexico, as a nation-state with distinct characteristics, has imagined itself into being since and through the Revolution by investing in a lively cultural industry. Integral to this is the film and television industries, and, as Monsiváis (2000) and, more latterly, Ignacio Sánchez Prado (2015) and Smith (2014) have explored, these often deploy forms sitting at the periphery of taste. From such scholarship it is clear that there is much to be gleaned from work that is deemed of low value. Where what has been produced is not fixed to any particular government nor to a consistent agenda, the imagined nation (cf. Anderson 1983) came into being through audiovisual narrative forms. The 2010 commemorations have been an opportunity to reflect on and measure the failures and successes of the Revolution, which make it a productive moment to examine how culture has been employed in tastemaking practices. To do this I look at an institutional curated film cycle (chapter 1) to examine their significance in the face of this commemorative moment and take neglected adaptations as reversionings of narratives of the Revolution (chapter 3).

Mexico has a large number of public institutions dedicated to culture and history. Much important work has been done to understand their significance at a national level and through comparison with other Latin

American countries. While there can be a privileging of prestige, in this field there is a well-established and vital thread of cross-disciplinary research working against rigid categorizations of taste and value. In particular, two notable scholars, Claudio Lomnitz-Adler (1993) and Nestor García-Canclini (1995), have examined the relationship between popular culture and the ways institutions manage articulations of Mexican modernity and nationalism. Lomnitz-Adler (1993) is most interested in the nation as a necessary but tentative category that requires a nuanced understanding. Through his unpacking of top-down articulations that imagine a nation stratified by race and gender, Lomnitz-Adler proposes a new way into understanding the nation as "intimate culture" that is "real, regionally differentiated manifestations of class culture" (1993, 28). The intimate is grounded in intersectionality and rearticulated through lived experiences. Such analysis counters any clear sense that cultural understandings are dictated by a set of institutions, rather that they are a question of negotiation. A single tastemaker does not decide how culture is consumed but is a node in this intimate culture. With a similar focus on consumption and experience, García-Canclini (1995, 5) has championed popular cultures and articulates top-down and bottom-up forms of cultural production that are consumed using "unstable, diverse strategies" by subjects who are simultaneously traditional, modern, and postmodern. Like García-Canclini (1995) and the television and media scholar Martín-Barbero (1987), I use the popular as a broad definitional category that includes a range of public and private actors and institutions and the work that they create, produce, and consume. García-Canclini (1995) has argued that institutions and cultural agents are integral to the construction of value in Mexico, which is tied to how the nation is articulated and inscribed.

Tastemakers and Tastemaking: Mexico and Curated Screen Violence builds on this work and analyzes how such institutions play a significant part in the imagined nation, thereby becoming tastemakers. At marked moments, when culture becomes ritualized through commemoration, the "conservation and celebration of the patrimony, its knowledge and its use is basically a visual operation" (García-Canclini 1995, 118) understood through mediated versions. As a consequence, film, television, and related media cultures are helpful ways into comprehending the nation through tastemaking; conversely, tastemaking operates as a means of understanding the nation through the creation and curation of film and television.

There is a recurrent demand for subjectivity, agency, and an ethical approach to the representation of violence in scholarship about mediatized violence. Taste does not recur as an overt concern, but it is implicit in much of the writing because of the inherently excessive nature of violence as spectacle. In turn, excess is one of the recurrent features of "bad" taste, and yet specularized violence is often highly revered. Violence bears comparison with the realm of kitsch, where knowing what is a "good" or "bad" spectacle is a marker of taste. Tastemaking as a paradigm, and as an analysis of an enactment of taste, sidesteps binary conclusions. For too long the canon of violent films analyzed have been shaped by a singular form of screen violence. Taking on ethical approaches imbued with an intersectional awareness invites reflections on taste as enacted by tastemakers.

Gendered Tastemaking: Intersectional Situatedness

Like Valencia (2018), my theorization of violence draws on intersectional feminisms informed by the challenges to European and US feminisms proposed by postcolonial theorists. This results in an acknowledgment of "geopolitically-situated systems of knowledge" and recognizes that these pluralized feminisms should be understood "as responses to [the] specific contexts in which they develop" (Valencia 2018, 9). Writing in the first-person plural, Valencia (2018) asserts a pluralistic, reflective, questioning, situated, and intersectional approach. These demands resonate with Butler's framing of war and its victims and foreground subjectivity, agency, and the question of how lives are valued. As I do not live in any of the locales I discuss, my perspective is as an outsider looking in, which makes the first person singular more appropriate. While acknowledging this outsider status, I aim to understand these works as situated interventions into global discursive and aesthetic patterns. Tastemaking violence involves thinking about how lives are valued through culture and its curation, recognizing that some lives—male, female, and gender nonconforming—are more vulnerable in this regard than others. My assessments of tastemakers and tastemaking practices keeps to the fore the understanding of Sobchack (1984), Sontag (2003), Butler (2009), and Valencia (2018) of how victims of violence should be given agency and be grievable. Discussions of agency—whether that of victim or perpetrator—are central to my analysis and are the focus of discussions in chapters 2 and 4.

Gender is a determining factor in how audiences are conceived. Women-centered stories are assumed to be of primary interest to women, thus narrowing how they are curated, marketed, and evaluated, whereas male-centered narratives are presumed to be universal. These assumptions come with presuppositions of their value that are further marked when attached to certain generic conventions, star persona, or media. Within this framing, it is easy to ignore masculinity and to read mentions of gender as coterminous with women or those who struggle with normative codes and presentational selfhood. To be male is to struggle with a series of suppositions and traditions that can limit at the same time that they provide privileges and access to certain fields of production. When discussing violence, masculinity is often established through heteronormative codes of strength, domination, skill, and responsibility for home and nation. These are heavy burdens and to be found in select individuals who are often idealized, or sometimes to be feared because their inherent violence can be excessive and needs to be contained.

Violence enacted by and on a gendered body is highly codified on-screen. Sometimes, gender-based violence is an overt concern of the films and television series I examine in this book; at other times, it is so naturalized as to be rendered invisible. Violent women or violence against women is differently understood than violence by men on other men. Central to my analysis is how gendered bodies conform to or deviate from standardized conceptualizations of violence as a person who enacts or has violence inflicted upon them. But, above all, I am concerned with the tastemaking practices that determine whose bodies are valued as grievable when violence is central to the narrative. This is strongly inflected by gender, but also by multiple other intersectional concerns such as class and race, as I will discuss. It also bears noting that the representations of violence I discuss in the following chapters are often quite disturbing. In writing about them, I have chosen to use an intentionally clinical tone, not to diminish the awfulness of the crimes being represented or the historical realities to which they refer. Rather, I mean to focus attention on the filmmakers' techniques in screening these crimes and how they engage practices of tastemaking.

Linked to how gendered bodies are valued is how the culture for and about men and women are valued. Emily Hind (2019) has made this case in relation to literary culture establishing the affiliative, affective, and taste networks that rewards culture by men and overlooks or denigrates culture by women. Despite attempts to upend high/low distinctions through an established pattern of analysis by highly respected scholars and writers' critical reticence with regard to what is deemed low-value culture is still circumscribed by anxiety about what national culture should be. Underscoring much of the anxiety around value and classification is the necessity for curatorial practices because of the sheer volume of production in Mexico.

A Curated Selection of Tastemakers and Tastemaking

The tastemakers considered in this book are the result of my curatorial choices. They are rooted in key moments and chosen to exemplify work across the value range, from high to low, as they are conventionally ascribed. Nonetheless, each tastemaker has unique characteristics. The tastemakers and texts chosen are five examples selected to provide a sense of how tastemaking practices vary across the taste range.

Chapter 1 is centered around Nelson Carro, the programmer at the national film institute, the Cineteca Nacional de México in Mexico City, and a film cycle he was tasked to curate in 2010 as part of a centenary commemoration of the Mexican Revolution. It would be easy to assume that as a government employee in a highly centralized state he would conform to a narrowly defined and conservative reading of the Revolution. However, the choices he made belie this and also reveal much about film culture in Mexico. This chapter draws on a 2011 interview I conducted with Carro and the growing field of film festival research to consider curatorship and tastemaking in a structured context. I propose that curatorship and discrete film cycles provide new ways of understanding film festivals.

Chapter 2 looks at questions of prestige filmmaking and considers how the auteur filmmaker Amat Escalante as tastemaker has employed and extended the aesthetic features of the festival film. In doing so, he references national and transnational aesthetics to create work that sits at the hinterland of taste. Escalante is heavily influenced by arthouse and festival film aesthetics, which signal legitimacy, and makes films that challenge audiences because of the duration and the hyperrealism of the violence, which prove difficult to categorize in relation to value. Research into slow cinema, sound studies, and editing informs the analysis of the violence in two of his films, *Los bastardos* (2008) and *Heli* (2013). Using videographic criticism and interviews with the filmmaker, the films are considered in relation to violence that is excessive and prompt ethical questions about perpetrator and victim perspectives and, consequently, Escalante's tastemaking practices.

Chapter 3 shifts attention to two adaptations of *Los de abajo* ([1915] 1997)/*The Underdogs* (2015), a *novela de la Revolución* (novel of the Revolution) by Mariano Azuela, an unstable text that saw many versions before it was assimilated into the literary canon. The first film version was by Chano Urueta in 1939 and the second by Servando González in 1976. These are distinct in approach and style, and the poor reception of these films is assessed with reference to adaptation theory and its preoccupation with a perceived top-down hierarchy of value between literature and film. I propose redirecting attention away from reflections on their high/low value and, by drawing on theoretical approaches from translation studies, consider adaptation as reversioning. Using videographic criticism, close textual analysis repositions the approach and proposes that considering the filmmakers as tastemakers and as nodes in a multilayered tastemaking landscape creates a new reading of the texts and contexts.

Chapter 4 centers on two poorly received films about the murdered women of Juarez, *Bordertown* (Gregory Nava, 2006) and *The Virgin of Juarez* (Kevin James Dobson, 2006), which opens up questions of who gets to tell stories of the abused and tortured women and how genre cinema can frame such narratives. The films were classed as failures, and my analysis focuses on the role of stardom and genre as framing devices in the narratives and considers how value can be measured using videographic criticism as a means of informing the analysis. The star texts of Minnie Driver, Jennifer Lopez, Ana Claudia Talancón, and Maya Zapata have distinct valences and create different meanings as tastemakers. These actors are considered in the light of the brutal stories of violence the films are telling and what that says of the limited legitimating paradigms of scholarship related to stardom and genre texts.

Continuing the focus on tastemaking and stardom, chapter 5 takes another actor, Kate del Castillo, and considers how her celebrity-star persona has been subject to misreadings that have had real world consequences for her including being threatened with imprisonment. It examines the television series *La reina del sur* (2011–), in which she stars, proposes that it should be read as an example of a new "quality" *telenovela*, and considers del Castillo as a node in an interrelated network of mediated practices. As a form that is placed in a low-value category, lacking in cultural salience, this chapter argues that del Castillo's television performance and persona challenge assumptions about the *telenovela* and considers her value as a tastemaker.

These case studies demonstrate how tastemaking is a productive means of understanding culture with a particular focus on film and television and its curation. The selections were chosen to exemplify the range and variety of material that can be examined through a focus on tastemaking and tastemakers. The practice of tastemaking in each instance needs to be understood through an engagement with the context of production, consumption, and the stories they tell as well as the profile of the tastemakers. These tastemakers are a mix of curators, filmmakers, and stars who have distinct renown inside and outside of Mexico. The work examined has been received differently in ways that are overdetermined by fixed ideas around taste.

Methodological Approaches to Tastemaking

The case studies in *Tastemakers and Tastemaking: Mexico and Curated Screen Violence* are all linked to moments of considerable violence in Mexico. Taking violence as a means of considering tastemaking is deliberate because it requires proposing novel mixed methodologies to facilitate the navigation of a vast range of material. Like all scholars and writers, I must strategically and carefully pick my way through the resources available across a variety of platforms and spaces in order to find patterns or differences. This results in a dataset that has potential to be expansive, cannot be exhaustive, and needs to be managed and contained. Nonetheless, selection is both necessary and subject to questions of value and taste. *Tastemakers and Tastemaking: Mexico and Curated Screen Violence* is about extending what should be studied in order to redraw the boundaries to knowledge and to reconfigure approaches to institutional curators through film cycles and festival studies; prestige film and extreme realism; adaptation studies and reversioning; star studies and genre; and star-celebrity and television studies, focusing on how these intersect with violence. Therefore, I am covering a range of material to interrogate how taste has been used, what it means for work to be valorized, and to challenge conventional modes of looking at culture as high or low value.

To a degree this is a question of curating a dataset that becomes its own archive, but also of proposing the expansive potential of this approach. I draw on *curation*, a term that has gained currency in the early twenty-first century. Its usage has widened beyond the exclusive domain of institutions, such as galleries and museums, to that of individuals in their curation of a digital self (see Marwick and boyd 2011 and Balzer 2015). *Tastemakers and Tastemaking: Mexico and Curated Screen Violence* examines a variety of uses across the taste range from high- to low-value work. Curation is about selecting what is shown and made, and has evolved through an intermediated discussion. I am drawing on the developing meaning of curation and extending it by naming it *tastemaking* to include all those who have agency in its application and enactment. Whether the individual is choosing from an archive, citing influences, or experimenting with new forms and methodologies, tastemaking is a task that is integral to how we comprehend violence at any given moment and how this becomes part of a means of understanding events of the recent or distant past. Through this tastemaking practice these social subjects become tastemakers.

The analysis of these varied tastemakers requires a mixed methodological approach because of the need to read against conventional attitudes to these texts and produce new conclusions. Therefore, an interdisciplinary theoretical frame and archival research at the Cineteca Nacional de México into understudied texts is supplemented with interviews and conventional close textual analysis combined with videographic criticism. I employ a range of disciplinary resources, adapting them to the needs of the study. These have included employing film festival studies to evaluate institutional practices, star and celebrity studies to consider a range of high-profile and lesser known actors, and, following the lead of recent researchers into Mexican film, such as Sánchez Prado (2015) and Tierney (2018), drawing on industry and production studies to comprehend the contexts in which these tastemakers are operating.

To supplement and inform these archival and interdisciplinary approaches, I have used videographic criticism in a selection of case studies as a mode of close textual analysis because it allows a distancing from questions of personal taste. Videographic criticism is an evolving form that involves cutting up films using editing software to seek patterns or idiosyncrasies. As a critical form of close reading it facilitates careful analysis of repetitions, motifs, or tropes within the film itself or enables comparison with other films in order to discover new readings. Although never free from my own biases and assessments of value, the careful and slow work required through editing an audiovisual essay gives space to unpack the detail and step back from prior evaluations. This is a mode of analysis coined by Christian Keathley and Jason Mittell (2016) that has an emphasis on play and collapses the critical distance between the object and the critic, making the critic a creator of a new work from the available film, televisual, or archival material. This results in "analysis . . . on the object's terms" emerging from its materiality and a "commingling of the object with the critical discourse about it" (Keathley and Mittell 2019, 13). It allows for experimentation through "opening up the film by cutting it up, reassembling it, and rearticulating it" (Velez-Serna 2017, 144). This can result in an open and imperfect form of creativity that leads to an exploration of film removed from traditional forms of analysis (Velez-Serna 2017 and Pisters 2017). In chapters 2, 3, and 4 this method has proven invaluable because of the baggage these texts carry and the challenges inherent in the analysis of audiovisual violence.

The audiovisual essay can follow a cinephilic regard for the aesthetically accomplished; select exemplary elements, themes, or patterns; or explore the anomalous or idiosyncratic. It is a methodology that has seen exponential growth in recent years. The variety of emerging practices can be found in the work published by such online scholarly journals as *[in]Transition*, *NECSUS*, and *Tecmerin*, and those compiled in the annual *British Film Institute/Sight and Sound* list of the best audiovisual essays. The labor and effort involved in the audiovisual essay results in rewarding new finds in texts whose merits may not be at first evident or externally validated. Controversial or uncomfortable texts suppose distinct challenges. The "*digital material thinking*" (Grant 2016, 1, italics in original) of videographic criticism allows a way into challenging texts through the mise-en-scène critical approach championed by Adrian Martin (2014, 40) that involves "a visceral, felt closeness to the frame-by-frame details and workings of cinematic style." To spend time altering, editing, and seeking patterns or anomalies across texts that are not easily read according to conventional analytical practice allows for novel readings and distinct ways of understanding texts that would be otherwise ignored or dismissed as lacking value.

Violence supposes specific challenges in videographic criticism. Where the temptation might be to look away or cover our ears when the screened violence pushes at the edges of our discomfort, paying greater attention to the detail of "certain inexplicable affects, a play of colour, an intensity of rhythm, all those pure (or not so pure), highly material and tangible signifiers" (Martin 2014, 41) distances us from our affective responses and can reveal much about the aesthetics of violence. As a scholarly tool and methodology, videographic criticism facilitates close analysis of scenes of torture (chapter 2), comparisons between the pacing in editing (chapter 3), and reflections on points of view in rape scenes (chapter 4) that reveal more than conventional methodology can. Videographic criticism can distance us from the immediacy of the affective or visceral response to violence and shift our perspective. Using this mixed methodological approach allows a new way into comprehending screen violence.

Videographic criticism as a methodology demonstrates how "different means of expression also constitute different instruments of contemplation" (Lavik 2012, n.p.). There is not a single approach when selecting scenes or cutting and reordering the material. It is research through (re)making. The characters, narrative, themes, or patterns suggest focus and the editing process posits its own conundrums, questions, and issues. Pace and rhythm are integral to editing and are best revealed through videographic criticism. This method reveals how duration can be distinct from attention and focus. Slowing down, cutting up, altering the sound, and shifting attention in scenes of extreme violence or torture examined in chapters 2 and 4 defamiliarizes the scenes and displaces the visceral, resulting in a more dispassionate response. Videographic criticism also poses dilemmas because it utilizes material that may have inherent flaws. While sharing common elements, each experiment results in different outcomes and reveals much in comparative study.

Videographic criticism can signal the exemplary in the text that is aesthetically pleasing or high value, or both. It is also a way into understanding work that falls into the interstices of taste because it is violent or lies beyond standard measures of prestige filmmaking for a multiplicity of reasons. To create an audiovisual essay using material thinking both facilitates and elicits prompts from works centered on violence. In turn, this approach demands that the critic rethink the ethical and cinematic challenges involved in audiovisualizing human capacity to inflict hurt or trauma on another. It places the critic in the position of having to find solutions to the problems audiovisual violence poses. What results is not a single solution, but one that the critic, like the filmmaker, must be able to defend. I explore these problems, the solutions, and my findings from these in chapters 2, 3, and 4.

Conclusion

The conceptualization of value as the realization of a series of decisions rather than a fixed entity is a useful paradigm to examine how prestige is ascribed in highly unstable and multinodal means in film and television. Nelson Carro's curation (chapter 1) ascribes value, but not canonical status. Amat Escalante's art films (chapter 2) aspire to prestige and evade clear attribution of value because of their hyperrealist violence. The historiography of the repeatedly reversioned *Los de abajo* (chapter 3) reveals that its value is ever-shifting, gaining and losing its prestige status. Jennifer Lopez, Maya Zapata, Minnie Driver, Ana Claudia Talancón (chapter 4) and Kate del Castillo (chapter 5) are high-status, low-value stars, which results in challenges to the prestige attached to their work.

Tastemakers and Tastemaking: Mexico and Curated Screen Violence considers how film and television have been deployed to signify markers of taste, that is, to illustrate the tastemaker's cognizance of the value and prestige attached to cultural productions, or the ways they play with these senses of value. It examines where scholars find deficiencies because of what they see as the apparent frivolity or populism associated with particular forms, tropes, and star persona or where they presuppose value because an object has been an established feature of the canon or ascribed high value through placement in a prestigious circuit. It draws on a series of case studies from across the value range—from high to low—in order to consider the ways in which film and television can construct and normalize state and nonstate violence in order to sustain and justify its enactment, and to challenge its discursive and audiovisual strategies. By looking at tastemaking as an action takes taste to task and allows a space to upend rigid gatekeeping practices around what is valued and legitimated.

Chapter One

Cultural Institutions and Gendered Taste Formation

Nelson Carro and the Cineteca Nacional in 2010

The curation of film cycles is tastemaking by an influential tastemaker. The year 2010 saw the commemoration in Mexico of the bicentenary, marking two hundred years of independence, and the centenary of the Mexican Revolution. These two events were the subject of many official celebrations and cultural activities. One of these was a three-month-long film cycle at the national film institute, the Cineteca Nacional de México (hereafter, Cineteca) in Mexico City. As part of this cycle a wide variety of Mexican and international films were screened. The cycle was curated by Nelson Carro, the assistant director of programming at the Cineteca, whose selection reflected his individual scholarly cinephilia, archival availability and permissions, and institutional demands. Having had the opportunity to discuss the process of selection with Carro (Thornton 2011), review the material shown, and consider the complex series of ideas behind such choices, this chapter considers the curatorship of this program and examines what it means to be an institutional tastemaker.

With a particular focus on the films of the Revolution, an event that has ongoing political and cultural significance, this chapter examines how film programmers can become authors and their program act as narratives, as proposed by Mark Cousins (2013, 171) in his film festival manifesto. Cousins demands that "the people who run film festivals must think of themselves as storytellers and stylists" and "challenge themselves to do things differently," so that festivals (or, in this case, cycles) "should be the conscience of the film world" (Cousins 2013, 171). I extend this concept and consider how curatorship can be a form of storytelling as metatextual paradigm. Picking up on Cousins's manifesto and drawing on research into film festivals, this chapter considers what Carro's curatorial role reveals about Mexican film culture's attitude to the Revolution, but also examines how he structured an alternative narrative of the Revolution and Independence through his programming choices as a tastemaker.

To some degree Carro is a "caretaker bureaucrat," a term conceived by David Balzer (2015, 24–26) to describe an individual who manages the legacy of an institution and has to grapple with the political, economic, and cultural demands and expectations of such a role. Carro clearly navigates all of these with an acute awareness of his responsibilities while curating a thoughtful and uncontentious film series of highly contested events. His work goes beyond Balzer's definition whereby, although he may be a government employee (bureaucrat), he is aware of the "cultural consecration" that is a consequence of his decisions, which "confer on the objects, persons and situations it touches, a sort of ontological promotion akin to a transubstantiation" (Bourdieu 2010, xxiv). Carro's curation is tastemaking. Curation is a question of the curator's taste and of establishing or reinforcing values attached to specific cultural objects or means of representation, which makes it a form of tastemaking.

For the commemoration of the bicentenary of Independence (1810) and the centenary of the Revolution (1910–20) Carro curated a three-month-long film cycle for the Cineteca. The choices Carro made reflect much about his taste, but also that of the institution, the public's expectations, and what is ascribed value in Mexican scholarship. He stretches Balzer's idea of the forms of caretaking a bureaucrat can do and acts as a significant tastemaker because his series captures an intersection of interests and concerns. Carro's work on this cycle is an instance of capturing a history of the present, as theorized by Lev Manovich, from among the "overabundance of information of all kinds" (Manovich 2001, 35). By homing in on Carro's selections I am considering a curation of taste by a key tastemaker whose work could be at risk of becoming ephemeral, temporary, and transient rather than part of an ongoing contribution to and commentary on a significant national commemoration.

The study of a single tastemaker can give insight into a much broader field. Homing in on a single subject makes it possible to explore how tastemaking draws from a critical and cultural context. By understanding Carro's role and its significance I consider the significance of programming commemorative activities within an institutional framework and reflect on Carro as a storyteller-curator. Given the controversial and highly contested status that the Revolution still has in Mexico and the sheer number of films that are set during this time period, it was not an easy event to curate.

1910 and 2010: The Long-Running Mexican Revolution

The Mexican Revolution started in 1910. Those who fought in it had a multiplicity of intentions and ideologies, from anarchists eager to overthrow a capitalist dictator, Porfirio Díaz, who favored foreign investors at the expense of local workers, to those opposed to his reelection who simply wanted a change in power. As a large, geographically, economically, and socially diverse country, the motivations of the civilians who took up arms and joined in the Revolution were varied. The Revolution was a brutal war that resulted in the death of more than a million people and the dramatic displacement of millions more, leading to a major population shift from the rural areas to the cities. These displaced people often favored nostalgic stories of the countryside and romances set during the Revolution rather than challenging confrontations with a recent trauma (see Monsiváis 2000, 2004). With few exceptions, Mexican film scholarship privileges more overtly political assessments of the past while overlooking genre filmmaking, in particular the Revolutionary melodrama.

The consequences of the Revolution on Mexico and its political and social landscape were significant, and in its aftermath the government had to unite a populace that had previously engaged in a form of civil war. This was done through a party structure that included highly centralized power, clientelism, and, importantly, putting the Revolution at its center as the defining national narrative (see García Canclini 1995 and O'Malley 1986). Evidence can be found for this in diverse activities and works including commemorative days and events, immense public monuments, the allocation of funding for art forms such as murals, literary prizes, and films, and in the eventual naming of the long-ruling party as the Partido Revolucionario Institucional (the Institutional Revolutionary Party, or PRI). Maintaining power for seventy-one years the PRI discursively institutionalized the Revolution and did so practically through support for events and activities (García Canclini 1995, 53). When the PRI lost power in 2000 and, again, lost the election of 2006 (at the turn of each *sexenio*, or six-year cycle, there is a presidential election), the new party, the Partido Acción Nacional (National Action Party, or PAN), didn't have the same ownership over the Revolution and there was some uncertainty over how they would claim it as their own for the centenary anniversary. Since the Revolution had been framed as the single defining national narrative of modern Mexico, it would have to be commemorated and reconfigured in a way that redefined it for a new century by the PAN with Felipe Calderón as president.

There were several commemorative activities supported by the government at the local and national level, which culminated in a series of planned cultural events between the 16th of September (the inciting moment of Independence) and the 20th of November 2010 (the beginning of the Revolution) at a variety of national institutions. One of these events was the film cycle that took place at the Cineteca, the National Film Institute, which holds an impressive archive of national and international films, has a well-stocked library and a multiscreen cinema, and other leisure amenities including cafés and a bookshop selling film-related goods, including DVDs and books. The Cineteca draws a largely educated, middle-class audience, many of whom live in the nearby neighborhood, and screens Mexican, Latin American, and international films of the sort that circulate in the arthouse circuit.

I am using the term *cycle* as a literal translation from *ciclo* to convey the particularity of the specific type of event or thematic curated series, or both, that the Cineteca regularly hosts. It is worth addressing here the sheer volume of films about the Revolution that have been made in Mexico to give a sense of the selectivity involved. There are more than 250 films produced to date. This is as a consequence of state support for such narratives through such interventionist means as direct financing or practical support such as the provision of army troops and weapons for battle scenes (see Thornton 2013a). That is not to say that all of these films are resoundingly positive representations of the Revolution and its aftermath. Many of these government-supported films were made in the studio system and varied in their approaches and readings of the Revolution. Other films were made after the studio system collapsed in the late 1950s and early 1960s that were intended to directly challenge the framing of the Revolution set out by the government. Some of these films were also made in the politically heightened late 1960s and 1970s, after students were massacred by government forces in protests leading up the 1968 Olympics and the subsequent harsh repression of dissenting organizations in Mexico's own version of the Dirty War (see Thornton 2013a). Therefore, many of these films were ostensibly about the Revolution, but really about the political, social, and cultural conditions of each distinct historical moment.

Film criticism also emerged during this latter period in the 1960s, while new modes of filmmaking were developing. Labeled the *Nuevo cine* group after a short-lived film journal, many of these new male film critics reviled the studio films of the 1930s, 1940s, and 1950s, picking out a few early exceptions, and celebrating the films of their contemporaries (see Thornton 2013a). It's an example of the sort of network Emily Hind (2019, 37–39) explores, one created by male film critics to promote and advance their own work and that of their contemporaries through the careful curation of antecedents. The *Nuevo cine* tastemaking selections have become an established canon in Mexican film criticism. Although the commemoration in 2010 reflects this bias, it does not fully explain all of the selections included in the cycle. Carro's programming choices reveal how he operates as a tastemaker within an institutional and scholarly framework that navigates a complex intersection of hierarchies of value, institutional exigencies, and political meaning. The fifty-six films shown as part of the commemorative *Dos siglos de libertad vistos por el cine* (Two Centuries of Freedom as Seen On-Screen) cycle included films about key figures of the independence movement and the Mexican Revolution, and films from other countries featuring revolution, class, or other major historical confrontations as a key theme or central narrative concern.

In *Cultural Studies and Cultural Value*, John Frow (1995) writes about intellectuals as mediators of cultural value with the power to frame and structure meanings attached to specific works. Touching on similar terrain, Hind (2019, 30) highlights how male this selection can be, whereby "mutual promotion, in addition to self-promotion, keeps male privilege functional," leading to a narrow and repeated canon. As someone who is aware of his power if not his gender bias, Carro drew on a reified canon established by these early male tastemakers that has been reinforced through scholarly work and has been expanded through engagement with a wider field of production. This makes him an important and powerful node in a complex intersection of institutional requirements, critical interests, and industrial exigencies.

When reviewing Carro's curatorship, there were few surprises in the national films chosen, most of which conform to the accepted canon. In contrast, the selection of international films, few of which reference the events in Mexico, provide scope for more radical engagement with the idea of independence and revolution. It was through these international films that the real dialogue about legacy took place. Before I discuss his choices, I want to turn to film festival research as a way of understanding Carro's selections.

Commemoration through Curatorship: Film Festival Research and Film Cycles

There is no clear methodological model for the analysis of film cycles, such as those that the Cineteca regularly curates. Therefore, I turn to film festival research because it provides useful frameworks for the analysis of these cycles. Film festival research is a relatively recent scholarly field that has grown since the 2000s in response to the "massive proliferation of the festival mode" in the 1980s and 1990s (Loist 2016, 58). The European-based Film Festival Research network, founded by Marijke de Valck and Skadi Loist in 2008, with its comprehensive website, has helped nurture and promulgate much of this work (see filmfestivalresearch.org). Research into film festivals is concerned with hierarchies of taste and value in the ways certain festivals and their curators act as gatekeepers of particular ideas of prestige and how others challenge these by framing a festival focused on alternate identities, political perspectives, or geographic locations.

To comprehend the evolution of the festival and pick up on the understanding of prestige and value that is shared with the curators at the Cineteca, I want to provide a brief history of the film festival. Founded in 1932, the Venice Film Festival was the first reoccurring festival (Loist 2016, 53). It was timed, deliberately, to coincide with the Arts Biennale to align the films being exhibited with artistic symbolic capital (de Valck 2016b, 102–3). Originally developed as a way of showcasing national cinemas, the curatorship of film festivals was often marked by political polemics associated with those nations. One such example lies in the plan to found the festival at Cannes in 1939 that was the result of a boycott of the Venice Film Festival because of its association with the Italian dictator Benito Mussolini (Loist 2016, 54). Initially delayed by the outbreak of World War II, the first festival at Cannes took place in 1946 (Ostrowska 2016, 19–20). Since the 1950s, Cannes and a reformed Venice Film Festival have dominated as top tier A-list film festivals, a category awarded them by the Fédération Internationale des Associations de Producteurs de Films (International Federation of Film Producers). Other European and North

American festivals have been admitted into this top tier including Berlin and Toronto, with only one Latin American film festival, Mar de Plata in Argentina, included. The A-list is an exclusive group and shares a common aesthetic approach, which has resulted in the "festival film" (Falicov 2016, 212–13). Such films, "no matter where they come from . . . are indebted to the modernist and realist aesthetics of the European arthouse" (Ostrowska 2016, 28–29). This aesthetic approach is evident in the films that attain success at festival competitions, favoring male creatives.

The year 1968 was a major turning point in the history of festivals. The student protests in Paris and attendant debates about culture and its significance among students and academics resulted in the cancellation of Cannes in 1968 and a demand for reforms to the festival (Ostrowska 2016, 24–27). Principal among these were the shift from national entries to auteur films being recognized as a category. As a consequence, sidebars (carefully curated selections) that privileged the auteurist film at Cannes, such as Un Certain Regard, were established by the then director, Gilles Jacob, in 1978. Dorota Ostrowska (2016, 27–29) credits his curatorial choices and influence with the creation of the "Cannes film," or the "festival film," that, while not a "uniform group," became a recognizable style by the 1990s. The year 1968 stands as an international shift toward the arthouse auteur film at the festival level (de Valck 2016b). It also coincides with developments in the Mexican film industry and with wider debates surrounding film culture in Mexico, as I consider later in this chapter.

The selection throughout the Cineteca's programming reflects an arthouse sensibility that owes much to the tastemaking of the A-list film festival. In common with festivals, the cycles at the Cineteca have a complex economic model. The Cineteca is government supported and receives a limited amount of private sponsorship but must supplement its income through ticket sales and the sale of other goods and services at the cafés and bookshop. This public-private model is typical of many festivals and is a determining factor in the curation of the cycle at the Cineteca, because it is dependent on audience attendance, the creation of a public through the discourses it produces, and a sense of collective identity (Fischer 2013). It also hosts talks related to screenings, such as question and answer sessions and expert discussions, to frame the cycles as an event with added value, and, like a festival, act as a "hub of exchange" (Iordanova 2016, viii) and provide an aliveness "in ways that are uniquely tied in with the space and time of the festival event" (de Valck 2016a, 3). The cycle has, therefore, much in common with the film festival and is also highly influenced by film festival circuits (see Loist 2016). The cycles the Cineteca organize are temporal, carefully curated events that are intended to cultivate taste and, in the case of the *Dos siglos de libertad vistos por el cine*, debate about the ability of film to approximate historiography.

Cineteca Nacional de México: Curating National and International Film Culture

Located in Colonia Xoco in Mexico City proximate to the largely middle-class boroughs of Coyoacán, renowned for its artistic and creative residents, and Colonia del Valle, where two of Mexico City's universities are located, the Cineteca plays a role in Mexican film culture and has strong symbolic as well as political significance. The Cineteca opened on January 17, 1974, with a screening of *El compadre Mendoza/Godfather Mendoza* (Fernando de Fuentes 1933), one of the films shown as part of the film cycle *Dos siglos de libertad vistos por el cine*. At its launch the Cineteca had two screens, a café, an archive, a screening space for researchers, a bookshop, and a climate-controlled store for its film collection. Due to financial constraints the storage facility went into disrepair and there was a major fire in March 1982, which destroyed a substantial part of the archive, in particular early films (Mora 2005 and Smith 2013). It was reopened in 1984, but the storage facility was not completed until 1994. After further renovation and expansion, by 2012, in addition to the well-resourced archives, the Cineteca had shops, restaurants, an exhibition space, and storage facilities, with ten indoor theaters screening films and special events daily and a free outdoor screening space. All but one of these screening spaces (Matilde Landeta) are named after male filmmakers: Arcady Boytler, Luis Buñuel, Juan Bustillo Oro, Fernando de Fuentes, Gabriel Figueroa, Alejandro Galindo, Roberto Gavaldón, Ismael Rodríguez, Jorge Stahl, and Salvador Toscano. With cheaper entry prices than the multiplexes, it has proven popular with audiences, reaching a peak of more than a million tickets sold in 2015 (Agencia el Universal 2016).

According to the Cineteca's website, it has two main aims: "preservar la memoria fílmica tanto nacional como mundial" (preserve national and world film memory) and "promover la cultura cinematográfica en nuestro país" (promote film culture in our country). Its stated mission is to rescatar, preservar, conservar, incrementar y catalogar los acervos fílmico, iconográfico, videográfico y documental, mismos que conforman la memoria cinematográfica de México, así como promover y difundir las más destacadas obras de la cinematografía nacional e internacional con el propósito de estimular el desarrollo de la cultura del cine [rescue, preserve, conserve, grow and catalogue the film, image, videographic, and documentary archives that make up Mexican cinematic memory, as well as to promote and distribute the most notable films of national and international cinema with the aim of stimulating the development of film culture]. (Cineteca 2019)

Memory figures large in these statements as does a clear sense of a differentiated agenda toward national and world or international cinema. The Cineteca's primary aim is to archive, preserve, and promote Mexican cinema and to nurture Mexican film culture through the exhibition of film from Mexico and around the world. While the Cineteca also shows a selection of mainstream films, the Mexican and global arthouse films shown are usually those that fit the definition proposed by Rosalind Galt and Karl Schoonover (2010, 6) of films that have an "overt engagement with the aesthetic, unrestrained formalism, and a mode of narration that is pleasurable but loosened from classical structures and distanced from its representations."

The Cineteca publishes monthly glossy booklets and has a well-organized website. The three booklets under consideration for the purposes of this study are from September, October, and November 2010 and number 322, 323, and 324 covering the period of the *Dos siglos de libertad vistos por el cine* cycle. Such supplementary archival ephemera, of the sort discussed by Ger Zielinski (2016) in relation to festival analysis, provide a useful key to understanding the cycle and the Cineteca's taste-making practice. The booklets help structure the narrative of the cycle and are integral to understanding Carro as a storyteller. The sections being tracked and analyzed are those that describe *Dos siglos de libertad vistos por el cine*. In addition to the *Dos siglos de libertad vistos por el cine* in 2010, there were nine cycles in September, eight in October, and three in November. The range of cycles conveys the sense that the Cineteca has ongoing selections of carefully curated films conforming to specific parameters that are often temporally and thematically finite.

Film Cycles: Mexico and the World

To give a sense of the scale and regularity of curated cycles I want to consider what was programmed alongside *Dos siglos de libertad vistos por el cine*. The twenty cycles across the three months included "Cinemundi," a regular selection of international children's films, on this occasion with a focus on Czechoslovakian films from 1972 through 1979; a European Union–funded selection of fifteen films; a selection of six Nordic films; and a selection of films by individual international filmmakers (Jonas Mekas, Kim Longinotto, and Amos Gitai). November had only three cycles because it has one major cycle, "52 muestra internacional de cine" (fifty-second focus on international film), which occupied most of the calendar. This is a selection of films from major A-list film festivals chosen to coincide with the sixty-year anniversary of the release of *Los olvidados/The Young and the Damned* (Luis Buñuel, 1950). The two selected for particular attention in the November booklet are *Loong Boonmee raleuk chat/Uncle Boonmee Who Can Recall His Past Lives* (Apichatpong Weerasethaku, 2010) and *Somewhere* (Sophia Coppola, 2010), because the former had won the Palme d'Or at Cannes and the latter the Golden Lion at Venice. These selections give a sense of the lively curation of a rich variety of films from across the world that cover a range of periods available to see at the Cineteca and of how the institution privileges the high-value taste of the A-list film festival. The Thai director Apichatpong Weerasethaku is a fascinating example of "a filmmaker with a clear festival flavour and career" (de Valck 2016b, 110). His films fit within the European arthouse aesthetic and have little commercial success outside of that circuit. His work neatly highlights how the Cineteca privileges the festival film over commercial concerns.

The films shown under the rubric of different cycles over the three months at the same time as the *Dos siglos de libertad vistos por el cine* are circumscribed by geography. Aside from Mexican film, the selections privilege European film and those that emerge from European film festivals. This is a pattern that Lindiwe Dovey (2015) has observed in African cinema culture because of how film financing and tastemaking privilege a narrow range of films whose financing comes from European sources. Dovey analyzes African film festivals in African nations and Europe, suggesting that they can function "as a heuristic device, film festivals can help scholars and teachers to keep the dynamism and heterogeneity of African filmmaking practices alive" (2015, 20). In retrospect, the study of film festivals allows space to analyze what has been chosen; using the concept of a cycle, with its narrowly defined focus, can invite close analysis as well as forward planning to imagining alternative inclusions. Dovey's emphasis on thinking through the value choices made as part of a festival opens up thinking around other curatorial practices. Therefore, despite the limited pool of films that form curated cycles, there is still capacity to confront singular frameworks of what national conflicts may mean. It is my contention that Carro's selection and curatorship of the cycle at the Cineteca goes beyond a checklist of a singular perspective of what independence or revolution mean at a local or international level. In particular, the non-Mexican films chosen reveal a desire to interrogate a singular approach to period filmmaking; when considered alongside the Mexican films, the cycle as a whole reveals itself to be a heuristic device with a storytelling function that accommodates multiple, dynamic, heterogenous, and open-ended accounts of national and global events. Underpinning this variation is a selection that reveals much about Carro as a tastemaker curating the cycle and the institutional tendency to favor high-status work.

Curating War: Europe and the US Are the World

The *Dos siglos de libertad vistos por el cine* cycle reveals a geographic privileging of European film common to the other cycles. Of the fifty-six films within this cycle, twenty-two are Mexican (I discuss these later) and twenty-five are European financed or coproduced with one or more European country: France (nine), the United Kingdom (seven), Spain (five), Germany (five), Italy (three), Belgium (two), the Soviet Union (two, both by Sergei M. Eisenstein), and Poland (two, both by Andrzej Wajda). Austria, Holland, Hungry, Norway, Romania, and Yugoslavia contributed financing for one film each. Two films are Cuban coproductions, one with Spain and the other with France, and one is coproduced with Venezuela and two European countries (Spain and Italy). This locates value in European film and favors European class struggles, conflicts, and the end of empires: the French Revolution, Napoleonic conflicts, World War I, the collapse of the Austro-Hungarian Empire, and the Russian Revolution. But the selection does more than just privilege European film; these historic points of reference are crucial to an understanding of both the Independence movement in Mexico and the Mexican Revolution. Mexico's history is bound up with that of Europe as a consequence of colonialism and the economic and political interests that fought over its considerable natural resources.

Instigated in 1810 by Father Miguel Hidalgo y Costilla who led poor farmworkers into revolt against the ruling creole class, Independence was attained in Mexico in 1821. Inspired by the French Revolution and in conflict with the French who made several incursions into Mexico, Independence was only the beginning of a long cycle of conflicts between Mexico, Spain, France, the United Kingdom, and the United States to establish the boundaries of the new nation-state and to attain rights over land and natural resources. These tensions continued right up to the Mexican Revolution in 1910. Therefore, film narratives that span the eighteenth, nineteenth, and twentieth centuries and consider the American War of Independence, the French Revolution, Napoleonic power, slavery, conquest, boundary conflicts, World War I, the end of empire, and immigration and belonging all function to explore the questions and geopolitical context of Mexican Independence and the Revolution.

The impetus for the Mexican Revolution originated in disparate political ideologies and motivations. Its start date was 1910, but the end date is subject to ideological interpretation and definitional issues. The year 1920 was the end of the bellicose period that led into a more protracted ideological struggle for the significance of the Revolution. There was a three-year religious war, the Cristero rebellion (1926–29), that is sometimes subsumed as an extension to the Revolution (see Bailey 1974 and Benjamin 2000). The year 1940 is also a date given for the end point of the Revolution because the land reforms brought in by President Lázaro Cárdenas (1934–40) were a central tenet of many fighting in the Revolution. The lack of success of these reforms puts this date into question, and the lack of specificity as to the end date gives a sense of the density of meanings of the Revolution in Mexico and the different causes for its outbreak. These varied from the specific desire to overthrow the despotic president, Porfirio Díaz, to a multitude of other theories taking hold around the world in the early twentieth century, including socialism and anarcho-syndicalism, that were combined with local concerns over landownership, poverty, and class inequalities.

The teasing out of some of these sociological issues and political concepts can be found in the European film choices that foreground class, in particular, which are concerned with struggles for equality or socialist ideals, or both. The seven films that fall under this broad rubric include Eisenstein's *Bronenosets Potemkin/Battleship Potempkin* (1925) and *Oktyabar/October* (1927), *Ziema obiecana/The Promised Land* (Andrzej Wajda, 1975), *Hauptlehrer Hofer/Schoolmaster Hofer* (Peter Lilienthal, 1975), *A Room with a View* (James Ivory, 1985), *La bella del Alhambra/ The Beauty of the Alhambra* (Enrique Pineda Barnet, 1989), and *Daens* (Stijn Coninx, 1992). The date range of the films, from 1925 to 1992, and the contextual and thematic reach convey the scope of this cycle. All these films were shown in either October or November, coinciding chronologically and conceptually with the Mexican Revolution and proving to be a highly nuanced selection. Eisenstein's films make for the most obvious choices among all of these given that they convey some of the similar motivations for revolution among the laboring classes in Russia as were present in Mexico, as does Pineda Barnet's film, which is set in a Cuban brothel and focuses on the conditions of poverty and inequality that lead to revolution. Alongside the other films that portray labor disputes (by Wajda, Lilienthal, and Coninx), there is one perplexing inclusion, *A Room with a View*, an uncritical portrait of period decadence that foregrounds class while indulging and privileging its affective qualities. Rather than read this choice as merely an outlier, Dovey's framing of film festivals as a heuristic device that informs my concept of tastemaking helps explain how *A Room with a View* works within this cycle as a way of examining class from multiple perspectives, which reveals a dynamic and heterogenous approach to questions of class on film.

Tastemaking is differently layered in the curation of US films. In the *Dos siglos de libertad vistos por el cine* cycle fourteen films are either fully financed by the US or are coproductions between the US and either a European country or Mexico. Lance Hool's *One Man's Hero* (1999) is the only coproduction between the US and Mexico. It portrays the role of the St. Patrick's Battalion in the Mexican-American War, which fought on the side of the Mexicans (1846–48) (Velasco-Márquez 2006). Only three of the US films are set during the Mexican Revolution: *¡Viva Zapata!* (Elia Kazan, 1952), *The Wild Bunch* (Sam Peckinpah, 1969), and *Reds* (Warren Beatty, 1981). One of a small number of biopics of the Revolutionary leader Emiliano Zapata, Kazan's *¡Viva Zapata!* was written by John Steinbeck and stars Marlon Brando. It is a much-discussed film that is as much about Kazan's controversial appearance before the House Un-American Activities Committee (HUAC), where he named fellow actors and directors as communists, leading to their blacklisting, as it is about the Mexican Revolution (Thornton 2013b and Pineda Franco

2019). None of the Mexican films about Zapata have been critically or commercially successful nor were they included in this cycle, therefore Kazan's film is a fitting exploration of this key figure and a choice that privileges high-value cinema.

Peckinpah has two films in the cycle, *The Wild Bunch*, and his least violent film, the comedy *The Ballad of Cable Hogue* (1970). Peckinpah's *The Wild Bunch* features the Mexican actor-director Emilio Fernández as the drunken, federalist General Mapache, who is obsessed with the trappings of modernity at the expense of his people; the Wild Bunch outlaws help defeat General Mapache. Peckinpah's films are similar to those of the Mexican filmmakers of the 1960s and 1970s because, where they turned to distant battles as ways of comprehending the present unrest, his ultraviolence has been read as a reaction to US national and foreign politics (see Thornton 2012). Choosing *The Wild Bunch* means that the cycle includes a fascinating late-period performance by Fernández and an outsider's unconventional representation of the Revolution. By programming it alongside *The Ballad of Cable Hogue*, it invites a look at what US filmmakers were concerned with in the 1960s and 1970s, a key period in the Mexican films of the Revolution shown as part of the cycle. Carro has constructed a dialogic story of revolution and independence through his curation of the film cycle.

Peckinpah is one of only two US directors who have more than one film included in this cycle. The second is Martin Scorsese, whose nineteenth-century dramas set in New York were screened: *The Age of Innocence* (1993), about the New York elite, and *Gangs of New York* (2002), about conflicts between Irish American immigrants and earlier settlers. Both of these films play a similar role in the cycle as *A Room with a View*—that is, they are films that complexify and challenge clear-cut narratives around independence and revolution. The third choice of a US film, *Reds*, is a biopic of the US journalist and socialist John Reed, author of a significant account of the Revolution, *Insurgent Mexico* ([1914] 2006). *Reds* is only briefly set in Mexico and stands in for another significant film about Reed by Paul Leduc, which I discuss later. *¡Viva Zapata!*, *The Wild Bunch*, and *Reds* are multilayered dramas about the Mexican Revolution told by outsiders that contribute to the cycle as a heuristic device. They reveal that Carro is a tastemaker who has curated a dynamic and heterogenous selection in dialogue with his institutional and formative context.

Nelson Carro: Curating Unruly Archives

Dos siglos de libertad vistos por el cine cycle exists within a complex ecosystem that relates to other cycles and programming decisions that took place within the same month(s) and, more broadly, in dialogue with the wider meaning of the Cineteca as an institution and its role in the commemoration of significant historical and political events in Mexico. As already mentioned, this cycle was included as part of the decadelong commemoration managed at a national level by the government of President Felipe Calderón (2006–12). Carro's curation is as a key tastemaker who carefully navigated his role as someone who has a long-term role at an institution, taking into account the Cineteca's needs and affordances, the political reverberations of 2010 as a date and synecdoche, and his capacity to form and draw on Mexican and global film cultures. Curatorship of this sort is misunderstood as rigid and stultifying in a period when the focus is on the highly mobile, busy, disruptive, transnational star curator, such as Hans-Ulrich Obrist or Carolyn Christov-Bakargiev (see Balzer 2015). A close look at Carro upends this simple binary analysis.

As well as being a full-time programmer, Carro is a learned scholar of Mexican and global arthouse cinema, making him a curator who is more than the mere guardian of the status quo, suggested by David Balzer's (2015, 24) term *caretaker bureaucrat*. While he has a caretaking role as promotor and curator of the rich archive of the institution, rather than the upholder of a singular perspective stultified by all that bureaucracy presupposes, Carro should be read as a curator who uses the cycle to structure a story of Revolution and Independence, resulting in a nuanced, albeit male-centered, account of national events. To look at this film cycle is a way to understand Carro's curatorial choices, the commemorations and their signification, and to learn from this example how market demands intersect with political and cultural requirements at the Cineteca.

There are numerous programmers attached to the Cineteca, such as Carlos Bonfil, who acted as guest curator for the Carlos Monsiváis cycle. At the time of the *Dos siglos de libertad vistos por el cine* cycle Carro was assistant director of programming and was tasked with curating it. Carro was born in 1952 in Montevideo, Uruguay. While at the university studying chemistry he became involved with what was a very active film society, and from this experience he developed film programming into a specialty. By the early 1970s he found work at the Cineteca Uruguayo in Montevideo, moving to Mexico City in 1976, where he now lives. On his personal website (https://www.nelsoncarro.com/, on hiatus since 2013), he presents himself as both a cinephile through his expression of an enthusiastic and lifelong love of film as an audience member and as a journalist and scholar writing regular reviews for national newspapers and cultural magazines as well as contributing to academic publications. He has held the position of assistant director of programming at the Cineteca since 2007.

His trajectory is reflective of the confluence of two key strands in Mexican film culture: the development of film journals by filmmakers and writers in the 1960s and 1970s, and the significant encyclopedic work carried out by a team of researchers under the aegis of the film historian Emilio García Riera who catalogued and synthesized Mexican film production (see Noble 2005). Therefore, Carro's curatorial practice is based on a deep and broad understanding of Mexican and global cinema. In conversation, it was clear that he is also highly aware of the dynamics of film culture in Mexico and the institutional exigencies of the Cineteca (Thornton 2011). He curates programs and cycles on the basis of what will attract audiences and what he values as worthy of inclusion. He favors high-value work and has a clear gender (male) bias, as I discuss later. To further understand his curatorial storytelling and his discursive framing, I want to turn to the accompanying booklets for the cycle.

In the absence of reviews or audience figures for discrete cycles, program booklets, although often treated as ephemera, provide another way into understanding the process of tastemaking. Carro gave a concise and carefully worded introduction to the cycle in the September program that reveals his philosophical approach to cinema and its uses as a commemorative tool as well as leaving much space for interpretation. For him, cinema "ha sido testigo de la historia" (has been a witness to history). This may suggest that film has an indexical quality. However, in his follow-on sentence his use of the word *registrado* (registered) suggests that cinema looks at history obliquely, acknowledging that it can observe reality although not always accurately. He continues by saying that the Revolution was a school for documentary makers learning their craft. Despite this assertion, there are no documentaries in the film series, although there were several made about the Revolution, including compilation films and interviews with survivors, for example, *Memorias de un mexicano/Memories of a Mexican* (Carmen Toscano, 1950) and *Los últimos zapatistas, héroes olvidados/The Last Zapatistas, Forgotten Heroes* (Francesco Taboada Tabone,

2002). Carro's reflection is an acknowledgment of how the Revolution was heavily mediatized and an affirmation that the documentary was integral to the foundations of early Mexican filmmaking. His language asserts his credentials as a curator with applied knowledge of the field and flags any gaps there are in the cycle.

Given Carro's foregrounding of the gaps, it is useful to think about the potential films available to Carro through archival analysis, because that is a key function of the Cineteca, and his approach had to be highly selective given the range of material available to him. As with festival programming, editing is integral to the curatorial practice of creating a film cycle (Rastegar 2016, 182). It is clear in Carro's commentary that he builds on a foundation of factual filmmaking and suggests that the archive can also function as a resource revealing past versions of history. After his three opening sentences, the remainder of Carro's introduction is concerned with how cinema has "reconstruido" (reconstructed) and "reinterpretado" (reinterpreted) history, thereby converting history into an "espectáculo" (spectacle). This brings into doubt cinema's capacity to convey facts precisely or accurately, but it also privileges fiction. He continues, "Y esas imágenes podrán ser falsas o tener muy poca relación con la realidad, pero tienen un enorme poder de convicción" (these images can be false or have very little relationship to reality, but they have an enormous power of conviction). In addition to detailing the range of material and the periods and figures included, he states that "en algunos casos, un mismo asunto podrá ser objeto de miradas diferentes e incluso contradictorias" (in some cases, the same event could be subject to different approaches that can even be contradictory). Different filmmakers or performers can give opposing versions of the same event or figure. He concludes, "*Dos siglos de libertad vistos por el cine* propone reflexionar sobre la relación del cine con la historia, una relación casi siempre conflictiva, muchas veces fallida y sólo afortunada en contadas ocasiones" (*Dos siglos de libertad vistos por el cine* invites you to reflect on the relationship between cinema and history, which is a frequently tense relationship, often flawed and only very occasionally successful). Such reflections underscore his awareness of films and the cycles' storytelling function.

Where archives can seem like exhaustive repositories, archival research reveals the "unruliness of archival objects" whose indexical nature is sometimes questionable but can be a useful way of rethinking historical certainties (Baron 2014, 3). Carro is conveying his sense of the unruly archive and both cumulatively and clearly articulates how flawed film is in conveying truth. Therefore, far from contributing to any solidified or stilted vision of history, this cycle should be read as a reflection on cinema as a partial and subjective look at the past. His careful framing of the cycle signals that there is more to uncover and more work that exists beyond what the Cineteca has in its archive. Carro does not take on this task reluctantly. It is clear from his introduction and in conversation (Thornton 2011) that this is an opportunity to invite new reflections as to how film operates as a system of meaning.

With many archives there can be a problem of excess where "there are always too many documents and too many possible ways of reading them" (Baron 2014, 3), which is labeled "noise" (Baron 2014, 4) because of the difficulty of sifting through the volume of available materials. As a consequence, each document becomes a "fragment of the vast trove" available to the researcher or curator (Baron 2014, 110). As a tastemaker, Carro's assertions about the choices he has made for this cycle allude to the range of material available, the limited capacity of any single film or even cycle to convey a historically accurate account of the events, and both how unruly and noisy the archive is.

Carro's nuanced language and careful presentation of the cycle can be contrasted with the more banal offering in the October overview by an unnamed author: "La revision histórica que inició el mes pasado con el ciclo Dos siglos de libertad vistos por el cine, continua como un asomo a distintos eventos mundiales que transcurrían de forma paralela a nuestras gestas de Independencia y Revolución" (The historic overview that began last month with the cycle *Dos siglos de libertad vistos por el cine*, continues with a look at distinct world events that took place at the same time as our own exploits during Independence and the Revolution). This is purely descriptive and factual and lacks the curatorial awareness of the complexity of the task Carro has undertaken and provides in his own September introduction.

Carro's curation reveals an applied awareness of "the connections of programming, product, and criticism that unite multiple nodes of cinephilia and films themselves" that Cindy Hing-Yuk Wong (2011, 4) has noted as a feature of film festivals. This suggests that festival analysis would be enhanced through reflection on cycles and similar events that are more closely defined and circumscribed by local parameters, such as commemorations. Carro's choices are more than what will draw in a crowd, they are also about received ideas of value and taste becoming a catalogue of a tastemaker and how his choices intersect with the exigencies of the institution. There is also a question of how programming is political with its attendant politics. Just as festivals originated in and are ever evolving as a consequence of political change, programming is subject to similar shifts. This is particularly acute when considered in the light of the Revolution on film by Mexican filmmakers. The Revolution was a conflict with no definitive end point, no easy resolutions, and a considerable volume of versions and reversioning, and this is reflected in multiple and varied versions on film.

Indispensable and Highly Selective: Curating a Tastemaker

Although *Dos siglos de libertad vistos por el cine* was launched in September to coincide with the date independence is commemorated, the cover of that month's booklet was given over to a cycle dedicated to the cultural critic and tastemaker Carlos Monsiváis, *Las imprescindibles de Monsiváis* (Monsiváis's indispensables). For my purposes, the Monsiváis cycle is worth pausing on briefly, although the cycle of twelve films from 1933 to 1950 merits its own deeper analysis and commentary elsewhere, given the significance of Monsiváis as a reviewer and chronicler of city life (see Brewster 2005 and Hind 2019), whose focus on the marginalized and popular was highly influential in canon formation and tastemaking. The film critic Carlos Bonfil, a friend of Monsiváis, curated the cycle, which he introduces by describing Monsiváis's comprehensive knowledge of film and his exhaustive ability to remember details about plots, characters, and gossip related to the films. Bonfil highlights the eclectic nature of Monsiváis's taste in film and, in Roya Rastegar's (2016, 192) words, demonstrates that "to curate films is to care for the films, their makers, and viewers, to guide their meanings and consequences within culture and society." Some of the selected films had required Monsiváis to champion them, such as the *cabareteras* (musical cabaret genre) *Aventurera/The Adventuress* (Albert Gout, 1949) and *Víctimas del pecado/Victims of Sin* (Emilio Fernández, 1950), but they have now long been inserted into the canon. Other choices were well lauded locally and internationally on their release as well as attaining considerable box-office success, when Mexican cinema dominated the Spanish-speaking market, such as *Enamorada/A Woman in Love* (Emilio Fernández, 1946) and *Nosotros los pobres/We, the Poor* (Ismael Rodríguez, 1947). By choosing only from the Golden Age of Mexican cinema and focusing on melodramas and the *cabaretera* genres, the cycle does not fully engage with Monsiváis and his legacy. To illustrate the conservative nature of the choices in this cycle, five of the films are by the much-celebrated Emilio Fernández during his period of collaboration with the cinematographer Gabriel Figueroa. These are uncontroversial and high-value selections that are not in the spirit of Monsiváis, a critic who kept up a lively engagement with contemporary film up to his death in 2010 and championed work considered low value and marginalized by mainstream critics, including work about women, homosexuals, and the disenfranchised. Given the timeliness of the choices, I focus on those films that overlap with the commemoration of the Mexican Revolution because of what it says about Bonfil and Carro as tastemakers working within the same institutional context.

Two films shown in September as part of the Monsiváis cycle directed by Fernando de Fuentes reappear in November as part of the *Dos siglos de libertad vistos por el cine* cycle: *El compadre Mendoza* (1933) and *¡Vámonos con Pancho Villa!/Let's Go with Pancho Villa* (1936), while the other film of the Revolution by Fernández starring María Félix, *Enamorada*, is only shown as part of the Monsiváis cycle. The de Fuentes films were flops on their release, but were revived by Bonfil and critics of the *Nuevo cine* group, while *Enamorada* was a critical and commercial success (see Tierney 2007). The former films are tragic tales of brothers in arms fighting for the greater good of the Revolution, while the latter is a melodrama. This gives some indication of how Monsiváis's interventions celebrating women, stardom, and the popular is still radical even when attached to long-established films and when compared with how Carro privileged male stories of battle over women's stories in the cycle commemorating Independence and the Mexican Revolution. Bonfil's selection is narrow, but it is still more woman-centered than Carro's retrospective cycle.

Mexico's Battles On-Screen

Under Carro's curation twenty-two Mexican films by twelve different directors were shown as part of the *Dos siglos de libertad vistos por el cine* cycle. There were five directors with two or more films selected from their oeuvre: Miguel Contreras Torres (five), Julio Bracho (three), Felipe Cazals (three), Fernando de Fuentes (two), and Gonzalo Martínez Ortega (two). Of the twenty-two films, ten deal with the period leading up to or directly related to the Mexican Revolution and the rest range from independence through the Napoleonic War and up to the Porfiriato. Given that there are fewer films to choose from covering this long nineteenth-century period, the choices made are more about availability than narrowly defined selectivity. In contrast, as already mentioned, there are several hundred films about the Revolution to choose from, therefore the tastemaking involved in the selection among this archival noise is revelatory of a particular kind of gendered canon formation.

There is a periodization at work in the selection of films: the so-called Golden Age (1930–50) and the *Nuevo cine* group (1960–70). The Golden Age is a much-discussed period and a highly contested label. As mentioned earlier, *El compadre Mendoza* (1933) was the first film shown at the Cineteca, which could suggest that it is a key marker in Mexican film as a commercially successful and culturally celebrated form. This is not the case and gives an indication of the taste of those who established the institution. It was not the films about the Revolution, but *Allá en el rancho grande/Out on the Big Ranch* (Fernando de Fuentes, 1936), a *comedia ranchera* (a rural-based musical comedy genre), that catapulted Mexican film onto the international market, in part as a result of awards at Venice (see García Riera 1995). As a result, Mexico became a successful production base for films whose primary market was the Spanish-speaking world, peaking in the 1930s and 1940s. Golden Age as a label is sometimes disputed and the precise beginning and end points are debated, but it has become part of conventional academic indicator of a highly lucrative period of studio-based filmmaking (see McKee Irwin and Castro Ricalde 2013; Ramírez Berg 2015). The Golden Age is not a marker of quality, but of popularity. The most popular films of the Revolution during the Golden Age were star vehicles often centered on romantic narratives and with strong musical numbers. These comprise those films included in the Monsiváis cycle and others featuring stars such as María Félix and Dolores del Rio (Thornton 2013a, 2017b).

As has been discussed elsewhere, neither of the de Fuentes films had commercial success on their release (Pick 2010; Thornton 2013a). Instead, they were recuperated by the filmmakers and writers who have become known as the *Nuevo cine* group (see de la Vega Alfaro 1999, 191, and Mora 2005, 105). This label is a convenient shorthand for an active film culture in Mexico that emerged at the same time as the studios were going into decline, the universities had set up new film courses, and there was a lively political atmosphere alchemized by worker and student protests. In tandem and in dialogue with one another, a new generation of filmmakers developed who came up through the university system or trained abroad (some of whom studied in the USSR or Italy), and through film clubs got access to a range of films from around the world (see Mora 2005). As well as a strong educational grounding, this range of new opportunities and exchange of ideas opened a new generation up to a distinct formation of taste. José Bolaños, Gonzalo Martínez Ortega, Servando González, Marcela Fernández Violante, and Alberto Isaac, whose films are included in this cycle, all fit into this grouping. As I discuss in chapter 3, González is both representative of and anomalous among this group and all but one of this selection are male. The Golden Age films shown as part of the *Dos siglos de libertad vistos por el cine* cycle have been filtered through the lens of a tastemaker formed by the *Nuevo cine* aesthetic.

There are two films by filmmakers who sit uneasily within this Golden Age/*Nuevo cine* framework and invite us to question the conventional academic boundaries: *La sombra del caudillo* (The Shadow of the Strongman) (Julio Bracho, 1960) and *La guerra santa* (The Holy War) (Carlos Enrique Taboada, 1977). As is well documented, *La sombra del caudillo* did not get a screening until 1990 because of a bureaucratic form of censorship (see Ibarra 2006 and Thornton 2013a). Based on an eponymous book ([1929] 1979) by Martín Luis Guzmán, it is a political noir thriller about corruption and assassination set amid a barely fictionalized version of the ruling party. Aesthetically and in its star casting, it is a glossy high-end film that conforms to studio production style, but ideologically chimes with the films of the late 1970s that form part of this cycle. The notoriety of its long-delayed release also adds to the sense of significance attached to *La sombra del caudillo*.

The horror genre filmmaker, Carlos Enrique Taboada, is an unusual inclusion because *La guerra santa* (1977) falls outside of conventional measures of value. Taboada had a trajectory that overlapped with Bracho. Unlike many of those lauded by the *Nuevo cine* group, both Taboada and Bracho worked as part of the studio system and had successes spanning the studio and poststudio periods. Taboada was a screenwriter working in film and TV from 1954 and directed his first film in 1964. The aesthetics of *La guerra santa* is similar to that of the other films from the 1970s that form part of this series because of the use of flat lighting, low-key performative styles, phatic and relational dialogue, and the use of outside spaces. These films are all reflective of a lower budget and less available infrastructure as well as a deliberate attempt to convey the Revolution in a realist style. But it is a film that has been overlooked because of the director's primary association with genre filmmaking.

The 1960s and 1970s were marked by political and social unrest, oppressive state action (including the massacre of student protestors), and a dirty war that resulted in deaths and disappearances. The aesthetics of filmmaking was marked by this shift in public and lived experience where the Mexican government became oppressor rather than protector. In a clientelist system this rupture was significant and played out on-screen, as evidenced in the films of Bolaños, Martínez Ortega, González, Fernández Violante, and Isaac.

The public cinema screening of both of these films is a rare event. *La sombra del caudillo* was in limbo for decades and has had occasional screenings since it was given permission for distribution. *La guerra santa* got poor distribution, was not a cause célèbre, and has had little critical attention. Unlike most other Mexican films set during the Revolution that use encoded means of criticizing the post-Revolutionary period, these films do so explicitly. They are also an uneasy fit with the other films that conform to the *Nuevo cine* canon. These choices demonstrate Carro's careful curation of the archive and reveal how he established a layered heuristic storytelling device through the cycle. *La sombra del caudillo* is consistent with the films privileged by earlier tastemakers, such as the *Nuevo cine* group, while *La guerra santa* reveals a personal selection from the available archive. Carro as tastemaker is more than simply following a prescribed route, he is guiding the viewer through his understanding of quality and value.

Opting In or Opting Out: Leduc, Calderón, and Estrada

In the historiography of the 1970s an exemplary figure recurs, Paul Leduc (see Ramírez Berg 1992; Pick 2010; Thornton 2013a). His film, *Reed, México insurgente/Reed, Insurgent Mexico* (1971) stands out as a gap in this film cycle. For the film historian García Riera, *Reed, México insurgente* is an authentic reimagining of the past that shakes off what he sees as the colorful excess of the studio Revolutionary melodramas (1994, 21) and is an exemplar of political filmmaking of this era. It would be an expected inclusion in this cycle. The absence of *Reed, México insurgente* is telling of what Carro has had to navigate in order to coordinate this cycle. The first of these is the broader political significance of the Revolution and Independence in 2010.

Commemorations of national formation are necessarily political, and because of the nature of how the Revolution, in particular, has been deployed in Mexico, these activities could only be political (see O'Malley 1986; Benjamin 2000; Joseph, Rubenstein, and Zolov 2001). The year 2010 was branded by Calderón's government as the Bicentenario de la Independencia y Centenario de la Revolución Mexicana (Bicentenary of Independence and the Centenary of the Revolution). As evidenced in his speech launching the events on February 10, 2010, Calderón (2010) placed emphasis on national pride, presenting Mexico as a pluralist and stable country capable of overcoming past adversity and current challenges. In this speech he refers to a selection of events that were planned to mark the commemoration, including a mix of cultural activities and the construction of public works with a full awareness of how "commemorations renew affective solidarity" (García Canclini 1995, 133). Calderón is a divisive figure who led a failed policy of increased militarization of those areas and cities most effected by crime related to the drug trade. In 2010 he was already two years into his presidency, and his appeal to unity and consensus clearly marked the events as projections of his presidential political project (Madrazo Lajous, Romero Vadillo, and Calzada Olvera 2017). Israel Cervantes Porrúa (2017) has assessed the performative nature of the Calderón presidency with reference to the security measures taken under his presidency and concludes that Calderón deployed ritual and spectacle as a means of political control. Such activities reveal how the commemorations form part of "an entire system of rituals" whereby "the original and 'legitimate' patrimony is periodically ordered, remembered, and secured" (García Canclini 1995, 112; see also Pérez-Anzaldo 2014). Performance and display have been part of a wider spectacle of violence related to the illegal drug trade taking place across Mexico. Therefore, Calderón's articulation of the significance of the 2010 events is wrapped up in his political actions and their performance by way of taking control of the narrative of Revolution.

For this reason, Leduc responded to Carro's request to screen his film and refused permission to have *Reed, México insurgente* shown as part of this commemorative cycle (Thornton 2011). Despite its power as a challenging and dialogic text, Leduc did not want *Reed, México insurgente* to contribute to a cycle that was included under this official and heavily politicized commemoration. Leduc opted out, but this does not suggest that opting in is necessarily a sign of conformity nor of giving legitimacy to the status quo. It reveals the strategic and situated choices that Leduc as a filmmaker with control over film rights and Carro as institutional curator have made within the logic of their respective positions. Such gaps in the program become meaningful only when informed by a clear understanding of the key films of the period and interviews.

Leduc's protest sits as a subtext to Carro's cycle as text. Dissent from within has been long practiced in Mexico. Many of the 1970s filmmakers who made films critical of the powerful were funded by government agencies (Treviño 1979, 26). Financial support was a government strategy used as a means of performing openness and democratic principles that belied other actions, such as the counterinsurgent policing practices, and facilitated the emergence of a new generation of filmmakers (see Ramírez Berg 1992). The filmmakers had creative freedoms that the government could claim they were nurturing.

In place of Leduc's version of Reed's Mexican experiences, Carro included *Reds*, a film about Reed that links the Mexican Revolution to the Russian Revolution, thus inviting connections across national boundaries and with other films that form part of the cycle. Leduc's decision to opt out was not widely publicized and lacked significant impact. It evidences the unseen and rarely registered terrain that tastemakers, like Carro, must navigate when curating film cycles.

A contemporary example of such dissent while opting in that sits alongside the film cycle is the screening of *El infierno/The Narco* (Luis Estrada, 2010), a film partly financed by the 2010 commemorative official funds. It carries the 2010 logo in the end credits. *El infierno* is about a decent small-town Mexican migrant deported from the US, who through happenstance, local corruption, and a need to survive becomes a drug trafficker. The memorable final scene preceding the 2010 logo takes place on the 16th of September during the *grito* (shout), an annual commemoration of Hidalgo's call to arms (the Grito de Dolores) in 1810 that subsequently led to the battle for independence. The *grito* is reenacted annually all over Mexico in public squares. Described by Guadalupe Pérez-Anzaldo (2014, 217) as a "cataclismo" (cataclysm), in the final scene of *El infierno* the mayor, bishop, heads of the army and police, and other local grandees are all gathered to proclaim the *grito* when the protagonist sprays them with bullets, brutally murdering them all in front of the gathered community. There is a sense of justice in the murders, as these are all corrupt and dangerous individuals, which is combined with the decline in the protagonist's character and the horror of the dramatic deaths. The mix of terror and celebration is shocking in a film supported by 2010 funding that so clearly references the commemorations.

El infierno is a deliberately provocative film by Estrada, who has made his name as a controversial filmmaker and whose work has previously experienced delayed release, similar to *La sombra del caudillo* (see Velazco 2005), and evidences his decision to opt in as a critical strategy, where Leduc opted out. *El infierno* was not included in the *Dos siglos de libertad vistos por el cine* cycle nor was any other film supported by government 2010 funding. This is an indication of the subtle distance placed between Carro and 2010 official commemorations and an assertion of his autonomy. Within this narrative of contestation, provocation, and the activation of a lively cycle, there are blind spots. The most noteworthy of these is the way the war story presented is dominated by male narratives.

Gendering War

The range of films in the *Dos siglos de libertad vistos por el cine* cycle is highly gendered. All but one of the directors are male. The one film by a female director, Marcela Fernández Violante's *Cananea* (1977), is a heavily male-centered fictional account of the formative experiences of one of the anarchist originators of the Revolution. This is a rarely told account of the lead up to the Revolution. Fernández Violante's gender could appear to be mere happenstance because the narrative is so male-centered. However, as I have considered elsewhere (Thornton 2017a), Fernández Violante makes for a fascinating inclusion because she is a paradoxically anomalous and representative figure in Mexican film culture and is further evidence of Carro's use of the cycle to engage with the narration of the national. Fernández Violante often gets overlooked when histories of Mexican women filmmakers are told because she falls outside of the patterns of how other women entered the industry and, conversely, is frequently overlooked when stories of the 1960s and 1970s generation are told because she is a woman. She was the first woman admitted to the director's union when her male peers were choosing not to join. During the 1970s she made studio-based films just as the studios were in decline, and yet, like her male peers, she told different stories to those of the conventional studio films of the Revolution. Her work has been largely ignored, while at the same time her male contemporaries were making films with a similar focus and aesthetic sensibility outside of the studio system and theirs have been lauded. As a filmmaker whose work has been supported through national film funds and university financing, her films are easily sourced at the

Cineteca. But this does not fully explain her inclusion. In this film, her presence is significant because the stories she tells are uneasy explorations of foundational moments and figures. Yet, *Cananea* is about two opposing male characters, which means that her gender may have influenced the stories she chose but does not cause a significant irruption in what is a predominantly male cycle.

There is one exception to the absence of female-centered narratives, *La soldadera/The Female Soldier* (1966) a little studied film by José Bolaños starring Silvia Pinal, an actress whose work has spanned seventy years (1949–present) and has ranged across genres and media. In *La soldadera* Pinal plays Lazara, a woman who falls in love with a Federal soldier and follows him into battle. He is killed and she takes up with a soldier from Pancho Villa's army, finding herself having to cope with the challenges of being a soldier's companion. The *soldadera* figure has been vilified and mythologized, but it has seldom been given feature-length treatment and it merits inclusion in a film cycle dealing with the Revolution (see Mendieta Alatorre 1961; Soto 1979; Slaughter 2010). Therefore, this film is exceptional among films made during the 1960s and 1970s, but it is not unique across Mexican film history. A studio superproduction costarring María Félix and Dolores del Rio, and cowritten by José Bolaños, *La Cucaracha/ The Soldiers of Pancho Villa* (Ismael Rodríguez, 1958) also tackles the experiences of the *soldadera*, but is a good example of the type of film excluded from this cycle.

None of what Deborah E. Mistron (1984) has described as "Revolutionary melodrama" are included in this selection, despite being the majority of films made about the Revolution. The fact that many of the popular studio films of the 1930 through 1950s are owned by private television corporations, in particular Televisa, is a factor in this selection. However, the absence of other films by or about women suggest that choosing female-centered narratives was not at the forefront when Carro curated this cycle. This was confirmed to me in an interview with Carro (Thornton 2011). His approach is about a perceived meritocracy and value combined with a need to draw in an audience. It is his contention that since the popular studio films can be seen regularly on television, his selection of films are those that are more difficult to source. Market demand, availability, and licencing do not tell the full story of what is left in or out of this cycle; tastemaking is key. Carro as tastemaker is drawing on a long history of privileging male directors and male-centered narratives about the Mexican Revolution.

There are serious implications for women directors when they are excluded from such retrospective curation structured around narratives of national formation. Their stories and creativity continue to be sidelined and women are missing from a vital historical moment. Primarily male directors are given the valorization that is accrued through curated cycles. Carro has power as a tastemaker because he is at a national institution. While the choices are his, his tastemaking is reflective of wider patterns within Mexican scholarship of whose stories are granted significance. The gaps are not because the films do not exist—there are films that fit with Carro's selection. The gaps reflect a consistent devalorization of women filmmakers. The story of this cycle is gendered, favoring male filmmakers and male narratives.

There was space for the inclusion of female-centered narratives or films by women as some male directors had several films selected across different historic events or within the same period, or both. This is the case with two of de Fuentes's trilogy of films about the Revolution, *El compadre Mendoza* (1933) and *¡Vámonos con Pancho Villa!* (1936), as are two of Bracho's films, one about the Cristero rebellion (1926–29), *La virgen que forjó una patria/The Saint That Forged a Country* (1942), and the second about the brutal struggle for political power in the aftermath of the bellicose phase of the Revolution, *La sombra del caudillo* (1960). If there had been a concerted effort to include more than one film by a woman, there are plenty to choose from that still fall within the parameters that appear to be in place. Given the emphasis on two distinct periods of filmmaking (the Golden Age and the *Nuevo cine* generation) films that could have been screened include a seldom-exhibited film by Matilde Landeta, *La negra angustias/Black Angustias* (1949), set during the Mexican Revolution or, another by Marcela Fernández Violante, *De todos modos Juan te llamas/General's Daughter/Whatever You Do It's No Good* (1975), a film about the Cristero rebellion. Landeta's work has been recuperated in recent years; as I have mentioned, she is the one woman with a screen named after her at the Cineteca. This is an indication of the value placed on her by the institution, and yet she was not deemed worthy of inclusion in this cycle. Such suggestions are put forward merely to highlight how a greater gender awareness could have resulted in a wider representation of women. Other films exist both within and beyond the parameters of taste evident in Carro's selection.

The exclusion of women in this way is not unique to Mexican curatorial practice. In 2018, there was a protest by eighty-two women working in film at the Cannes Film Festival representing the eighty-two women whose work has been put forward for the Palme D'Or over its seventy-one-year history, the foremost award at the festival (Women and Hollywood 2018). This compares to 1,688 men. Therefore, the paucity of women or women-centered narratives as part of the Cineteca's commemorative cycle is indicative of a wider malaise in festival curation. In the Mexican context, it is also reflective of the omission of melodrama, a mode most associated with a particular type of excess and often linked to surface pleasures and the glamour of stardom. The star-filled films of the Golden Age have been dismissed as mere extravagant romances that use the Revolution as a convenient backdrop (see García and Aviña 1997, 79). Carro's choices are in keeping with this approach. Another neglected period is the 1980s and 1990s when there was an upsurge in films directed by women who sought to address grand narratives in new modes. Films such as *Entre Pancho Villa y una mujer desnuda/Between Pancho Villa and a Naked Woman* (Sabina Berman and Isabelle Tardán, 1995) sought to reflect on how cultural nationalism ignores women's stories. Such exclusions or oversight is reflective of a tendency to overlook women as subjects of war or as creatives capable of telling war stories, and it reveals much about Carro as a tastemaker and the tastemaking context at the institutional and national level.

Conclusion

The cycle is a festival curated by a singular tastemaker set within a particular national context and provides an opportunity to explore how the analysis of festivals can be extended through understanding tastemaking practices. The paradigms used for the analysis of film festivals are helpful in understanding small sequences and curatorial practices that consider how the festival can act as curator of national commemorations. Film festivals are often narrowly defined closely following the model of the so-called A-list, such as Venice, Cannes, Toronto, and Berlin. These provide significant opportunities for filmmakers and producers to market their work or garner publicity for their offerings. Such annual global marketplace gatherings have been well studied. What are neglected in this field are the event festivals that coalesce around a theme or historical commemoration, which are usually more local in flavor. Examining the *Dos siglos de libertad vistos por el cine* cycle helps complicate this picture of what programming means more broadly and how curation operates in the light of the national 2010 commemorations of the centenary of the Mexican Revolution. From September to November of that year the national film institute presented a film series that included a canonical selection of mostly male Mexican films alongside a number of international films that touched on similar themes, an intersection of the national and the global. Festival theory presupposes a global and highly mobile audience of journalists and critics. Thus, the national focus of such an event provides new insights into local curation and tastemaking that intersect with festival aesthetics. When the national event draws on the international, it provides a new attention on the local. The analysis of the cycle has potential to comprehend its function as a storytelling tool because in its entirety it gives a more heterogenous account of Independence and Revolution than any single film could.

The cycle provides an opportunity to focus on a single node in a complex intersection of taste and tastemaking practice. It is the outcome of the labor of a single tastemaker whose curatorship draws on a wider context. Taking the commemoration as the moment of analysis allows space to consider cycles and film festivals as a vehicle for narrating the nation. As a narrative thread the Revolution is more than the local versions; it is placed in an international framework through the strategic decisions of a tastemaker. In a deliberate tastemaking strategy, the story of the nation is told through national, transnational, and international films. The curated cycle invites interrogation and analysis of whose stories are valorized through inclusion. Studying cycles expands the definition of what a festival is, contributes to rethinking programming as a form, and challenges the narrow understanding of caretaker bureaucrats.

At the Cineteca curatorial practice in the film cycle has been built on an ever-evolving national narrative by a thoughtful bureaucrat navigating academic, audience, and institutional understandings of cultural value. More than "simple warehouses of the past," Mexico's institutions have long indulged and financed contestatory positions, and how they do so on each occasion is worthy of comment (García Canclini 1995, 116). These decisions become tastemaking.

The events commemorated suppose certain challenges. They are commemorated physically and architecturally through monumental buildings, in the naming of streets, buildings, and metro stations, and in annual events on key dates. Where there are hundreds of films about the Revolution the selection becomes highly meaningful and reveals much about the biases and hierarchies of value placed on film by Carro and the Cineteca, which are informed by scholarly film culture. Carro's tastemaking is an instance of how individual decision-making illuminates and nuances national and institutional historiography. His programming evidences how "the curator is someone who insists on value, and who makes it [value], whether or not it actually exists" (Balzer 2015, 26). Carro's choices form taste and are informed by the taste of others. But, more importantly, his careful curation demonstrates how a selection of fifty-six films can prompt and provoke, allow space for reflection and consideration, and provide a simultaneously iterative and dialogic understanding of events that can seem closed and overdetermined. His is a fascinating engagement with national, international, and transnational films that articulate a polyphonic story of Revolution and Independence that opens up new readings because of this and yet is narrow because of his gendered selections.

Given the scale of commemorative activity surrounding events that were grand in scale and have been grand in impact, focusing on one individual's curatorial practice provides a way into understanding a wider context. Carro as a tastemaker is a scholar with a cinephile's approach to film and its culture. Demonstrating a deep and extensive knowledge of Mexican and global cinema enabled him to curate a cycle that acts as a wide-ranging commentary on Independence and the Revolution. Unraveling the nuance and significance of Carro's curatorial process, with its contingent mix of autonomy and institutional responsibilities, is a way of understanding tastemaking as practice. The gaps in the cycle are subject to practical issues, such as availability and permissions, but also to his and the contextual tastemaking network he inhabits. As a tastemaker whose decisions must fit with institutional demands and carry external expectations from scholars and audiences, Carro makes selections with care and consideration that reflect his own biases and assessments. The overrepresentation of male filmmakers and male stories and the dearth of women creatives and women-centered narratives are an example of this. Understanding his tastemaking becomes an act of discovery and a way into comprehending a wider field. Carro and the 2010 film cycle *Dos siglos de libertad vistos por el cine* is an example of how a single tastemaker can be a window into a broader film culture.

Chapter Two

Commonplace and Routine

Amat Escalante's Extreme Realism
in *Los bastardos* (2008) and *Heli* (2013)

Auteur directors are tastemakers. Variously hailed and reviled as they circulated at the prestigious international film festivals and arthouse cinemas, Amat Escalante's first two feature films, *Los bastardos* (2008) and *Heli* (2013), explore structural and physical violence. Using elements of the horror genre with realist aesthetics, violence, when it happens, does so at a pace that appears mundane, sudden, and, therefore, simultaneously banal and shocking. The mixture of the slow and the shocking gives the victims of violence agency and invites reflection on the consequences of such brutal actions on all involved including those committing these acts. Escalante's films explore the terrible consequences of a form of violence that is supported by transnational actors and which co-opts the young to partake in it. In *Los bastardos* and *Heli* Escalante demonstrates his fluency in prestige filmmaking, employing slow cinema editing techniques and paying careful attention to sound and music. The violence is manifold and sonically nuanced. Clearly attuned to arthouse taste and the artistic symbolic capital of the film festival that is valorized by tastemakers, such as Nelson Carro (examined in chapter 1), Escalante pushes at the edges of what is acceptable in his representation of violence perpetrated by men in prestige arthouse cinema in ways that have been acclaimed and rewarded. There is a gendered inflection to how this violence plays out differentially against men and women. Excessive, because his representation of violence is hyperrealist, and reflective in his use of the techniques of slow cinema, both films require a careful understanding of the relationship between gender, representation, and prestige cinema. Drawing on his press interviews and examining the techniques he employs, I propose that he is a countertastemaker who deliberately employs prestige cinema and pushes against its taste boundaries This chapter considers what hyperrealist violence in a prestige production suggests about tastemaking and explores the relationship between points of view and aestheticized brutality in Escalante's work. Using videographic criticism in order to unpack the detail in the uncomfortable realm of hyperrealist violence, it will explore where to place work that is often contentiously read as residing in the boundaries between high- and low-value tastemaking.

Therefore, central to this analysis is prestige, a term used by Bourdieu (1993, 113–16) to describe high-value cultural capital that an object or work accrues as a consequence of an inherent quality attached to it. Prestige is a slippery term that has evolved, changing as the canon is disputed and challenged, and can be difficult to categorize at this present moment when there has been little consensus over what constitutes good and bad taste. Markers of esteem, through awards and inclusion in festivals with symbolic, cultural, and economic capital, result in prestige. But, as Colleen Kennedy-Karpat and Eric Sandberg (2017, 4) state, "prestige is the heart of a . . . systematic cultural trick designed to conceal an absence of reality. The concept of prestige thus carries within itself a recognition of its intangibility, its impermanence." If taste is difficult to pin down, prestige as higher order taste is even trickier. I use prestige to refer to work that is granted prestige through external validation, not as an inherent value. In this chapter, prestige is to be understood as the recognition conferred on Escalante's work through awards and inclusion in A-list festivals, and the aesthetic choices he makes in order to appeal to these. This chapter considers prestige as a tentative label because it relies on external validation rather than inherent qualities, all the while still being determined according to codes, tropes, and aesthetic techniques that Escalante, as a tastemaker, is playing with and pushing against in his films. Underlying his tastemaking practices is the privilege that his gender affords him to navigate prestige film.

Amat Escalante: Prestige Filmmaker

Amat Escalante was born in 1979 in Barcelona, Spain, but grew up between Guanajuato, Mexico and the US, spending his late teens in Austin, Texas. He has a primary attachment to Guanajuato, which he either references in his films or uses as a location. Escalante worked as assistant director on *Batalla en el cielo* (Carlos Reygadas, 2005) and, subsequently, has been mentored by Reygadas, an auteur whose work has been well received and distributed through these same international circuits (see Shaw 2011 and Paz 2015). A director with considerable cultural capital thanks to critical and festival reception, Reygadas has leverage in the field and produced Escalante's first three feature films. This form of apprenticeship to a prominent male auteur gave Escalante considerable cultural capital through access to prestige festivals.

Escalante's debut feature *Sangre* (2005) and *Los bastardos* (2008) were shown as part of Un Certain Regard at Cannes, a mark of prestige, as discussed in chapter 1. Un Certain Regard is a curated selection of twenty films that the festival committee consider to "have an original aim and aesthetic, and are guaranteed to make a discreet but strong impact on screens around the world" (Frémaux 2019, n.p.). Further evidencing the prestige attached to his work, Escalante received the best director award at Cannes in 2013 for *Heli* (2013) and the Silver Lion for best director at the 2016 Venice Film Festival for his horror film *La región salvaje/ The Untamed* (2016). These high-value awards at A-list film festivals all mark him as a high-status filmmaker who attains international arthouse distribution for his work.

This reading is bolstered by Escalante's self-presentation as an auteur. Such framing is evident in interviews when he is speaking about his work and through comparison to other male Mexican directors who, like him, since the late 1990s/early 2000s primarily make films in Mexico with an eye to the international film festival and arthouse circuits. These include auteurs, such as Reygadas, as well as other such contemporary male directors as Michel Franco, Fernando Eimbcke, and Alonso Ruizpalacios (Solórzano 2017 and Matheson 2018). Escalante shares Reygadas's tendency to place his work in this field of transnational male auteurs rather than market it through Mexican or US multiplex distribution networks. Although Escalante's films are either set in Mexico or have a significant Mexican narrative concern there is not a large market for arthouse film or a robust independent distribution network in Mexico (see Mantecón 2013; MacLaird 2013; Sánchez Prado 2015; Tierney 2018). Therefore, aiming at the transnational prestige arthouse circuit has been the most financially viable option for the style of films he makes. In addition, as I will discuss, while Mexico-centered, his films reference global arthouse cinema rather than national cinema.

Escalante has written and produced all of the films he has directed and his other credits include editing on *Sangre* and *Los bastardos*. This is evidence of an auteurial approach to filmmaking and has led to him being described as having a "distinctive filmic voice," which Kristy Matheson (2018) has identified through an aesthetic consistency including "the use of non-actors, muted colour schemes, direct shooting style, minimal cutting and bursts of violence." For the Mexican film critic Fernanda Solórzano, his intellectual concerns are "violencia, impunidad, machismo, corrupción—no como un espectáculo sino buscando recrear el clima de esa realidad" (violence, impunity, machismo, corruption—not as a spectacle but as an attempt to re-create the atmosphere of that reality) (2017). These are all large issues that Solórzano identifies as national in scope with a focus on realism.

Despite the validation he has attained through prestige circuits, Escalante is a filmmaker who is as yet understudied and lacks substantial critical assessment. This chapter focuses on *Los bastardos* and *Heli*, because they simultaneously draw on prestige filmmaking techniques yet, when they were screened at festivals, they divided audiences because of the hyperrealism of the violence, which has been variously read as excessive or authentic, subject to the critic's understanding of Mexico. Drawing on the groundwork laid out in chapter 1 on the film festival aesthetic and using audiovisual criticism, this chapter explores how Escalante's films share an aesthetic approach with slow cinema filmmakers that is hyperrealistic, durational, and concerned with authenticity, in order to propose that this provides victims of violence with agency and subjectivity. In this regard and building on the conceptualizations of Sobchack (1984), Sontag (2003), and Butler (2009) of how lives should be apprehended and given subjectivity, it considers how Escalante's approach can be framed as ethical tastemaking.

Los Bastardos: Good/Bad Victims

Escalante (Matheson 2018) explains that the locations for *Los Bastardos* were inspired by James Benning's documentary *Los* (2001), a film composed of thirty-five two-and-a-half-minute static shots of the greater Los Angeles area. Drawing on this slow observational style, *Los bastardos*, which was also filmed in Los Angeles, has been described as "una historia lenta, elíptica, de poco diálogo y escasa explicación" (a slow, elliptical

Figure 1. Slow cinema inspired by James Benning in *Los bastardos*.

story with little dialogue and limited explanation) (Lie and Mandolessi 2012, 111). The film is concerned with twenty-four hours in the life of two undocumented Mexican workers in Los Angeles, Fausto (Rubén Sosa) and Jesús (Jesús Moisés Rodríguez), dwelling on the banal details of a day that culminates in tragedy.

It opens with their journey on foot to a corner where they and others wait to be picked as laborers. It observes their day's work preparing foundations for a house and follows them as they walk through the park to drink and while away the time after work. While there they receive racist abuse from a group of white youths. They initially walk away only to return later when only one of the youths is left sleeping off the effect of alcohol. Implicitly, they enact revenge. In this scene they are filmed from below, with Fausto holding a sawed-off shotgun and looming over the perpetrator/victim, whose point of view we share. Although there are some hints in the dialogue that they have plans for their day beyond the construction work, this is the first visual confirmation that they are disposed to violence.

Without revealing what they do to the youth, violent action is implied through a hard cut. This cuts to a change in location to a mother, Karen (Nina Zavarin), preparing food for her monosyllabic teenage son, Trevor (Trevor Glen Campbell), in a bland suburban home. Trevor has dinner and leaves to hang out with friends. Karen takes down a hidden stash and smokes heroin. This activity is intercut with Fausto and Jesús making their way to this middle-class Los Angeles suburb, having been paid by Karen's ex-husband to scare Karen. Jesús and Fausto break in as

Karen slumps in a drug-induced stupor watching television. What follows is a series of quietly ambiguous incidents where Karen's consent in the action is unclear. They smoke heroin with her and swim in the pool. Jesús performs a sex act on Karen, during which her passivity is left open to interpretation. While tense and ambiguous in tone, the low-key drama of these incidents is disrupted in the final minutes of the film. Fausto and Karen watch television in the sitting room and Jesús snacks in the kitchen. Fausto calls out that he is bored and wants to leave. While Fausto and Karen sit on the sofa, watch television, and smoke heroin, she notices that he is distracted and moves to grab the sawed-off shotgun on the coffee table. Her opportunity to revenge the home invasion and assault is denied. He picks it up and shoots her. Her death is hyperrealist and gruesome. Fausto's apparent motivation is his vulnerability at having been emotionally moved by the reality television cop show they were watching. He goes to vomit in the bathroom while Jesús cleans his ear, which is bleeding as a result of the sound of the gun. Meanwhile, Trevor comes home, grabs a snack and shortly realizes that his mother is dead. He shoots Jesús on finding him in the bathroom. Fausto escapes through the window, runs down the road, slows to a trot, and walks away as it becomes clear that no one is pursuing him. The film ends with Fausto arriving at a farm to pick strawberries. As he starts to pick the fruit the camera slowly zooms in on his face and his attempt to hide tears by covering his eyes with his T-shirt.

Through editing, emphasis is placed on the mundane elements of Fausto and Jesús's day—walking, working, eating—giving less time over to the violence. At times, it is implied rather than shown. While there are moments of emotional intensity and action, the film is marked more by "el carácter más bien inexpresivo de la actuación" (the inexpressive nature of the action) (Lie and Mandolessi 2012, 112). Nadia Lie and Silvana Mandolessi (2012) compare *Los bastardos* at plot and audiovisual level to another prestige film, *Funny Games* (1997) by the Austrian auteur Michael Haneke. They provide a substantial list of common aesthetic and narrative elements including long takes and the use of static cameras; sudden bursts of high-energy music, which they categorize as violent; correspondences between mediatized televisual violence and what happens on-screen; and the recurrence of the color red (Lie and Mandolessi 2012, 113). They also identify a type of "extraña solidaridad resignada entre los perpetradores y su víctima" (strange resigned solidarity between the perpetrators and victims) over the course of the narrative (Lie and Mandolessi 2012, 114) that "borrando la inicial oposición entre buenos y malos para convertirlos a todos en 'víctimas'" (erases the initial opposition between good and bad rendering them all "victims") (Lie and Mandolessi 2012, 116). Therefore, Karen's death, with its shocking force and visceral impact, is indicative of the gendered nature of structural violence.

Los bastardos uses the aesthetics of prestige cinema to create an ambiguous identificatory position. Where the home invaders in *Funny Games* seem to be rich disaffected psychopaths with no apparent motivation beyond a mixture of boredom and malevolence, Fausto and Jesús in *Los bastardos* are hired by Karen's ex-husband as workers; thereby, he has outsourced his emotional and violent labor. Fausto and Jesús are not identifiably "bad." Their motivations may even be interpreted as "good." This job is more lucrative than their day shift and may help pay for medical care for a family member alluded to in the dialogue. This means that Karen's harassment and subsequent murder is motivated by contrasting impulses: her malicious ex-husband's financial capacity to outsource labor and Fausto and Jesús's caring responsibilities and virtuous intentions. Yet this does not lessen the impact of the violence nor absolve them of responsibility; instead, it renders Karen's suffering, her son's distress, Fausto's trauma, and the unplanned murder all the more tragic.

This assessment is supported by Escalante's stated aim:

> I didn't want to make something about Mexicans as victims or showing only one side of the situation. The inspirations are just the feelings I had of how it felt being in the United States, the landscapes, the marginalisation of not being able to speak the language, isolation and this clash of cultures. These guys (Jesus and Fausto) are there to find comfort, to find warmth; the house serves as a metaphor for the United States. (Matheson 2018)

Escalante is foregrounding his awareness of filmic representations of Mexicans as either victim or villain, thus framing his work as serious and reflective filmmaking. Similarly, his description of the source of inspiration for the title of the film as coming from his lived experience as a bicultural migrant with a primary affective attachment to Mexico suggests an intentional ambiguity: "Cuando te vas a otro país extrañas mucho al tuyo, y lo idealizas. Te sientes huérfano porque no tienes madre patria. Fue mi experiencia, y también de ahí viene el título" (When you go to another country you miss your own and you idealize it. You feel like an orphan because you don't have a motherland. That was my experience and the title came from that experience) (Solórzano 2017). In addition, he extends the possible interpretation of the title to other, less privileged migrants, such as those portrayed in the film, as well as suggesting that it could be open to multiple other readings: "Los 'bastardos' podrían ser los migrantes, la estadounidense a la que secuestran o su esposo. Podría ser quien sea. Gente cercana a la producción de la película dudaba si debía llamarse así porque es un nombre agresivo, pero la película también lo es. Su violencia viene de su ambigüedad" (The "bastards" could be the migrants, the US woman who was kidnapped or her husband. It could be anyone. People involved in the production of the film doubted whether it should be called that because it's an aggressive title, but so is the film. Its violence comes from its ambiguity) (Solórzano 2017). There are shifting identificatory positions in the film and little is explained, which reinforces this sense of ambiguity.

Violence, Ambiguity, and Arthouse Prestige Cinema

The absence of a definitive bad guy character means that in *Los bastardos* the blame lies elsewhere, on wider structural issues within the Mexican state that disenfranchises marginal subjects. Lie and Mandolessi identify *Los bastardos* as representative of a shift in the representation of violence from "sus antiguos agentes (El Estado, el sujeto criminal)" (its former agents [The State, the criminal element]), to more pervasive forms, whereby "las fronteras entre los buenos y los malos se borran y la violencia se hace inescapable" (the lines between good and bad are erased and violence is inescapable) (Lie and Mandolessi 2012, 117). *Los bastardos* is part of a new tendency in Latin American film, which sets out to critique structural violence, such as that of the Argentine film *Carancho* (Pablo Trapero, 2010) that also employs European arthouse techniques evident in work by Haneke (see Lie and Mandolessi 2012). Such analysis chimes with that of Sayak Valencia (2018) and underpins Escalante's attested aims, which is to portray a new form of violence that is pervasive and, for a distinct majority, unavoidable.

As a consequence, *Los bastardos* invites reflection on the causes of violence, but "los responsables se vuelven 'invisibles,' están 'fuera de escena,' su estatuto es incierto, sus móviles inaprensibles" (those responsible become "invisible," they are "offscreen," their status is undefined, their movements indescribable) (Lie and Mandolessi 2012, 118). Although violence is made visible through the actions of the characters on-screen, it is clear that there are factors beyond their control that influence the characters' behavior.

Lie and Mandolessi (2012, 118) also pinpoint a key concern I share about these films on the nature of identifying who is responsible for committing the violent acts, that is, whether the pervasive nature of these forces renders them invisible and beyond critical understanding. This is a question that Escalante addresses in a 2017 interview with Fernanda Solórzano in the Mexican cultural journal *Letras Libres*, when he suggests that he would not make *Los bastardos* now during the presidency of Donald Trump because it is not a time that allows for nuance or ambiguity regarding identificatory positions. For him, the film invites the audience to shift between identifying with the home invaders and Karen in ways that require an audience with sufficient cultural capital and a contingent liberal worldview to be able to read it correctly (Solórzano 2017). Ambiguity is a marker of taste and value that can undermine a film's political message as well as complicating it.

Nonetheless, ambiguity is a significant feature of global art cinema and identifies *Los bastardos* as high-value filmmaking. Extending David Bordwell's analysis of art cinema, Rosalind Galt and Karl Schoonover (2010, 16–17) suggest that ambiguity in art cinema results in a "hybrid form that allows realism and modernism to co-exist within one text" and is "a composite mode, a rubric that is able to yoke together disparate modes of expression and, hence, may be uniquely equipped to address equally incommensurate modes of experience and engagement." Escalante's insistence on ambiguity, his aesthetic concerns, and his attention to lived reality throughout his interviews is his way of inserting his work within consistent trends in recent global art cinema. As a consequence, his work invites comparisons with prestige productions and established filmmakers. He engages in tastemaking practices that harness high-value aesthetics, but his approach to violence challenges a comfortable reconciliation with "good" taste, as I will discuss. He continues this mode in *Heli*.

Heli: Routine and Commonplace Torture

Heli was shot in Guanajuato, central Mexico, a state Escalante describes as peripheral and conservative (see Bautista 2016 and Marric 2017). *Heli* tells the story of a young factory worker, Heli (Armando Espitia), and his family who become victims of extreme violence and have to live with the traumatic aftermath. Heli lives with his wife, Sabrina (Linda González), their baby son, as well as his sister, Estela (Andrea Vergara), and their father, Evaristo (Ramón Álvarez). Twelve-year-old Estela is seeing a seventeen-year-old young special forces army recruit Beto (Juan Eduardo Palacios). Beto finds a stash of cocaine and asks Estela to hide it in the water tank at her family home for a day until he can find a buyer. Heli finds and destroys the drugs. The army raids the house looking for their drugs, kills Evaristo, and dumps his body in wasteland. They take Beto and Heli to a house in an informal settlement to be tortured and they take Estela away to a separate location. We do not discover her fate until later in the film. What follows is a sequence that divided many reviewers, as I will discuss, and is why Escalante's work fits uneasily within paradigms of taste. Beto is killed and hung from a bridge, and Heli is left on the walkway seriously injured. Meanwhile, Sabrina returns home to see the house in disarray and splattered with blood. Heli returns home, is taken in by the police and questioned. They try to coerce him into implicating his father. He refuses and continues to do so when he is taken into police custody repeatedly. His recovery from his physical and psychological injuries is slow. He returns to the car factory where he works, makes mistakes, and is fired. In addition, the trauma has affective consequences at home, Sabrina and Heli are shown, at times, to be tense and violent and, at others, caring and tender toward each other. After doing all that is in his power to find her and after the police tells him that her case has gone cold, Estela returns home, pregnant, traumatized, and unable to speak. She draws a map of where she was sequestered. Heli seeks out the cabin where Estela was held and kills the man he finds there. In the closing sequence of the film Heli and Sabrina have sex while Estela and the baby sleep peacefully in the next room. This suggests that there is potential for a positive future, albeit tainted by all of the trauma that has preceded it. The ending is highly ambiguous because Heli and his wife have no significant source of income, Estela is still traumatized, and the justice Heli has enacted has strong potential to provoke a revenge attack. There is a little space for optimism, but it may be short lived.

The torture sequence is the most commented upon of this film and is where Escalante's representation of violence lays bare questions of taste in relation to prestige filmmaking. In spite of the political intent integral to his filmmaking, neither the durational nature nor the ambiguity with which Escalante imbues the violence in his films is always well received. After its Cannes premiere, at which he won for best direction, the press reviews for *Heli* revealed a common thread. In otherwise positive reviews the extreme nature of the violence is emphasized. For example, Mark Kermode (2014) in the *Guardian* describes it as "harrowing and often unbearably grim," while A. O. Scott (2014) in his review for the *New York Times* states that it "is at once extreme and unspectacular, a grisly and lurid slice-of-life drama." Similarly, in her succinct and largely negative review for the *New York Post* Farran Smith Nehme (2014) states that "the torture is supposed to be unflinching and bold, but it's just deadening. The real unflinching truth is that an average newspaper reporter can do a more artful, compassionate job with a drug-war story than this movie does." What all of these reviews signal is their own preoccupation with assessing how authentic the film is and whether it matches their understanding of Mexican reality. That is, their tolerance of the torture is based on how authentic it is, not with how graphic it is. Kermode and Scott, in this instance, believe it to be difficult but worth enduring because of its realism, while Smith Nehme is disgusted because it does not measure up to her expectations. A question that Smith Nehme's review prompts is about the nature of audiovisualized torture and why the fact that it is deadening is a fair criticism. It is deadening. Rather than a failing, its slowness is the precise point. It eschews the spectacular, and through slowness makes torture something to be endured by the audience.

In contrast with Smith Nehme's suggestion that it is unrealistic, when describing the negative reaction to the torture scene Escalante emphasizes its realism:

> Cuando la película provocó esa reacción allá sentí una especie de decepción. Si eres de México, o de cualquier lugar donde pasan tales atrocidades, es difícil no sentirte responsable. Habla de cosas que ves en la calle o que le están pasando a gente cada vez más cercana a ti. Por eso quise tocar el tema. (When the film provoked that kind of reaction I felt let down. If you are from Mexico, or anywhere else those sorts of things happen, it's difficult not to feel responsible. It shows things that you see in the streets or that are happening to people close to you. That's why I tackled this theme). (Solórzano 2017)

The challenging aspect of the torture sequence is the slowness of what is done to Beto and Heli through the use of long takes and the shifting points of view. Intentionally challenging to audio-view, its slowness creates discomfort that makes it demanding to sustain looking and listening.

There is critical consensus about how difficult the torture scenes are to watch, but little consensus on their value. Escalante makes recourse to his own Mexicanness as a source of authenticity, contrasting it with outsiders' miscomprehension. In order to sidestep any such claim to insider/outsider readings and to fully comprehend its detail, I have used videographic experiments in Final Cut Pro X to carry out close textual analysis on the torture sequence. Although already slow, I edited the sequence by cutting the image up and isolating the perpetrators' activities and the shots of the victims; it facilitates a more attentive looking and listening to points of view.

In the room, there are three adults, three children, and Beto and Heli. There is only one master shot halfway through the sequence. For most of the sequence, Beto is either unconscious or in extreme pain, so his point of view is never taken up. Given the busyness of the action and its disturbing nature, the wide shots on the body of the individual being tortured are privileged in the reviews and analysis of this film. Lasting over six and a half minutes, the torture sequence is composed of long static takes intercut with reaction shots of those in the room. Less durational than the reviews or, indeed, the sensation of audio-viewing this sequence suggest, there are fourteen cuts in total and two pans. When Beto is being tortured it cuts to Heli, the men on the mattress, and the children. Heli looks away, clearly disturbed, and one of the children plays a handheld console, whereas the others do not divert their gaze. Our point of view is either as a seated onlooker in the room tilted up as if looking up at Beto or Heli's body, or standing, which is likely the point of view of one of the torturers. When we are invited to take up the perpetrator's point of view it can muddle the message of the film. In *Heli* the constantly shifting point of view is about making us uncomfortable and inviting us to consider our responsibility for these crimes. Videographic criticism reveals point of view and the real time or actual rather than experiential duration.

The torture is carried out with routine efficiency clearly by people for whom this is a commonplace activity. In his assessment of the significance of *Heli*, César Albarrán-Torres (2017) emphasizes both the mundanity and the banality of the labor involved in this torture scene: "The hitmen act monotonously, like slaughterhouse workers who kill on a daily basis." This is conveyed through minimal dialogue and a coordinated series of effortless movements. On arrival in the room two men tie up and gag Beto and Heli. The mise-en-scène is limited to a television on which three children are playing video games, a long sofa, and a mattress. The children move to the sofa without being told by the adults, which is evidence of how habitual this activity is in this space. There are three men in the room and a woman is occasionally seen in the background through a door, apparently preparing food. When not involved in the action, the men sit on the mattress smoking out of what looks like a crack pipe or casually sit on the sofa drinking beer, observing the activities and joining in the taunts. At first, two men hang Beto off a hook on the ceiling and take turns hitting him with a bat until he loses consciousness, and then set his genitals on fire. Using homophobic slurs, they goad one of the children to hit Beto in what is clearly a form of apprenticeship for continued involvement in this form of labor. Once the flames subside, they throw Beto on to the floor and hang Heli from the hook and beat him. They stop short of burning him, because it is not a prescribed part of his punishment, but he is clearly also seriously injured by this beating.

Videographic criticism facilitates a shot-by-shot analysis and a further slowing down of the action. By removing the shock of the sequential effect through cutting it up into its discrete shots and removing the soundtrack allowed a shot-by-shot analysis. Looking closer rather than looking away reveals that this sequence is shot using long takes and the editing, while minimal, is used to emphasize the acts of looking by onscreen characters.

For Escalante, the long takes and minimal editing were deliberate ways of making the experience durational and true to life: "Siempre me ha interesado mostrar el lado de las cosas que no solemos ver, sin editarlo. De ser posible, que los únicos cortes sean los parpadeos. Alguien puede decidir taparse los ojos, pero también puede descubrir qué pasa si lo ve representado sin glamur." (I always want to show the side of things that we don't normally see, without editing. If possible, the only cuts are the blink of an eye. Anyone can decide to cover their eyes, but you can also find out what really happens if you watch it shown to you without glamour.) (Solórzano 2017). There is a suggestion in his comments that there is an indexicality to his realism that is emphasized through a form of editing that focuses on looking and seeing something hyperrealistic. These are all techniques privileged in slow cinema. Slow aesthetics are integral to this tastemaking practice and aesthetics.

Slowness, Ethics, a\nd Point of View

In his pick of the top 10 films of all time for the British Film Institute (BFI) Escalante nominated two slow films, *Jeanne Dielman 23, Quai du Commerce, 1080 Bruxelles* (Chantal Ackerman, 1979) and *Landscape Suicide* (James Benning, 1989), indicating that his choices "are the ones that influenced me the most at an early age and shaped the kind of filmmaker I want to be" (2012). Where most other films on his list get brief annotations—for example, Luis Buñuel's *Los olvidados/The Young and the Damned* (1950) is limited to metonyms of its oneiric and sexual elements, "the chicken, Meche and the milk"—the two slow films get more detail (Escalante 2012). He describes *Landscape Suicide* as "so haunting and affecting. I saw a 16mm projection of it when I was 16 years old. It has become part of my subconscious for sure." *Jeanne Dielman 23, Quai du Commerce, 1080 Bruxelles* "deeply impressed and influenced me" (Escalante 2012). These selections give an insight into the sort of filmmaker he has become. He mixes long takes of the mundane and banal with unexpected action that he de-dramatizes through slowness, thus playing with the durational experience.

Although slow cinema has predecessors, such as 1950s modernist filmmaking, 1960s durational cinema, and 1970s feminist experimental film, it is a new "moniker, appropriated as it is to describe a still-in-the-making and shifting canon" of art cinema that has grown from the mid-1990s up to the present day and is privileged by awards at film festivals (de Luca and Jorge 2016, 3). In part, as Escalante has acknowledged, this growth has been the result of developments in digital technology (Solórzano 2017). However, what this periodization also reveals is the simultaneous and interrelated emergence of other slow movements that critique capitalism. Unlike one of the best-known examples of these, the slow food movement, which produces manifestos, creates archives, and has a coherent political agenda (see slowfood.com), slow cinema has no such consistency or unifying principles. What it shares with these other slow movements is a consciousness of slowness as "a mode of temporal unfolding and as an awareness of duration" (de Luca and Jorge 2016, 4). As a political mode of filmmaking slow cinema can be a means to "actualise and negotiate conceptually different temporalities and competing visions of time" (de Luca and Jorge 2016, 15); it can also be a way of focalization on time as endurance. In his analysis of Béla Tarr's aesthetics of slow cinema, Jacques Rancière (2016, 248) explores how Tarr's shots take "too much" time, "their length always exceeds what is required to select the visual elements which make the story intelligible." He adds that Tarr's use of the sequence shot "embraces too little space. It introduces the viewers into a space that cannot be embraced from a privileged point of view" (Rancière 2016, 249). Similarly, Escalante frequently takes too much time indulging in an excess of slowness as a means of reflecting on the ethics of the perpetrator/victim point of view.

Revealing his discomfort from the absence of a privileged point of view in the torture scene in *Heli*, César Albarrán-Torres suggests that "Escalante bears witness to this hideous act in a fly-on-the-wall, almost detached manner. The camera stands back as executioners and victim share the dehumanising intimacy of violent death" (Albarrán-Torres 2017). This assessment ignores how the detachment is disrupted, if we attend to the shifting points of view and the multiple cuts in this sequence. Escalante does draw attention to temporality through the long takes and minimal editing in the torture sequence, but this does not mean that there are no cuts that disrupt an easy identificatory position.

The slowness of the sequence has ethical implications. Separately analyzing documentary and fiction film, Julian Ross (2016) and Asbjørn Grønstad (2016) reflect on the ethics of slow cinema. For Ross (2016), in the documentaries he analyzes the aim is to narrow the distance between the subject and audience. His case studies are documentaries about serial killers whose crimes have been sensationalized by the popular press, *AKA, Serial Killer* (Adachi Masao, 1969) and *Landscape Suicide* (James Benning, 1989). The aims of these landscape films are relational, "slowness creates an opportunity for sharing a durational experience with their audience" (Ross 2016, 262), and the aesthetics are ethical, "long takes, stationary camera positions and the de-dramatised sense of motion in these images allow space for contemplation by the audience to reach their own conclusions" (Ross 2016, 265), where the salacious details of the popular press had blocked identification between subject and audience. The analysis of Benning is salient with regard to an analysis of Escalante's filmmaking given that he has cited him as an influence on more than one occasion and explicitly stated that the wide shots of *Los bastardos* are inspired by Benning's *Los*. *Heli* is a similarly significant film because, like *Landscape Suicide*, it counters the dramatic tabloidization that is familiar in representations of drug-related violence and invites us to consider the commonplace and routine experience of traumatic death.

In his analysis Grønstad asserts that slow cinema is "inherently political" (2016, 277), but may not be innately ethical. He places a similar emphasis to Ross on the experiential and affective response to slow cinema: "it nevertheless provides a condition of possibility for intrinsically ethical acts, such as recognition, reflection, imagination and empathy" (Grønstad 2016, 274). For Grønstad, slow cinema "spatialises duration and thus it makes something invisible visible. By evacuating all but the most infinitesimal action from the frame, by bracketing inaction, what the extreme long take visualises is the passing of time itself" (2016, 275). The emphasis in these analyses is on realist cinema that in its durational de-dramatization can be hyperrealist and require the audience to endure long shots with little action. The durational regard of the blood and flesh splattered aftermath of Karen's murder in *Los bastardos* is intentionally uncomfortable. The slowness of the torture sequence in *Heli* is in keeping with the pace of the rest of the film, which means that we have been primed to expect it to last longer than is comfortable. Necessarily, it is the nature of what we are seeing that makes it deeply uncomfortable coupled with the slow unfolding of the aftermath of the traumatic experience on Heli and his family.

Editing: Rhythm and Eye-Trace

Heli opens on a medium close shot of an unidentified man's bruised and beaten head being held in place by an army boot. His mouth is gagged with duct tape. Also in the shot beside his head there are two feet belonging to someone else, one with a dirty sock on and the other bare. From the soundtrack and the texture of the surface underneath the man's head it is evident that they are on the flatbed of a heavy all terrain truck. Given the army boot on the man's head, there is a suggestion that it could be an army vehicle, or at least a boot worn by someone associated with it. After forty seconds the camera tilts upward, showing the rest of the man's body in the back of the truck and out through the front windscreen between the driver's shoulder and that of the front seat passenger, resting there until they reach their final destination, the bridge. This means that from a potentially neutral observational position the camera movement and the duration invite us to consider the point of view of this shot. Although it is not clear at this point because there is no master shot of the truck, as the narrative continues and when the sequence is repeated later in the film, it is evident that the point of view is that of one of the men in the truck who is implicated in the violence. On arrival one of the men is carried from the truck and hung from the bridge in a way that is a part of the visual communicative strategies of those involved in the recent violence in Mexico (Campbell 2014 and Valencia 2018, 162–64). He is only partially clothed, his trousers are around his ankles, he has considerable bruising and other scarring, and falls as a dead weight with no apparent struggle. Therefore, he has died before being hung. As the truck drives away, the camera occupies the point of view of one of the men in the truck, thus implicating us in this crime. This is underlined through slight camera movement caused by the men getting back on the truck. The truck drives away with no apparent urgency down an urban road with unremarkable markings and signposts. The complete opening sequence lasts exactly four minutes.

Pace and point of view play a significant part in this opening sequence of *Heli* that establishes the tone and its ambiguous identificatory position. It is a sequence that is repeated with some variation later in the film. To understand this repetition and variation, I want to turn to the editor and sound designer Walter Murch's *In the Blink of an Eye: A Perspective on Film Editing* (1995). He suggests that there are six criteria to consider when editing: emotion, story, rhythm, "eye-trace," "two-dimensional plane of screens," and "three-dimensional space of action" (1995, 17–20). For Murch, emotion is the hardest to define yet has primacy over the others. He attaches percentage importance to each subsequent feature on the list in descending order. While all of these have a bearing on the cuts in this sequence, the editing choices favor rhythm and eye-trace. Murch (1995, 18) describes the rhythm of a cut as one that "occurs at a moment that is rhythmically interesting and 'right.' " The editor of *Heli*, Natalia López, stretches the moment to a point that makes the sequence uncomfortable to watch and bends, rather than breaks, Murch's criteria. The sequence does not lack emotion, but it is given lesser emphasis over rhythm and eye-trace.

In order to understand these repeated sequences, I placed them side by side in Final Cut Pro X, thus allowing a clear understanding of similarities and differences in the edit. The second version takes place later in the film after the torture sequence when it is now clear that the head under the boot is Heli's and the dead man is Beto. This time it lasts two minutes and eleven seconds. The shot in the truck is flipped by 180 degrees with Heli's head on the left hand of the frame and Beto's feet on the right. These differences defamiliarize a shot that was familiar because of its duration in the opening sequence. In the second sequence, the point of view of the truck driving away is that of Heli on the bridge, or possibly Beto. Although a high angle is usually one of power or domination, because it takes up the position of a dead or severely injured person this point of view sets up the sense of fear and tension that dominates the final third of the film. According to Murch's proposed model, the rhythm of these sequences are off, insofar as they create a sense of unease and estrangement as well as drawing attention to the ambiguous point of view. This eschews a clear identificatory position or clear emotional signaling. In the service of the story and to establish the tone of the film these cuts are "right" because they do it clearly at the opening and later in its second iteration.

The cut also "acknowledges what you might call 'eye-trace'—the concern with the location and movement of the audience's focus of interest within the frame" (Murch 1995, 18). In these repeated sequences, through eye-trace and duration in the first, López and Escalante invite us to speculate on whose bodies these are and who the perpetrators are who caused them to be in this state. In the second sequence it is clearer who the perpetrators are and that the two victims are Beto and Heli, and we are conscious of the violence we have just witnessed enacted upon them. The scale of those involved in this chain of events is also made evident. These men in the truck are neither the soldiers who kidnapped Beto and Heli nor the torturers. The full horror of Beto and Heli's injuries have been revealed and it prompts us to recall the awfulness of how Beto's body is displayed in the opening sequence, which is repeated in the second from a different point of view.

As a trope in films about the recent violence in Mexico tortured and disfigured bodies on display have become so commonplace that mainstream films such as *Sicario* (2015) by the French-Canadian director Denis Villeneuve have hanging people as part of their mise-en-scène as if they were simply décor to incite fear in the US visitors or metonyms for the generalized barbarism south of the Mexico-US border. A transnational film that had considerable global success, resulting in a sequel, *Sicario: Soldado* (Stefano Sollima, 2018) displays hanging men in ways that demonstrate a lack of understanding of the codes that are employed by the *endriagos*, that is, the workers who carry out the labor of gore capitalism (Valencia 2018, 63–65, discussed in the introduction) and, more egregiously, uses the men's bodies as elements in the mise-en-scène that allude to how disposable and lacking in subjectivity Mexican lives are for the filmmakers. In *Sicario*, the first experience of Mexico for the protagonist, Kate Macer (Emily Blunt), is a horrorscape full of danger and threat. Ominous drone music by the Icelandic composer Jóhann Jóhannson accompanies Macer and the team as she is driven in one of a convoy of secure military vehicles through a largely derelict space and past bodies hanging from a bridge. In reality, the public displays of these cadavers are a deliberate "semiotics of violence" with a "*signature* specific to each mafia organisation" and to each supposed transgression of mafia rules (Valencia 2018, 154, 162–64, italics in original; see also Franco 2013). In *Sicario* the hanging people are objects without subjectivity and are only meaningful in the threat of violence to those moving through the space. The message is that key characters could become victims of similar fates, but those on display have potency only as symbols of terror (see Albarrán-Torres 2017). It is an instance of repeating the codes of the cartel as a semiotics of terror without acknowledging the humanity of those murdered. In contrast, in *Heli*, showing the hanging first as a slow and meditated act that forms part of the labour of the perpetrators, then repeating it in a defamiliarized fashion enacted upon a character we have come to know, counters the use of the body as mere propaganda and shows the consequences of this violence on those who witness and experience it.

Hanging has its particular semantics in the context of the recent drug-related violence in Mexico. Those who have written about it have highlighted its use as a spectacle with specific signification and associated signaling (see Franco 2013 and Campbell 2014), yet there is little written about what it means to look at the hanged person. In order to understand what happens when the hung person, normally denied its agency, is given back its subjectivity through an ethical act of looking, it is useful to turn to Courtney R. Baker's work on images of lynched black lives in the United States. Clearly, the public torture and murder by hanging of the individuals Baker discusses carry distinct meanings because their lynching "ritualizes and performs white racial dominance" and are specific to a particular cultural context (Baker 2015, 37). Commonality can be found in the hanging individual used as a spectacle that is intended to be looked at by others as a warning and assertion of power over others. When hung in a public space, victims can be robbed of their subjectivity and become a mere spectacle in their death if we do not recognize "certain bodies as human" (Baker 2015, 67). Escalante's slow approach works to recognize these as people, invite reflection and positive affective correction, and foreground the perpetrators' and lookers' shame. Looking at the hanging person evokes "an imagined community of fellow onlookers." When presented in a thoughtful manner, this is an attempt to counter simple propaganda or dehumanization, which has the potential to proffer "an identification of what constitutes the unacceptable treatment of a human being, starting with an identification of the unacceptable treatment of *this* human being depicted here" (Baker 2015, 104, italics in the original). Baker's (2015, 51) "*this*" is about subjectivity and agency and acknowledges that these are individuals who can return the look. In *Heli* the focalization and emphasis on the hanging man is about simultaneously establishing and destabilizing the point of view as well as reminding the audience of their looking and the individual's look. It also presupposes our horror at a hanging person because its banal and slow rhythm presents a violent act assumed to be extreme and unpacks its mundane nature. A side-by-side comparison of the points of view and duration of these sequences, like the slow shot-by-shot analysis of the torture sequence using videographic criticism, facilitates a close understanding of the controlled editing that pushes at the edges of high-value taste and prestige filmmaking.

Speaking about the action and shot length in *Los bastardos*, Escalante explains his intention behind using duration as a mode of filmmaking:

> I want to challenge the viewer, get them to a point where you almost want anything to happen because the tension has been so high. The shots were quite long and I was conscious of this feeling, of wanting the shots to be over, then the explosion happens. This idea of showing [the shooting], I didn't imagine it as a provocation, but I wanted people to jump, to feel like you're on a roller coaster. (Matheson 2018)

Working alongside the Turkish editor Ayhan Ergürsel on *Los bastardos*, Escalante pushed the tension so that the violent action of Karen's shooting was both a form of relief and shocking in its realism. In part, this is as a result of the camera positioning. We observe and hear Trevor return home and go to the kitchen for a snack in the background of a wide long shot that has Karen's body and her splattered remains on the sofa and the wall of their sitting room. This focuses on the consequences of violence rather than the drama of the action. Rather than follow Trevor's decision to pick up the gun and find the murderers, there is a hard cut to Fausto and Jesús in the bathroom. When Trevor shoots Jesús we see his blood and hear the shot before we see Trevor standing in the bathroom holding the gun. Each cut is a blink.

The question of focalization and blinking are central to Murch's discussion of editing: "in film—a shot presents us with an idea, or a sequence of ideas, and the cut is a 'blink' that separates and punctuates those ideas" (Murch 1995, 62–63). As mentioned earlier, in collaboration with his editors, it is Escalante's deliberate strategy not to create a blink; instead, he generally uses deliberately long takes that require the audience to create those cuts either by blinking or looking away. When he breaks Murch's ideal blink cut it makes the film sometimes difficult to endure (for example, in the torture sequence in *Heli* or the shooting in *Los bastardos*) and is an invitation for the audience to create their own meaning through duration.

Videographic experiments make clear that Escalante does not always stick to the same pattern in editing. In the repeated sequences just discussed in *Heli*, in its first iteration the cuts are minimal. There is no cut in the shot of Beto and Heli on the bed of the truck; instead, the camera pans up until they get to the bridge. The cuts happen when the camera is positioned outside the truck following the men carrying Beto and Heli onto the bridge and then back onto the truck. This follows the action. In the second iteration the shots are considerably shorter and do work as blinks moving us through the events with differing perspectives and points of view. Blinking and not blinking are used to alternate between action and movement and focalization. The moments to be endured are those to be reflected upon, providing the time to consider our point of view in the narrative.

In these films slowness invites reflection and an affective response. For some critics this made *Heli* unbearable because it demands looking at brutal assaults carried out as part of a mundane daily enterprise. This is not violence for pleasure. Even those committing it appear to carry it out as routine labor, work that requires relief from it through intoxication. The violence is more random and impulsive in *Los bastardos*, but its affective consequences are also heavily felt. It is clear that the two teenagers, Fausto and Trevor, will carry the weight of the murders as trauma. Rhythm and eye-trace humanizes the victims and perpetrators of violence. Slowness may have a reality effect, but if we were to encounter this reality we may wish to look away from these scenes and we may also want to cover our ears.

The Sound of Slow Violence

In the analysis of slow cinema visual aesthetics are privileged. Shot length and editing are the most salient features that recur in the literature as does a sparse mise-en-scène and minimal action (de Luca and Jorge 2016, 5).

This emphasis on visuals can be found in Lie and Mandolessi's (2012) analysis of *Los bastardos* where they do mention music, but not the other elements of the soundtrack. Reviewers of *Heli* react to what Lisa Coulthard calls the "unwatchableness" of the violence, thereby foregrounding their disgust at the excessive time spent observing the violence (Coulthard 2016, 183). Sound is either ignored or limited to music in these assessments. In her analysis of over 100 violent scenes in film and television, Coulthard challenges this sole focus on visual disgust and discusses the significance of sound in eliciting audience responses toward violent scenes. She considers the "sonically unbearable: acoustic disgust" that has "the potential to create a kind of violent revulsion in the viewer, attaining an affective and sensation-based impact beyond that of the violence depicted" (Coulthard 2016, 183–84). Coulthard has found that there is a tendency to use "overwhelming music cues" whereby "diegetic sound is eradicated entirely" in such scenes (Coulthard 2016, 184).

Escalante employs such musical and sonic cues, but also takes a different approach to those studied by Coulthard. In *Los bastardos*, in the moments immediately preceding Karen's shooting, Fausto tries to switch off the television using the remote; frustrated, he kicks the television, thus silencing it. He stands, taking a beat, and aims the gun at Karen, while Jesús looks on through the door frame. Fausto then shoots Karen, takes another beat, slowly places the gun on the coffee table, and goes to the bathroom to throw up. The only sound accompanying this is ambient diegetic sound. Rather than using music or effects to amplify this moment, Escalante allows the fact of Karen's killing, the visual effect of her remains splattered behind and around her body, Jesús's shock, and Fausto's reaction to dominate this scene.

The lack of extraneous music or sound effects is deliberate in a film that earlier had used music to dramatic and disruptive effect. For example, Jazkamer's Nordic death metal track, "The Worms Will Get In," used over the opening credits, has a sudden and impactful chord played on an electric guitar with a sustain and feedback pedal that gives it indeterminate duration. Trevor is introduced as he loops the high-tempo hardcore techno track "Ecstasy Motherfucker" by the Venezuelan musician KID606 on decks in his bedroom. In a videographic experiment in Final Cut Pro X, I cut these uncomfortable scenes and separated out the sound and visuals. I experimented with the effect of using music because, as Coulthard indicates, it is most conventionally used to heighten the "sensation-based impact" in such scenes and its absence was notable. Using only the music on the soundtrack because it fits with the characters and the tone of the film, I synced up both of these tracks alongside these two killings. Neither track worked with Fausto's killing of Karen. His steps are too awkwardly slow. He moves unevenly and with reticence. There is little deliberation to his actions. After the shooting, Fausto and Jesús move with little urgency. This mitigates against using either of these tracks. The first is too ambient and droning, almost devoid of a distinct rhythm, while the second is too fast paced and high tempo. Syncing the KID606 track alongside Jesús's blood spattered on the bathroom mirror against the sound of the gunshot works rhythmically and as a leitmotif for Trevor as if announcing his appearance mere seconds before we see him. It communicates Trevor's anger and confusion as well as the urgency with which Fausto leaves the house and the neighborhood. This experiment is not about determining the ideal music choice as much as it is about exploring the alterations music makes to the tone and mood of the sequence as well as what emerged through their juxtaposition. Neither experiment augments the film; instead, they detract from the quiet emotional isolation of these individuals and indicates why Escalante chose to use ambient sound rather than music in these scenes.

The ambient sounds of a quiet house in a suburban neighborhood dominate the soundtrack after the shooting, which emphasizes the awfulness of the violence in a commonplace domestic setting. The overturning of the television, the subsequent violence, and the quietness of the aftermath is an implicit critique of mediatized violence, according to Escalante: "En *Los bastardos* quise que la violencia en la pantalla realmente llegara al sofá de una casa" (In *Los bastardos* I wanted the television violence to literally bring it home to the sofa) (Solórzano 2017). The quietness accompanying slowness is used deliberately to focalize on the violence and its consequences on those involved as a form of tastemaking.

According to Coulthard, sounds of the body being wounded "can be over-amplified or incongruous, turning the human form into object, thing, or mass by an act of violence," adding that "the sound of the body itself, its materiality and moisture is where sonic disgust thrives" (2016, 185). Technological innovation has facilitated this shift toward sonic disgust in cinema. In their continued attempt to emphasize the banality of this activity, by avoiding the objectification of the tortured bodies, in *Heli* Escalante and his sound designer Sergio Díaz opted for a dull sound effect for the bat hitting against Beto and Heli's backs combined with their muffled screams as they are being tortured. Instead of foregrounding the sounds of torture, equally dominant in the mix is music from the video game the children had been playing (now on pause in the background) and the dialogue between the men. Their dialogue is a mix of a well-rehearsed script delivered in a flat tone, issuing threats, homophobic taunting, and phatic exchanges about drink and drugs. Mixing the horrific and the banal at similar levels has an equalizing force and renders torture a part of their everyday soundscapes.

De-Dramatized Violence: The Tedious Labor of Torture

In *Los bastardos* and *Heli,* when the men sit they convey the tiredness that is a result of the labor of this violence. They have to self-medicate with drink and drugs to inure themselves against it and are training up a new generation to take their place. All this detail nuances the practices and routine nature of this violence and its consequences. Rather than being a way of exonerating the actions, it goes some way to explicating the process and machinations that make such horrific violence possible. Abused by the soldiers when they dropped off Beto and Heli, these men are highly disposable and are clearly on the lowest end of the hierarchy of the drug trade. *Heli* reveals the hyperspecialization of the work that is integral to the multilevel organization of the drug trade (Valencia 2018, 146–54). The violence is an enactment of the numbing nature of this latest iteration of neoliberal capitalism as it manifests on the border between the US and Mexico. According to Sayak Valencia's analysis, the torturers are examples of the "new proletariat of violence" she calls the "gore proletariat" (2018, 160), laborers required to enact extreme violence in routine fashion. Given that the torturers are different men from those who hang Beto off the bridge, there is an implication in the film that what is captured in this scene is one of many incidents of this sort of torture that they will inflict. Beto and Heli are but two of several people they will torture on a given night. By pausing on the torturers as well as the tortured and de-dramatizing the audiovisual effect of the sequence, Escalante portrays how all levels of this trade is de-humanizing to perpetrators and victims.

There is a gendered nature to this violence. These are men inflicting pain and training the next generation of boys to continue this labor. The only woman in the frame during the torture sequence is carrying out the traditional domestic work of preparing food. The video game that the boys play and that continues to drone in the background of this sequence can be read as related to their apprenticeship as torturers. Through the game and the everyday violence they witness and participate in they are receiving their training as part of the gore proletariat. This rank within the hierarchy of the multilevel workforce is the one available to these men and boys, but it is not glorified. Given the despondency of the men carrying out the torture and the need they have to self-medicate through alcohol and drugs, there is little hope of escape from this form of labor.

Both sonically and visually the videographic experiments reveal that the torture sequence is much more nuanced and muted than is typical for violent scenes (see Thornton 2020b). The slow pace, ambiguous points of view, and realist violence make *Heli* a challenge to watch and resulted in negative responses on its release. What this style achieves is to humanize the victims and perpetrators and explores the consequences of violence across many layers of society. Both *Los bastardos* and *Heli* lay bare the consequences of labor in societies that have no duty of care toward workers other than to make them productive and to discard them when they fail to match that promise.

The affective responses the techniques in these films elicit, such as shame and disgust, reveal elements of what Jeffrey Sconce (1995, 374) describes as a "paracinematic sensibility" in Escalante's approach to filmmaking. In his knowing evocation of excessive emotional responses his films pose intentional challenges to an elite conceptualization of taste. Adapting Sconce's (1995, 380–83) discussion of "counter cinema," a term he uses to describe films that draw on excess in practice and aesthetics in a deliberate and self-conscious fashion, I propose that Escalante's approach is a form of countertastemaking. Employing the codes of high/low art, there is a dualism taking place in *Los bastardos* and *Heli* through the collision of excess and slow cinema that appeals to the prestige marketplace. Combining slow contemplation with the sonically unbearable of the torture scene simultaneously appeals to an elite stylized tastemaking and disruptive excessive tastemaking. In addition to these aesthetic practices, the performances in the films sit in a liminal space in between style and excess, making them integral to Escalante's countertastemaking.

Another indicator of Escalante as countertastemaker are the ways he reflects on violence in his films. He asserts that he makes films that are provocative, but he clearly distinguishes his style from those that are merely gratuitous:

> No me interesa mostrar cosas "shockeantes"—[el] internet está lleno de eso y ahí puedes encontrar cualquier imagen

que busques—. Prefiero recrear la violencia en la imaginación. Creo que la violencia se experimenta de una forma personal y profunda—es una sensación que te invade todo el cuerpo—y que el cine no expresa eso. Muestra mucha violencia, pero solo como herramienta o como valor de producción. He querido explorarla desde otro ángulo. [I am not interested in "shocking" display—the internet is full of those sorts of images, if you care to look for them. I prefer to prompt the audience to imagine the violence. I believe that violence is experienced in a profound and personal way—it's a feeling that invades your whole body—and cinema cannot express that. Films show a lot of violence, but only as a tool or an aesthetic approach. I wanted to explore it from another angle.] (Solórzano 2017)

Escalante comprehends the limits of cinema's ability to portray realist violence and aims to provoke a response from the audience. In his films violence is consciously structured so that it does not induce "meaningless sensation" (Charney 2001, 48) and, instead, directly addresses violence as experienced structurally and personally by the disenfranchised majority world in the global south and by those marginalized by capitalism in the minority north. He states, "I think [that] what I've been addressing throughout my movies is where violence comes from, where hate and rage come from" (Matheson 2018). The culpability for this violence lies not with good or bad characters on-screen, whose motivations for their actions are ambiguous, but with everyone: "Nadie [en la pantalla] es culpable porque todos son culpables. Y como es difícil señalar a un solo responsable resulta más sencillo culpar a quien sea. Por eso en *Heli* no hay un 'malo.' Me interesaba más mostrar un sistema podrido desde adentro" (Nobody [on-screen] is to blame because we are all to blame. As it is difficult to identify who is responsible it becomes easier to place the blame at random. For that reason, there is no "bad guy" in *Heli*. I am more interested in showing a system that is rotten to the core) (Solórzano 2017). Escalante uses ambiguity as a deliberate strategy that aligns him with a particular strand of prestige filmmaking akin to that of the Thai filmmaker Apichatpong Weerasethaku, mentioned in chapter 1, that deploys arthouse aesthetics and pushes at the edges of the audience's tolerance for violence and disgust. Escalante as countertastemaker is as an insider invited to present his work at festivals at which he receives mixed critical responses because of his approach to violence.

Conclusion

Escalante uses audiovisual techniques that are observational, durational, and encourage ambiguous interpretation. In his description of his directorial style he reveals his approach as hyperrealist: "I would like to become invisible when I'm making a movie, I don't want to be reminding people that me in-particular made it. I want people to get lost and forget maybe that they are even watching a movie" (Matheson 2018). These comments, and his references to documentary as a source of inspiration, all suggest that Escalante is aspiring to create an authentic realist portrait of contemporary Mexico. Despite these protestations, it is clear that Escalante in particular did make these films. He has developed a consistent aesthetic and stylistic approach that is common to prestige auteurist filmmaking. The salience of the films lies in his deliberate deployment of global arthouse conceits with its attendant cultural value.

As a prestige filmmaker, Escalante employs identifiable features of contemporary arthouse cinema such as slow cinema techniques, including minimal editing and endurance, all to convey a realist portrait of violence. If arthouse cinema is a genre with a relatively narrow audience, it is one that has potential to explore violence in ways that other well-established genres may not. This is not an appeal to the singular power of an elite form of culture over more commercial forms. Such narrowly defined fields of production should be challenged at every turn. What it does is consider how the arthouse can be a privileged site allowing for experimentation that places a high demand on the audience. However, as evidenced from the reviews and analysis of his films, within this field Escalante has had mixed responses, in part because he has pushed at the edges of what is deemed good taste in the representation of violence and tested the appeal to this audience.

Realist extreme violence can be ethically and politically attuned, as Escalante demonstrates in *Los bastardos* and *Heli*. The violence that is shown is graphic, lacking individuation, and challenges the audience's endurance. Karen in *Los bastardos* is assaulted and then killed on impulse by hired hands with no apparent prior motivation. Beto is murdered and Heli is tortured as part of a rolling cycle of violent enactments by a vertically disintegrated flexible workforce. Through the slow observation of and quiet listening into violent scenes, Escalante induces disgust and aversion that form part of an aesthetic approach that asks questions of the capacity of high-value techniques to interrogate wider sociopolitical issues. My videographic experiments facilitated a close audio-viewing of these challenging sequences. By laying bare the banal nature of this violence through durational pacing and subtly shifting points of view, Escalante invites reflection on the source of and responsibility for the violence, and the labor involved in its enactment. There is capacity in the use of fast-paced techniques and genre filmmaking to demand more from the representation of the tragic deaths and injuries caused as a result of the illegal drug trade. He mixes prestige cinema aesthetics and those of low-value cinema. Slow cinema aesthetics, which Escalante combines with quick cuts and edits, facilitate high-value tastemaking amid low-value extreme violence, making him a countertastemaker. Counter is understood as operating within a site of male privilege that is celebrated by film festivals and those who value experimentation with rhythm, duration, and genre. Escalante's gender facilitates his success, but does not guarantee it, as can be seen in the films examined in chapter 3.

Chapter Three

Reversioning and Thick Contexts
The Cinematic Adaptations of *Los de abajo*

Adaptation is tastemaking. Choosing a source text ascribes value and prestige to the novel and film within a hierarchy of value. To adapt is to translate from one medium into another with attendant suppositions about quality depending on the value attached to the author, auteur, or creative teams involved. There is still some tendency within adaptation studies to privilege the novel because of the origins of the field in literary studies, but this is shifting because such suppositions ignore how unstable measures of quality are and how dependent they are on taste. When they are adapted texts evolve, shift, and are rescripted according to the context that produces them. Therefore, it is better to think of them as moving from version to version.

 I consider adaptations of *Los de abajo* (1997)/*The Underdogs* (2015) because they allow for new reflections on tastemaking through adaptation. In the Mexican school curriculum, it is a novel that is firmly established as part of the canon, as evidenced by the multiple commemorative talks and activities that took place for its one-hundred-year anniversary, and yet it is highly unstable and lacking a fixed source text. Originally published in serialized form in 1915, redrafted and published as a novel in 1920, then adapted twice to film in 1939 and 1976, its fluidity allows space to rethink adaptation as reversioning and to consider how tastemaking has determined how these versions are read. Subject to tastemaking practices in the literary field, on its publication the novel was lauded as a realist testimony rather than as a literary account of the Revolution. Although later acclaimed for its literary merits, it sits uneasily within the conventional frameworks of high/low work. Neither film was included in Nelson

Carro's curated film cycle. Largely ignored as texts, these versions invite side-by-side videographic criticism to help nuance and map out cinematic adaptation.

The novel *Los de abajo* by Mariano Azuela is a narrative of derring-do, drama, and pathos. Demetrio Macías, a peasant farmer, leaves his wife and child and gathers a band of unlikely soldiers from among his neighbors, impelled by a shared desire to fight injustice. Inspired by his leadership, his troop grows to become a force of considerable size that moves through the countryside on its way to the infamous and bloody Battle of Zacatecas (1914) to fight against Pancho Villa and Venustiano Carranza's army. After their success at Zacatecas, Macías and his army become excessive in their behavior: holding debauched celebrations, killing with little purpose, raping women, and looting the houses of the wealthy with little sense of the aims of the Revolution. After these interludes, the war-weary and much depleted troop journey homeward. Shortly thereafter, they are killed in an ambush by the Federal army. Macías is the last to die.

This brief sketch of the plot gives an indication as to why this novel has been an appealing source text for two film adaptations. It also hints at the variables in the film versions. Impelled by the need to protect home and family, Macías rises up the ranks in the army. Initially, he is full of hope that the Revolution will deliver security and land rights for him, his family, and community. Gradually, through encounters with those in power and as a consequence of the brutalizing effects of battle, his idealism fades and his behavior declines. Family, place, and community are consistent concerns in films of the Revolution. While novels of the Revolution tend toward pessimistic readings of the possibility of success in attaining the aims of the Revolution, films tend to be more variable in their optimism according to the period when they were made.

Víctor Díaz Arciniega (2010, 20) describes the early text versions of *Los de abajo* as "deficientes" (deficient), that is, lacking literary merit. This deficiency makes for a productive case study in intertextual flows because it lacks the primacy of the idealized version. The narrative was first serialized in 1915 in *El paso del norte*, a Spanish-language newspaper, while Azuela was living in exile in El Paso, Texas. He redrafted and edited the novel, altering it considerably. *Los de abajo* was published in 1920 in the version that is widely circulated today (Portal 1997, 25). The novel had little critical or commercial impact until a 1924 article by Julio Jiménez Rueda decrying the "afeminamiento en la literatura mexicana" (feminization of Mexican literature) in *El Universal* led to a literary spat that prompted another critic to cite Azuela's novel as an exemplar of "literatura mexicana viril" (virile Mexican literature) (Portal 1997, 25–26). From that moment *Los de abajo* was given the distinction of being the first in what has become a long-standing focus of Mexican novelists and critics, the *novela de la Revolución* (novel of the Revolution).

The range and variety of these novels of the Revolution has led Claudia Arroyo Quiroz (2009, 58) to refer to them broadly as a corpus, thus avoiding limiting the scope of this label and alluding to its always already polysemy and indeterminacy. Within this corpus, *Los de abajo* has been imbued with an auratic quality (pace Benjamin 2002) because of the simultaneity of its publication with the events taking place, which has been read as authenticity. Yet it lacks the singularity of many canonical novels because of its own evolution, mixed reception, and multiple reversioning.

For Marta Portal (1997, 28), *Los de abajo* responded to a need to find meaning in the Revolution and its promises. Its resurfacing in different forms has had a similar function: to understand the Revolution and its contemporary relevance. Before being adapted to film, there was a stage version. Azuela was not happy with this first 1929 attempt, while he approved of the later version in 1950 (Portal 1997, 30). As well as the stage plays, there are multiple translations, at least five into English (1992, 2002, 2006, 2012, and 2015), and two film adaptations: a 1939 version by Chano Urueta, a popular filmmaker of the Golden Age, and a 1976 adaptation by Servando González.* The absence of an urtext complicates analysis, as the source text is not the clearly fixed entity that adaptation studies presupposes, and the films have had their own peculiar histories and aesthetic differences that allow for rich critical analysis.

Therefore, *Los de abajo* bears the distinction of being the foundational text of the Revolution, with all of the contingent critical attention and auratic quality of genius this supposes. By implication and despite the repeated efforts of adaptation theory to argue against such hierarchical thinking (see, for example, Chávez 2016, 135), this relegates the film versions as necessarily secondary and derivative. Yet, when the source texts have their own contingent and rocky history, marked by early oversight, revisions, and

---

*I have chosen the most recent translation of the novel because its choices are infused with a contemporary worldview. The dialogue quoted from the film is taken directly from the source text. As I was working with films without subtitles, and to avoid adding my own translation to the extant versions, I use the 2015 translation of the novel by Ilan Stavans and Anna More.

political agendas, it proves sufficient cause to shift away from top-down analysis of the films' fidelity to a fixed original, because there is more than one potential source text. Therefore, this chapter proposes moving beyond like for like comparisons between the source text and adaptation, because such an approach makes assumptions that labels one as an original and the other as mere copy (Leitch 2007, 6). The multiple sources, versions, and reversionings make such paradigms impossible. Furthermore, this study will go deeper into the texts through a close comparative analysis using videographic criticism as a research methodology, and uncover a new and generative comparison of the 1939 and 1976 film adaptations of *Los de abajo* in order to consider the significance of the contexts in which the many versions of this text were made.

Like Robert Stam (2000, 62), who suggests that adaptation is the process by which "art renews itself through creative mis-translation," I will draw on both translation and adaptation studies in my analysis. With its potentially negative connotation, albeit with a playful intent by Stam, creative mistranslation suggests at intentional error. The adaptation must be bound to some degree by the original, but can allow for the other medium to determine the new form the adaptation takes. To sidestep the negative connotation in the prefix mis- and to fill out the available gaps in his wordplay, a more productive term for my purposes is Kwame Anthony Appiah's (2000) concept of "thick translation," as the eponymous title to his essay suggests. Thick translation is one that is respectful of the grammar and lexicon of both the source text and the target text that should not be literally rendered (Appiah 2000, 419–25). Further, his position chimes with the assertions of Stam (2007), Scholz (2013), and Yau (2016) that ideology must be taken into account when examining adaptations. Building on Appiah, I want to propose that adaptation should be read as thick, that is, it should be considered with reference to its source and target conventions in ways that allow for a nuanced understanding of the context of production of both the source text and the adaptation(s). Therefore, thick adaptation studies as an act of tastemaking requires a careful unpacking of the contexts and production teams involved in the making of each version as well as a careful close reading of the texts themselves.

Origins, Intertexts, and Transformations

Neither film was critically or commercially successful (Tuñón 2011, 63). As adaptations of *novelas de la Revolución*, they are not unique in this regard. As I discuss in chapter 1, few of the hundreds of films set during the Revolution have been granted the prestige of acceptance into what is a select canon. The exclusion of many films from the canon says much about tastemaking, the gatekeepers who determine what is legitimated, and the demands made of adaptations, which is further complicated by the contextual production histories of both films. Analyzing these films can help formulate new ways of reading adaptations as versions that have thick contexts, that is, ones burdened by polysemous historical, aesthetic, and political concerns that deserve careful unpacking.

Ignacio Sánchez-Prado (2016) has drawn attention to the significance of the historical moment at which Azuela wrote the first version of the text. The year 1915 was mid-Revolution at a "moment of ideological undecidability" when the outcome was not yet foreseeable (Sánchez-Prado 2016, 50). Sánchez-Prado goes on to consider some of the changes that took place in the different editions of the novel as it was reedited post-conflict to become the "significantly revised" 1920 edition (50), the most significant of which was the shift in tense from present to past. This alters the immediacy and reportage of the text and resulted in a "change of the novel's 'reality effect' from the experiential sense of the present to the preterit's connotation of established history" (51).

A similar, and almost inverse, shift takes place between the 1939 and the 1976 adaptations. Made during an optimistic political period, the 1939 adaptation employs melodramatic elements, in particular in performance, pacing, and musical accompaniment, to create an affective response that is intended to seduce the audience, make war palatable, and reinforce the nobility of the Revolutionary struggle. In contrast, the pessimism of the 1970s loomed large in the 1976 adaptation, which uses realism and subtleties in performance that are emphasized through longer takes and isolating shots to unsettle the audience and convey the chaos of battle. As I will discuss, all this evokes a present and alludes to a recent past where the Revolutionary ideals are far from attained and underscores the pessimism that can be found in the novel. The 1976 adaptation was made at the height of political tensions by a director whose career was deeply marked by perceived complicity in recent horrific violence.

Clearly, therefore, there are temporal and medial shifts in the novel's publication history followed by reversionings that happen at distinct historical moments in very different production contexts. As novel, plays, and films, *Los de abajo* is a prime example of the type of text that Robert Stam suggests is "caught up in the ongoing whirl of intertextual reference and transformation, of texts generating other texts in an endless process of recycling, transformation, and transmutation" (2000, 66). I call such adaptations tastemaking. This ever-shifting reversioning, which is marked by cultural and political interests, makes *Los de abajo* a fascinating case study in tastemaking that displaces the originary prestige normally attached to a source text and frees the researcher to follow its patterns and traces.

Embedded in the idea of fidelity to an original in adaptation studies is a hierarchy of prestige and value (pace Bourdieu 1993). Up to the 2000s, the field of adaptation studies was bedeviled by the tendency to attempt to map out a value-laden taxonomy where faithfulness to the literary source text is fashioned as an indicator of merit and hierarchy. Although this can still be found in some theoretical analyses (such as, for example, Desmond and Hawkes 2006), the more fruitful approach is to move the focus from "literary texts not as primary sources but as 'intertexts,' one (albeit dominant) of a multiplicity of perspectives, thereby freeing adaptation from unprofitable 'eye for and eye' comparisons" (Cartmell and Whelehan 2007, 3). This is a more fruitful approach in a global overview of cinema's relationship with literature, as it moves from the particularities of privileging one text over another and allows for a more productive teasing out of the multifaceted interrelationship between the two. This is reversioning as tastemaking.

In their preoccupation with taxonomy, John Desmond and Peter Hawkes helpfully address the language of adaptation studies and its fixation with fidelity:

> For the most part, the language of fidelity uses neutral-sounding terms that are buried metaphors or, more technically, personifications.... When a reviewer says an adaptation is "faithful," he or she personifies the film by attributing to it the human quality of loyalty. (2006, 41)

They consider "fidelity" to be a dubious lexical choice that leads to inaccuracies and misdirection. Adaptation studies is a field overburdened by attempts at categorization and labeling. In Desmond and Hawkes's study, they get knotted up in trying to distinguish the forms that adaptations can take through the creation of lists that they recognize cannot possibly be either completist or defining (2006, 86–95). Such is the tension between taxonomies and indeterminacy in adaptation theory that although it is an area marred by "requirements and prohibitions" (Geraghty 2008, 1), it "continues to lack a presiding poetics" (Elliott 2013, 22). In a review of fidelity in adaptation theory and criticism, Casie Hermansson (2015, 147) identifies critics such as Desmond and Hawkes as part of "a growing resurgence of (pro-)fidelity criticism since the turn of the millennium," one that she supports because it is of concern to the reader/audience. This balancing of reader/audience expectations is a focus of many scholars who suggest that despite repeated attempts in the past to ditch fidelity as a paradigm it returns because of the readers' impulse to compare the two (see, for example, Geraghty 2008; Stam 2007; and Yau 2016).

The desire to upend fidelity as a means of evaluating adaptations means that it too often lends to a privileging of the source text in an up-down hierarchy where the film can only ever be an inferior form of "parasitism" (Stam 2007, 7). Stam challenges this by drawing on the poststructuralist "interrogation of the unified subject . . . which fissured the author as point of origin of art" (2007, 9). Thomas Leitch continues along this line and asserts that all reading is a form of rewriting, therefore adaptation is but an "intertext designed to be looked at through like a window on the source text" (2007, 17). With this de-privileging of the source text, it gives agency to the team of people who create the film as tastemakers as well as the audiences who watch it.

Scholars of adaptation studies use discussions of authorship and fidelity as points of departure to propose other ways of examining adaptions. Lawrence Venuti also disavows the "romantic assumptions about authorship" (2007, 26) and uses terms familiar to translation studies, "interpretants" and "equivalence," which allow the critic to look at what lies between the source text and its adaptation while taking into account the conditions of its production (2007, 31–33; see also Yau 2016, 256). This in-betweenness has been proposed by others in different ways. Kamilla Elliott (2013, 36) prescribes "drawing 'promiscuously' on random theories," while Leitch suggests using fidelity as a productive means of thinking deeply about the adaption in terms of "what it leaves out" (2007, 17). Hermansson (2015, 152) advocates Stam's (2000) use of translation as a means of understanding the shift from page to film. Therefore, I want to turn to how this discussion around fidelity in adaptation studies chimes with those in translation studies.

In translation studies, there has been a tendency to write about the primacy of the original text in a fixed hierarchy where the translation is necessarily seen as inferior. This has been countered by critics who challenge the use of the word *fidelity* as containing connotations that are dubious in terms of race and gender. Feminist translation theorists, such as Lori Chamberlain, assert that attention to fidelity, and even the use of such language, "reveal an anxiety about origins and originality, and a power struggle over the meaning of difference" (2002, 93). Furthermore, it can fester and rear an ugly discourse that is as much gendered as racialized. Chamberlain has identified that "translators have worried that the process of translation may violate the purity of the mother tongue, and that bastards would be bred" (2002, 94) and that the translation can be read as "derivative" (2002, 95). In light of the weight of this history, translation has been judged as both lesser and distorted in the process of transference. Just as with adaptation studies, there is a need to move away from the sense of superiority that is ascribed to a source text and to embrace difference and the necessary alteration that happens between languages and the cultural and historical baggage they carry, in the case of text to text translation or the similarly complex alterations that take place from book to film.

In order to convey the impossibility of a pure notion of fidelity in her discussion of the shifts between and across cultures that are involved when translating, Gayatri Spivak suggests that "meaning hops into the spacy emptiness between two named historical languages" (2000, 397–98). The "spacy emptiness" acknowledges that there are two artifacts, for our purposes—in adaptation, the film and the book—and there is an in between where meaning and interpretation can happen. Rather than embrace this interpretive space, the downfall in much adaptation theory is to see filmmaking and literature as belonging to different creative planes. Just as Ilana Dann Luna calls for "lateral readings" that consider "the actual operations taking place in the *process*" in order to comprehend "the cultural value of the final *product*" (2018, xviii, italics in original), close reading opens spaces that thick understandings further inform. With its multiple versions, *Los de abajo* provides challenges as the "spacey emptiness between" carries a thick burden of context, history, and culture.

Falling Out of Taste: Chano Urueta and Servando González

In order to understand why these films have not been included in the canon, it is worth taking a brief look at their biographies and filmographies. Chano Urueta (1904–79) was a genre filmmaker whose career was primarily within the industrial studio system. He occasionally acted in secondary roles and has fifty-five writing credits in a system that often credited the director as a writer irrespective of their involvement, but he is primarily known as a director, having directed 115 films between 1928 and 1974. His career bridged the Golden Age and the later period of low-budget B movies. Aside from films about the Revolution he made thrillers, horror films, and wrestling films with a melodramatic sensibility and with varying success. As was common at the time, several of these were adaptations including *El conde de Montecristo/The Count of Monte Cristo* (1942) and *Aves sin nido/Birds without a Nest* (1943). Highly influential in establishing genre filmmaking in Mexico, his work has yet to receive the critical assessment it merits, with a few exceptions (see, for example, Velázquez-Zvierkova 2018). Therefore, given that genre cinema is deemed low-value work and gets little attention, it is no surprise that his version with its deliberate appeal to popular taste has been overlooked.

Servando González's work has been ignored for entirely different reasons. González began his film career as the coordinator of the Departamento de Documentales de Gobierno (Government Department of Documentaries), a kind of propaganda wing of the government. There, he was responsible for innocuous films such as *Expo 59* (1959), a film for the World Fair held in Brussels, Belgium. It was his later involvement in filming the student movement on behalf of the military on October 2, 1968 in Tlatelolco, Mexico City, when an as yet unconfirmed number of students were killed and disappeared, that looms large in his biography (see *Milenio* 2008). González claims that the fourteen film rolls he shot were confiscated, but this compromised action alienated him from many of his contemporaries and marked his career and the consequent reception of his films (Molina Ramírez 2007, n.p.).

His 1976 version of *Los de abajo* employs aesthetic techniques that conform to prestige productions. It avoids melodrama in favor of a realist approach to storytelling, and the paratextual elements signal attachment to tastemaking institutions. All of these choices would appear to indicate that González's work should have appealed to his contemporaries, who were influential tastemakers. However, this was not the case because he worked for the government filming the student protests in 1968. Therefore, while he claimed ignorance over what was done with the footage, he was unrepentant up to the end of his life for this role. For his contemporaries, filming on behalf of the perpetrators aligned him with the murder of an indeterminate number of students by the army. Such a judgment was heightened because many of his contemporaries filmed or trained students to use cameras to bear witness to the rolling protests that took place in the months leading up to the Olympics held in October 1968. Therefore, for his contemporaries filming was clearly aligned with activism and solidarity with the students, who had been subject to repressive police and army tactics, and González's decision marked him as acting on behalf of a repressive state. As a consequence, his work has received little attention. His version of *Los de abajo* has not been considered alongside the work of his contemporaries because they were the tastemakers who established the early canon of Mexican film through journals, such as *Nuevo cine*, as well as through awards and curated cycles and festivals. All of these functioned as a primarily male network that promoted and helped promulgate each other's work.

These details tell us that neither film conformed to tastemaking assessments. Urueta's was assessed as a low-value production, while González's appeal to prestige high-value taste did not guarantee him a place in the canon. This is because key tastemakers excluded both. Therefore, examining tastemaking is a more useful tool to understand their work than evaluations of taste in considering the two versions of *Los de abajo*.

Videographic Criticism: Differences and Repetitions

As a means of finding my way through the thick and multifaceted layers surrounding these adaptations as tastemaking, I created an audiovisual essay and used videographic criticism as a methodology. Using Final Cut Pro X I found that the placement of the opening and closing sequences of the two films in split screen, fading out or removing the sound of one while I played the other, proved to be the most fruitful means of analysis for this chapter (Thornton 2020a). This experimentation led to close readings of the actors' movements, the lighting and camera work, the sound design, and editing, as will be discussed later in this chapter.

The audiovisual essay is usually descriptive of an end product, a form that allows for the sharing of a creative exploration of preexisting texts and "digitally generating new audio-visual frames" (Grant 2016, 1). Such essays are more than evidentiary outcomes (film and textual accompaniment), they are also a process that is described as videographic criticism, as discussed in the introduction to this book. This chapter is a close textual analysis of the opening and closing sequences of the film using this methodology. These sequences are of the same duration and they begin and end with congruent plot points, which provide an opportunity to compare and contrast the aesthetic and technical choices made by the filmmakers.

Differences and Repetitions

In general terms, both films are episodic in nature just as the source text is, but, where the 1976 film uses continuity editing, the 1939 version uses ellipses, wipes, and fades. This creates clear cuts between the episodes and also harkens back to a silent era of filmmaking. In this way and through the varied performances of the featured actors, there is a temporal discontinuity that is disjointed in the 1939 version. Given the actors' studio approach to the 1976 version, there is a clearer flow and coherence in performances. Analysis of the opening and closing sequences of both films demonstrates how consistencies and variations can illustrate how videographic criticism as a methodology is a worthwhile approach to understanding both versions as thick adaptations.

Beginnings

A close look at the opening scenes of both versions of *Los de abajo* provides a valuable insight into the differences and repetitions in these texts. On first viewing, the 1939 film appears to zip through the opening as if in a rush to establish the narrative and get the action started. The opening sequence of the 1976 film establishes mood and tone, and appears to be considerably longer in duration, yet hits similar narrative markers. In order to get an accurate reading of these establishing sequences, I placed both of these films in a timeline in Final Cut Pro X. At approximately seven minutes' duration, both are the same length from opening credits to the moment when Macías leaves home to join the Revolution. The different styles of performance, musical accompaniment, and other aesthetic choices lead to an impression of very distinct pacing that reveal much about the eras in which they were made and the directorial decisions that were made.

The 1939 version opens with the full credits, as was customary in Mexican film at the time. This is accompanied by a medley of Revolutionary *corridos* performed by an uncredited orchestra under the direction of Silvestre Revueltas. These are jaunty and sweeping choices that "romantiza y dulcifica los avatares de los villistas" (romanticize and sweeten the proxies for Villas soldiers) (Arroyo Quiroz 2009, 60), thereby establishing a light tone that draws on the Mexican audience's familiarity with *corridos* and their association with the Revolution (Mendoza 1954, xiii). This sequence lasts for just under two minutes. Necessarily, then, given that both films cover the same narrative detail and key dialogue over the course of the full seven minutes, the 1939 version has less screen time to cover the same ground.

A revealing split screen in the Final Cut Pro X timeline is an early instance of the thick potential of videographic criticism. Figure 2 shows the 1939 version on the left and the 1976 version on the right. The text on the left credits the union employed by the studio in the film. Up to the 1980s Mexican film was controlled and organized through the craft unions. Workers were not on continuous contracts with the studios; instead, they were employed via these unions. This gave the unions considerable power in negotiations and as employers. Every film of this period credits the main union in this way, revealing a peculiarity of the Mexican industry and establishing the film as a studio production rather than as the work of an auteur. In relation to evaluations of taste, this places the film as one of hundreds for wide international distribution and broad consumption, not a high-value work.

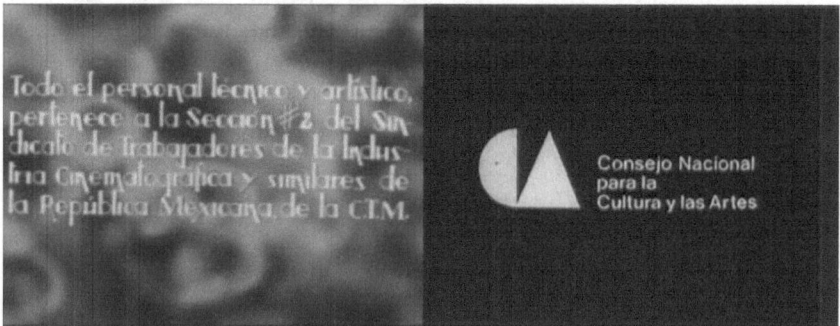

Figure 2. Opening credits (1939, left and 1976, right): The left-hand image reads "Todo el personal técnico y artístico pertenece a la Sección #2 del Sindicato de Trabajadores de la Industria Cinematográfica y similares de la República Mexicana, de la CTM [Confederación de Trabajadores de México]," which translates as "All cast and crew belong to Section 2 of the Union of Film Industry Workers and associates from the Mexican Republic, under the Confederation of Mexican Workers." The right-hand image reads Consejo Nacional para la Cultura y las Artes (National Council for Culture and the Arts).

In contrast, there are markers of prestige production in the opening credits of the 1976 version. At the same point in the timeline, it reveals the evolution in film production history, which was shifting away from a model that was largely dependent on the studios and the unions to one that worked relatively independently of these. There are a number of cultural institutions and sources of government funding named. The national arts funding body, the Consejo nacional para la cultural y arte (National Council for Culture and Art), is given first credit as the principal source of finance for the film. This is the first of three credits that opens the 1976 version, the second for the Instituto Méxicano de Cinematografía, the national film funding body, and the final one stating that this is a film by Servando González. This sequence is significant in several ways. It follows the standard practice of the time, which signals that this is an auteur film with the imprimatur of national funding bodies. González's credit was a risky move given that he was a controversial figure. At the same time, González is conferred with artistic credentials through the explicit support from such prominent named arts funds for this project. The confluence of arts bodies and directorial credit are indicators of prestige, markers that made little difference to its subsequent reception.

The credits for both films are acts of tastemaking. In the 1939 version it is an implicit tell that indicates period conventions and industrial practices of popular films. The 1976 version is a more explicit signaling of prestige and quality and invites an auteurial reading. That neither garnered attention is the consequence of distinct tastemaking practices. This is where the curatorial selections of the *Nuevo cine* group as tastemakers can be found. As discussed in chapter 1, their establishing legitimating legacy can be found in the gaps in the canon. The 1939 version was omitted because it did not match their high-value measures of taste and the 1976 version because of judgments about its director's actions.

In the 1976 version, a lone mouth organ begins to play over the Instituto Mexicano de Cinematografía credit and continues into the first wide shot of the humble house in which Macías (Eric del Castillo) and his family live. The music stops as the camera slowly tracks in on a small crack in a shutter at the front of the house through which Macías can be glimpsed. Lighting is low and the only visible light source in the mise-en-scène is a candle and the open fire. A dog barks. This cuts to inside the house on a close-up shot of Macías eating. His eye movements and rapid blinking indicate that he has heard the dog and that something is afoot. He looks to the left of the frame and there is a cut to his wife

(Regina Herrera; the wife is not named in any of the texts). She looks up from making tortillas, indicates with her eye movement toward the door outside of the frame that she is also concerned that there is unusual activity outside. There is a sound of rope on wood accompanying these micromovements that is soon revealed to be their child's (uncredited) bed rocking to and fro. The baby also looks up as if sharing the parent's suspicions. This is followed by a series of quick cuts from Macías' eyes, his wife's hands making the tortillas, and the dog barking outside, then back to a medium shot of Macías's wife from above. She says, "Te digo que no es un animal. . . . Oye cómo ladra el *Palomo*" ("I'm telling you that isn't an animal. Listen to how El Palomo is barking.") (Azuela 2015, 3).

The opening shot of the house in the 1976 version establishes these individuals as a family unit. The cuts identify them as having agency, but being framed alone also isolates them. Even the baby, who is more akin to a prop in the 1939 film, visible only swaddled tightly in blankets, is established as an autonomous figure whose eye and head movements mimic those of his parents. Like the novel, the wife is the first to speak. Her line is the same as that of the opening of the novel. Through camera, editing, and del Castillo's performance the filmmaker has established Macías as the principal character, with his family as significant characters. The centrality of this family unit as a foundational infrastructure for Macías is clearly established, so the tragedy of its loss is more poignant. The pacing, sparse dialogue, and minimal gestures create tension, allow the audience time to dwell on these characters—especially the mother and child—and their meaning for Macías and, symbolically, their value as subjects in the Revolution.

The 1939 version opens with a medium shot of Macías's wife making tortillas. Her back is to the camera and she turns to speak to Macías, who is out of the shot. Beatriz Ramos delivers the same lines above, with an added "debe ser algún cristiano" ("It must be a person") (2015, 3). The camera pans left to a wide shot of Macías (Miguel Ángel Ferriz) who responds to her "y que fueron siendo federales" ("And what would we care, even if they're Federales?") (2015, 3). She/Ramos moves over to him, holds his arm and says, "Sería bueno que por sí o por no te escondieras, Macías. Tu rifle está debajo del petate" ("You had better hide, Macías, just in case. Your rifle is under the petate") (2015, 3). These lines of dialogue are delivered in quick succession. At the same time point in the 1976 film Herrera delivers the lines, "Sería bueno que por sí o por no te escondieras, Macías" ("You had better hide, Macías, just in case") (2015, 3). In contrast to the 1939 film,

Figure 3. The wife (1939, left, and 1976, right).

she/Herrera pauses midsentence and looks up from her work to Macías/del Castillo knowing that what she is saying could be understood by him as an affront to his manhood. Macías/del Castillo looks at her, looks toward the window, stands up, picks up his rifle, and, in an act that appears to be a means of (re)claiming his masculinity, he cocks it and walks outside. At this point in the 1939 version, the wife/Ramos has gone to the mat, picked up Macías's rifle and ammunition and handed it to him, urging him to go out the door. There is no pause to reflect on what this act means other than a loyal wife protecting her husband.

In the audiovisual essay this is the first time the couples in both films are seen in the same shot. Where the 1939 film suggests unity of intent, the 1976 film alludes to tension and violence between the couple. In the 1939 film the two figures occupy the same amount of space in the visual frame in a wide shot. In the 1976 film the camera is positioned at Macías's/del Castillo's crotch level, he has the rifle on his left hand side and the action is accompanied by a loud sound effect of the rifle being cocked. His wife/Herrera is just visible in the background on her knees, making and cooking tortillas with her head bowed. There is an implicit threat in Macías's/del Castillo's gesture toward his wife that is also alluded to in her posture. Furthermore, Macías/del Castillo is posited as a threat to the intruders outside. In the 1976 version, the separate shots at the opening of the film also allude to how isolated the characters are from one another. Through the audiovisual prominence of the apparently small matter of cocking the rifle, the pauses in the delivery of the dialogue, and the wife's/Herrera's body language, it is suggested that home is not necessarily a place of safety, but potentially one of violence.

The family dynamic in the 1976 version is a radical departure from the 1939 film. There is considerable meaning attached to the home as Macías/Ferriz leaves to fight on behalf of his wife and their child, who are clearly associated with this space. His aim is to protect them and provide a better future. In films and novels set during the Revolution, home is a highly resonant space that occupies an idealized locus for the warrior who leaves it in the hope of return. Deborah E. Mistron has discussed the centrality of the family to the Revolutionary melodrama where the female character embodies tradition and the male Revolution and their union guarantees their stability and that of future families (1984, 52–55). As the locus of this unit, home has considerable resonance. One of the first tragedies of *Los de abajo*—this is more explicit in the novel—is the almost immediate loss of this home. The first chapter ends, describing Macías, "Cuando después de muchas horas de ascenso volvió los ojos, en el fondo del cañón, cerca del río, se levantaban grandes llamaradas. Su casa ardía . . ." (1997, 79) (When, after many hours of climbing, he looked back, he saw huge flames rising at the bottom of the canyon, near the river. It was his house on fire . . .) (2015, 5). This loss is implied in the red sky that profiles Macías/del Castillo in the 1976 film as he goes to gather his troop, whereas in the 1939 film Macías/Ferriz overhears a federal officer tell a cacique that they have burnt his house down. The men are in a two shot and it is unclear where they are situated in relation to Macías/Ferriz, just that he can hear their conversation. This then cuts to Macías/Ferriz and holds for a few beats as sweeping orchestral music underlines the tragedy of the moment. The shadow of death hangs over the opening sequence and its imminence makes the brief insight into the family structure all the more resonant.

The 1939 adaptation was made when Mexican film was experiencing a boom and the Revolutionary film was coming into being as a genre whose parameters as a popular form was not yet fully realized. Fernando de Fuentes had made *¡Vámonos con Pancho Villa!/Let's Go with Pancho Villa*, the last of his trilogy in 1936, which had yet to attain the canonical status it now enjoys, as evidenced in its prominence at the Cineteca's cycle. Other canonical films, such as *Flor silvestre/Wild Flower* (1943) or *Enamorada//A Woman in Love* (1946) by Emilio Fernández, would not be made until the 1940s. Therefore, Urueta's film bears many of the hallmarks of a genre in progress. He draws on generic markers of other forms, most particularly the melodrama, which has family at is center and, as Ramírez Berg (2015) has identified, was a genre that was foundational for Mexican film. The same unevenness in the film can also be identified in this genre in formation.

The analysis of these opening sequences provides the opportunity to follow the ways in which fidelity is a loose concept, one which has much of Spivak's spacey emptiness. In both versions similar elements of the plot are retained, such as the inevitability of Macías heading off to battle and the thematic significance of the family. The violence they portray is distinct and the familial relations are freighted with the context in which they were made. Each version has adapted the narrative, adhering to the aesthetics and political concerns of the time of production, yet these apparent similarities also reveal differences. The tastemaking involved in establishing the tone, mood, and style of the film rests in pacing and performance.

There is considerable scope to draw lessons from the enormous potential of comparative studies of versions and reversioning. More broadly, split screen can be a useful tool in videographic criticism to compare and contrast films by different directors. For example, Cristina Álvarez López uses split screen in her audiovisual essay examining *La Double vie de Véronique* (Krzysztof Kieślowski, 1991) and *Inland Empire* (David Lynch, 2006), describing it as a "poetics of doubling" where "the simultaneous montage of sequences from both films . . . helps us to become aware of striking similarities between the two films, but also offers evidence of the singularities of each director's particular poetics of doubling" (2012, n.p.). A similar poetics of doubling can be found in split screen experiments with the two very different versions of *Los de abajo*. Covering the same plot points and key moments across these versions, the split screen reveals how technological shifts, industry changes, aesthetic turns, and varying performances all result in films that convey subtly and notably distinct readings of the Revolution. My exploration of a reversioning of the same source novel through a split screen comparison and cross-cutting brings up a thick poetics of doubling that evidences shifts in pace and tone in the opening sequences and more markedly political elements in the closing sequence.

Endings

The final sentence in the novel ends with ellipses, "Y al pie de una resquebrajadura enorme y suntuosa, como pórtico de vieja catedral, Demetrio Macías, con los ojos fijos para siempre, sigue apuntando con el cañón de su fusil . . ." (Azuela 1997, 209) (And at the bottom of an enormous and magnificent crevice like a portico to an old cathedral, Demetrio Macías, his eyes fixed forever, continues to take aim with the cannon of his gun . . ." (Azuela 2015, 91). For Sánchez Prado, this is both a "utopian moment, placing Macías ephemerally in a foundational position, but ultimately freezing him in time," and a "prophetic moment" because Macías's unblinking eyes look to a future in which liberal rather than revolutionary ideals win" (2016, 60). The two film adaptations use this same ending, but to different effect and with considerable differences in the final sequences.

In the novel Macías returns home, greets his wife fondly and reaches out to his son, who hides in her skirt (Azuela 1995, 206). Feeling shunned, he leaves to return to war. When his wife asks why he is fighting, he replies, "Mira esa piedra cómo ya no se para . . ." (Azuela 1997, 207) ("Look at that pebble, how it keeps going . . .") (Azuela 2015, 90). This line clearly signals a fatalism on his part and suggests his lack of agency. It also indicates how pointless and directionless his involvement in the Revolution has become. This is a pessimistic view of warfare and the Revolution and is an episode that neither film includes. However, both films address the inevitable pessimism of the ending in distinct ways.

In order to analyze the ending of both films I placed the final sequence of both versions side by side, starting from the point at which Macías and his much diminished troop decide to return home to Juchipila. Like the opening sequence, this is just under seven minutes long. As with the opening sequence, the pace, performance, focalization, and editing are different. There are also considerable variations in terms of plot points and key moments in each.

In the 1939 adaptation, one of Macías's troop goes to Macías's wife to announce Macias's impending arrival. The house looks identical to the one that was reported to have been burnt to the ground, which upends the earlier loss as no explanation is given for this. Holding the wife's hand is their son, now five. The mother's face is lit from above, giving her a pure and saint-like appearance. The director of photography, Gabriel Figueroa, favored classical framing and lighting and would have deliberately shot her in this way (García Riera 1992, 124). The sweeping orchestral score in a major key underpins the optimism of this moment. That she is untouched by war despite the ravages of the Revolution on the land and its people is unrealistic, but to judge melodrama for its lack of realism ignores the conventions of the genre. The wife's purity has greater significance as it is both highly resonant symbolically and has parallels with other films of the Revolution, most notably *Flor silvestre*, also shot by Figueroa. Figueroa, within the constraints of the studio system, drew on his repertoire of canted camera angles, careful composition, and key lighting in ways that reflected his construction of a Revolutionary aesthetic that both glorified battle and those who participated in it (see Figueroa 2005 and Ramírez Berg 1994).

The ambush in the 1939 film individualizes the death of the key members of the troop who have been fleshed out over the narrative. They are framed centrally in medium shot, and get lines of dialogue reflecting key aspects of their character. This individual death is like that of the five deaths of the band of brothers who went to war in ¡Vámonos con Pancho Villa!, although in that film the deaths take place at different moments and for distinct causes. The deaths of the principal characters in ¡Vámonos con Pancho Villa! ar enacted as individuated, distinct, and given appropriate melodramatic pause. Similarly, the individual deaths in the 1939 version of Los de abajo are in keeping with the melodrama where we are invited to have an affective response to the deaths of characters with whom we are invited to identify. It also gives meaning to conflict, narrativizing it as comprehensible. Each man has had an honorable death that is marked separately, and the audience can name each character. Their deaths are therefore countable, knowable, remembered, and grievable.

In contrast, in the 1976 version there is no return home. The troop has been told that Pancho Villa has lost, and on their way home they are ambushed. Macías/del Castillo talks to another soldier about his longing for home and speculates on how big his son must have grown since he has been away. The ambush is depersonalized. The action happens largely in wide shots using multiple angles, pans, and quick cuts to give a sense of the chaos of the attack. There are some medium shots of individuals but little dialogue, and no time to dwell on their deaths. This is death brought about to quell the Revolution and rob the characters of their individuality.

González's biography reads as significant in how this sequence is constructed. As the filmmaker who shot film for the government in 1968, this sequence carries echoes of the student deaths. The lack of clear facts about the student deaths nor of a precise cause for their shooting are parallels for the deaths in the 1976 version. Additionally, the mise-en-scène is worth close consideration. The 1968 massacre may have taken place in a distinct urban locale, but their anonymity and the bloody nature of those deaths can be read into this ambush in a walled space in rural Mexico. The presence of the wall recalls the brickwork of the ruins in Tlatelolco where the students were killed. These structures are more redolent when compared with the mise-en-scène of the ending of the 1939 film, which has no wall or built structures. The graphic evocation of the wall and the anonymized and arbitrary nature of their demise all invite comparison between 1968 and the 1976 version of *Los de abajo*.

Unlike the 1939 version, the 1976 version of *Los de abajo* has complicated origins and associations. In a DVD extra to the 1976 version, "13 apuntes dispersos para la reconstrucción del pasado" (13 random notes on the reconstruction of the past), the principal actor, Erick del Castillo (he is credited as Eric in the film), discusses the origins and development of the film from novel to stage to screen. He asserts that a systematic, yet random, methodology was in play with the creation of this adaptation. At the same time, there are common patterns and fidelity to the source evident in both. Del Castillo's intervention is an important indicator of how those attached to this film disavow any assumed auteurist ownership over this project by González for specific contextual reasons.

In the "13 apuntes dispersos para la reconstrucción del pasado" del Castillo is keen to emphasize the prestige attached to the project so he describes how, as part of a cooperative of actors, he was successful in getting the Azuela family's approval for the adaptation first to stage and then to screen. As a significant agent in these discussions, he describes how he was instrumental in the decision to bring González on board. The framing of this production story has a particular function. His assertion of the family's approval, his inclusion of the success on stage and the cultural capital attached to that, and his foregrounding of the actors' cooperative— all are mentioned to lift some of the dubious political associations that have been attached to the film as a result of its director, González. The fact that del Castillo chose to highlight his own credentials and that of the source text(s) is an indicator of his concern and eagerness to place González's auteurial role as secondary to his own, to Azuela as author, and to the dramatic text. Del Castillo's contribution in the commentary becomes an act of tastemaking through signaling the features of high-value productions and emphasizing his contribution as taking primacy over that of the director.

It is not possible here to explore the full implications of González's politics in a reading of the film, but, if we are to be guided by del Castillo, we should avoid a purely auteurist reading of this text. In the light of this decentering of the director in an analysis of the 1976 version of *Los de abajo*, it is worth considering the screenwriter, Vicente Leñero, who is credited alongside González as having adapted the novel. Leñero was one of a number of left-wing novelist-screenwriters, including José Revueltas and José Agustín, who critiqued the government in their writing. They were part of an energetic, experimental period in Mexican writing that was often reflected in the choices and variety of cinematic projects they undertook. These multiple film adaptations form part of a "kind of multileveled negotiation of intertexts" (Stam 2000, 67). Attention should be paid to these authors as active participants in the filmmaking process, an area that has heretofore been overlooked or sidelined in the discussion of their output (see also Thornton 2016). Their work is indicative of thick adaptation where the source text works as intertext rather than privileged source.

Such patterns can be found in Leñero's adaptations of his own and others' novels, which are marked by a careful attention to form that privileges what he has called "elementos fundamentales" (essential features) of the source text and demonstrate an applied understanding of the form into which they are being adapted (Vega Zaragoza 2011, 10). This has involved losing significant features of the original novel that may be fundamental to that text and pushing it in other directions that suppose similar, yet form appropriate, experimental results. In his participation in other film adaptations, Leñero demonstrated a similar awareness of the need to retain key features of the narrative and to cut or expand elements as required in the adaptation, including when adapting his own novels to film (Thornton 2017a). This shift can be found in the adaptation of the 1976 version of *Los de abajo*.

Decentering the auteur is another important component of reading this adaptation as thick, which opens up other potentialities: adaptation as palimpsest, mnemonic device, and archive that Anna Westerståhl Stenport and Garrett Traylor (2015) see as integral to the remake. A remake is a reversioning of a film using an earlier film and its thick contexts as the source text. Their focus is on remakes in the digital context. However, for my purposes their discussion is highly resonant. The different versions and the textual and audiovisual archival material the films draw upon can be understood to "serve the functions of both cultural memorialization and information preservation" (Westerståhl Stenport and Traylor 2015, 78) because each new version recalls prior versions, draws on the conceits of the films of the Revolution, and references the recent past in ways that would be easily understood by the audience. For Westerståhl Stenport and Traylor, because remakes are understood not to have "an individual existence," they form part of a "database" of objects that "are not tacked

Figure 4. Macías in death (1939, left, and 1976, right).

on at the end of the hierarchy: they are inserted into the collection" (2015, 90). This thick database of objects necessary to understand the 1976 version include the first version, the many films of the Revolution, and the audiovisual record of 1968.

In the 1976 film even Macías is denied his screen death. He is shot at, runs behind a part of a ruin, and then is shown shooting back at the attackers in medium shot. The edit cuts between Macías/del Castillo being shot at and wide shots of others being killed. This cuts to a shot of the top of trees accompanied by silence. The shooting has stopped. From a high angle the camera pulls back to reveal smoke, dust, and the bodies of the dead horses and soldiers. Through tilts and pans the camera reveals the full extent of the devastation as a military drumbeat starts to play. The drumbeat gets louder as the camera focuses in on Macías/del Castillo. As the camera continues to zoom in on a close shot of Macías/del Castillo staring directly at the camera with his gun pointing toward the camera, the final lines of the novel appear on-screen, "con los ojos fijos para siempre, sigue apuntando con el cañón de su fusil" (his eyes fixed forever, continues to take aim with the cannon of his gun) (2015, 91), with Mariano Azuela's signature underneath. This shot has a very forceful impact as the camera continues to pull in on an extreme close shot of Macías/del Castillo aiming at the viewer for the duration of the credits.

In contrast, the 1939 film shows Macías/Ferriz slumped over a rock with a rifle by his head. This death lacks the same impact. It is the final shot of the film but is brief in duration. The melodramatic ending comes earlier with the scene in which a messenger tells Macías's wife that Macías is dead. She/Ramos appears to take this news as an inevitable sacrifice.

Figure 5. Macías's wife after his death (1939, left) and Macías in death (1976, right).

Looking beatific thanks to the use of key lighting, she/Ramos holds her son closely and asserts her hope for the future. Thereby, a terrible loss is turned into a positive ending (figure 5).

Over the 1976 sequence an, at first, slow orchestral version of the *corrido* "Si Adelita se fuera con otro" (If Adelita Went with Another) quickens to a jaunty pace as the credits continue. The pacing and the choice of music is significant. The *corrido* is one that recurs in Revolutionary films. There are two films called after this song, which describes a soldier's love for a beautiful camp follower, Adelita: *La Adelita* (Guillermo Hernández Gómez and Mario de Lara, 1937) and *Si Adelita se fuera con otro* (Chano Urueta, 1948) (Mistron 1984, 50). In the *corrido* the soldier vows to follow her wherever she goes and states that he will buy her lovely clothes and other luxuries. The film is about the privations of war and about the woman as a figure for whom the soldier is fighting, thereby displacing the ideological conflict onto a yearning for enduring love (Herrera-Sobek 1993, 104–8). It also reveals the courtly nature of the balladric tradition from which the *corrido* originated (Mendoza 1954, ix).

In the 1976 film, the slowed-down version also makes allusion to an earlier sequence in which this song is used over archival footage of the Revolution. Taking the place of footage of the characters fighting in the battle of Zacatecas at a turning point when their faith in the Revolution is waning, this sequence is a switch to documentary realism that is disturbing and metatextual. Originating in a variety of sources with no apparent connection to the linear narrative and cut together using a montage technique, it creates a sense of discontinuity. There are scenes of troops of diverse affiliation in different spatiotemporal relations and only a few of the cuts obey the 180-degree rule, which evokes confusion and the terrible repetition of battle. There are shots of dead people and animals that foreshadow the ending of the film. This documentary realism simultaneously has an indexical quality in its archival nature, but it also is unattributed and in its montage effects disrupts the apparent realism of the feature film into which it is spliced. To use the slow version of "Si Adelita se fuera con otro" in this earlier sequence and, again, in the closing sequence is to draw parallels between the fictional and factual worlds. By changing the song's tempo to a jaunty pace, it serves an ironic and critical function. The positive, albeit bathetic, mood such *corridos* provide Revolutionary melodramas, such as the sweeping orchestral medley used in the score of the opening credits to the 1939 version, is altered by the self-referential use of the shift from slow to fast pacing of the *corrido* in the 1976 film. The *corrido*'s changed tempo becomes more tragic through the particularity of the mix and in the ways it both references its earlier use and prompts the audience to recall the popular song as an auditory synecdoche for the Revolution.

The differences in the deaths of the battalion in the closing of both films lie in the evolution in warfare and its representation. In the 1939 adaptation, the Revolution conforms to "traditional warfare" as "a 'military act,' with its theatre, its music and its sense of patriotic duty," as war is imagined in the early twentieth century according to Paul Virilio (2005, 49). For Virilio, in this period the battlefield was effectively "a film set out of bounds to civilians" (1989, 16), and this is mirrored in the 1939 version. Macías's wife's exclusion from this zone marks it as separate from her life. How she is lit and acts, free of the trauma of conflict in the 1939 adaptation, underlines how apart she is from the horrors of war. It is an example of how "women became the *objective tragedy* in the wars from which they were excluded" (Virilio 1989, 29). The combination of her purity and the pain expressed on realizing that Macías is dead enacts this tragedy. The child beside her represents a more optimistic future, as he too experiences loss but is untouched by witnessing war. No such resolution is provided in the 1976 version, where the space in which the death occurs is a ruin that is evocative of lost glory and of contemporary tragedies.

Death is enacted by unseen forces in both films, and yet the moment of death is difficult to isolate in the 1976 film. The shift is in the move from an "industrialized warfare where the representation of events outstripped the presentation of facts" (Virilio 1989, 1) to a "logistical era of war . . . [when] destruction has been transferred from the armed population to weapons systems" (Virilio 2002, 10). The 1939 version captures the first, dramatizing the events to convey a coherence and encourage identification with the loss of these key characters. The 1976 version was made at a point when information warfare was still at a nascent stage with its mediatized instantaneity (see Virilio 2002, 10), but it captures some of its confusion and the depersonalization of the deaths that took place in 1968. Apart from Macías, it is difficult to name the dead in the final scene in the 1976 version, just as the dead in 1968 have not yet all been named (Brewster 2010). The de-narrativization of death is an effect of how the total annihilation of the troop in the ambush is shot and edited.

Both adaptations of *Los de abajo* reveal the ways the adaptation of violence goes beyond a simple analysis of page to screen transformation. It is historically determined and a distinct aesthetic decision. The 1939 version may display less blood than the 1976 version, but the realism effect is not the most powerful difference. The strongest indicator of the cultural and political context is the space for a glorious and acknowledged death in the 1939 version that contrasts with the anonymity of death and the contingent dehumanizing effect that this has on the characters in the 1976 version.

Videographic criticism reveals that adaptation is a thick form of translating a novel to film with considerable capacity for the collaborative filmmaking team to create distinct meanings in the space between the text and screen. The versions of *Los de abajo* reveal the acts of tastemaking involved in these representations of violence. The 1939 version is melodramatic, emphasizing affect and loss, while the 1976 version presents the deaths as isolated and part of a never-ending cycle of violence. Adaptation is tastemaking. Looking at the process of tastemaking and the tastemakers involved provides new ways into understanding violence on-screen.

Conclusion

The history of Mexican cinema is told as successive and distinct periods dominated by local and international factors with significant periods of high production and short periods of few outputs. It shifted from having a robust and successful film industry during its studio era (from the 1930s through the 1950s), attracting considerable national and international audiences, with an occasional exceptional auteur, to a period of auteur filmmaking in the 1960s and 1970s that was less well received commercially. This tension between periodization and auteurship is dominated by questions of taste and the prestige that is awarded to works of distinction. In Mexican film criticism, those films that circulate only in the local commercial marketplace, which have been deemed to have poor production values or employ generic and formulaic approaches, or both, are ignored in favor of films that conform to inter- and transnational arthouse notions of value. In this model, the 1939 adaptation was part of the great expansion of film production and a form of industrial filmmaking that is generally described as the Golden Age, while the 1976 version was made during a period of independent political filmmaking. Both of these periods were heavily supported by government incentives and finance and have garnered considerable scholarly attention. Up until recently, critical research into the Golden Age of Mexican cinema tended to consider a relatively narrow selection of films deemed to have high value because of international awards, auteur traces, star presence, high degrees of commercial success, and contemporary critical acceptance. Focus on the independent period is (sometimes erroneously) framed as a countermovement to the studio system, where recent film graduates created largely low-budget auteur cinema that had critical acclaim but little commercial success. The Revolution was a recurrent setting for films from both of these periods.

Adaptation and translation studies are perennially preoccupied with unpacking and dismissing fidelity as a centrifugal focus with the same frequency and with overlapping concerns in both. Looking at the opening and closing sequences of these two versions of the films allows for direct comparison to how fidelity can be a productive point of departure that leads to deeper and thicker reflections on violence on film. Much of the original dialogue, plot points, and tone are retained in both versions, but the creative and pragmatic decisions that are made result in significantly different films. The 1939 version was made in a studio under working conditions that determined particular aesthetic choices including pacing, performance, locations, lighting, and music. Greater creative freedom was afforded to the filmmakers in the 1976 version and they strove for a heightened realism effect, an aspiration of many of their contemporaries. Where the priority in the first version was reconciling the population with a stable political enterprise, in the second it was about confronting the reality of a recent turbulent confrontation.

When considering films that have attained little critical and commercial success it is easy to assume that they are of lower value. One possibility is to assert their value as forgotten masterpieces. This would be erroneous given that this is too burdened with having to match them against measures of value and prestige that privilege a narrow spectrum of qualities. Another, more useful way is to assess them first against specific generic markers as Revolutionary films and, second, as products of a particular set of sociopolitical, industrial, and cultural contexts. This provides a refiguring of tastemaking practices across a range of media and texts. The versions that are examined become part of a new form of thick adaptation studies that allows for the consideration of multiple factors in the making of a film.

For this project, the "digital material thinking" of videographic criticism has helped to collapse the distance between the object and its analysis. Although it has resulted in the creation of an audiovisual essay, the methodology rather than the final outcome is the primary focus. It is in this adoption of the audiovisual essay as process that I found a way to rethink the film as tastemaking. This process resulted in close textual analysis through my reversioning and, metacritically, enabled an assessment of the thick adaptations of *Los de abajo*.

Videographic criticism is integral to this analysis and has proven to be an invaluable tool in forging a new understanding of both versions, a methodology I continue in chapter 4 with very different film texts. In its potential as a means of carrying out close textual analysis, I am proposing that it should be employed more widely in order to enrich our understanding of films that have otherwise been devalued. The aim of this chapter, therefore, is not to confer legitimacy on one film over another nor to elevate the versions in order to attain an "ontological promotion" and ensure their entry into an accepted canon (Bourdieu 2010, xxix). Rather, it is to challenge their dismissal and draw attention to how these two versions of *Los de abajo* can serve as instances of layered and multidimensional films that merit more than the mere dismissal they have largely received. They reveal themselves as acts of intermediated tastemaking and thick translations.

Chapter Four

Bodily Excess and Containment

Bordertown (Gregory Nava, 2006) and
The Virgin of Juarez (Kevin James Dobson, 2006)

A hand reaches out from a grave at dusk followed by a figure sitting up gasping for breath. Separately, a face emerges through rubble and dirt followed by a hand in another grave. Excessive and nonrealist, these resurrections are central scenes in both *The Virgin of Juarez* (Kevin James Dobson, 2006) and *Bordertown* (Gregory Nava, 2006), two films focused on the dead and disappeared women of Juarez. In reality, when women in Juarez are taken, assaulted, sometimes mutilated, and murdered, they do not return. Often their bodies are never found despite efforts by family, friends, and allies. In contrast, the women in these films defy death to return from the grave and their survival is fantastical. Their assault, burial, and return from the dead has dramatic potential and carries the possibility that the victim could seek vengeance and attain a form of resolution in line with horror and rape revenge genre conventions.

Both *Bordertown* and *The Virgin of Juarez* involve US-based journalists crossing the border to write stories about the lives of the murdered women of Juarez that are not normally acknowledged as "grievable" (Butler 2009 and Driver 2015). Renowned female actors are the protagonists of the films—Jennifer Lopez as Lauren Adrian and Maya Zapata as Eva in *Bordertown* and Minnie Driver as Karina Danes and Ana Claudia Talancón as Mariela in *The Virgin of Juarez*. These women have distinct star texts with variable levels of fame and tastemaking influence. While ostensibly the central narrative concerns are the assault, abuse, and murder of women, the bodies of the stars are foregrounded in ways that create an uneasy tension that neither film can resolve. This chapter considers the significance of the bodies of Lopez, Zapata, Driver, and Talancón as markers of taste and value in films depicting violence.

Lopez/Lauren as Latina is to be understood as imbricated in Mexican culture and her "excessive" body is integral to the plot of *Bordertown*, while Driver/Karina's contained white body and lack of understanding of what, to her, is a foreign culture is equally important to the narrative of *The Virgin of Juarez*. Zapata/Eva is a star in Mexico, but relatively unknown outside of Spanish-language film and television. She is doubly marked as Mexican and indigenous in *Bordertown* in order to create a distinction between her and Lopez/Lauren. Mexican film and television star Talancón/Mariela's racially marked body as victim and cult leader in *The Virgin of Juarez* is an ambiguous and shifting signifier because, like Zapata, her recognition as star outside of Mexico is limited. For both Zapata and Talancón their assaulted bodies carry the burden of prior meaning, where Mexican women are framed as victims of violence whose lives are barely grievable.

Using theoretical analysis of the signification of the women's racialized bodies and how they are fashioned (Dyer 1997; Molina Guzmán and Valdivia 2004; Burns-Ardolino 2009; and Calefato 2010), this chapter looks at how star texts are used to draw attention to a terrible reality while simultaneously masking it, and considers how the women's ethnicities are imbricated into the narratives as a way of negotiating difference and otherness. Having failed to convince critics and audiences, *Bordertown* and *The Virgin of Juarez* cannot be easily analyzed using conventional approaches. Therefore, this chapter uses a mixed methodology of star and genre studies and videographic criticism to carry out close readings of the films despite their perceived failings and uncover what can be learned from stars as tastemakers.

Distasteful, Sickening, and Vulgar: Juarez as More Than Mere Crime

Although a number of films have been made about the murdered women of Juarez, *Bordertown*, because of its high-profile star, is the best known and most excoriated. It was booed at its press release at the Berlin Film Festival and described by the German tabloid *Berliner Zeitung* as "pretty distasteful," suggesting that "one can't take La Lopez seriously in her role for a single moment: She is simply too cute and too J-Lo!" (Spiegel 2007, n.p.). "La Lopez" is a nickname commonly used in the popular press that gestures to her Hispanic origins and her celebrity (read frivolous) persona (see, for example, Dijkstra 2013). Revealing the ways surface is not taken seriously, the reviewer finds that Lopez's appearance gets in the way of the gravity of what has happened in Juarez. Similarly, in *Variety* Leslie Felperin finds fault with Lopez's acting, describing it as "passable" but criticizing her appearance as "too fussily groomed" (2007, 15), thereby suggesting that she has an excessive star persona and because of that should not be taken seriously. Jean Franco takes issue with the genre choices and is even more critical. She dismisses *Bordertown* as a "sickening vulgarization of the murders" (2013, 1) that reduces the killings to "a single heroine and villain to tell a story where the murderers and victims are a multitude" (2013, 233). These assessments are interesting, yet they are incomplete and reveal much about what is considered legitimate in the representation of brutal violence. Comparison with *The Virgin of Juarez*, which received little distribution and has had no academic attention to date, provides an opportunity to get a more complete understanding of the questions of taste and curation when representing sexual assault, violence, pain, and death. These are films with high-profile transnational stars and less high profile actors (in the transnational arena) whose presence is an act of tastemaking. The intersection of real-world events, star performances, and hybrid genre conventions merit interrogation and is a way into understanding taste and value in film more broadly.

To get some insight into how these assessments draw on questions of legitimacy, it is worth taking a brief look at films that have attained wider acceptance among critics on this subject including the documentaries *Señorita extraviada* (*Missing Young Woman*) (Lourdes Portillo, 2001) and *Bajo Juárez: La ciudad devorando a sus hijas* (*Bajo Juarez: The City Devouring Its Daughters*) (Alejandra Sánchez and José Antonio Cordero, 2006), and the fiction film *El Traspatio* (*Backyard*) (Carlos Carrera, 2009). All of these films have attracted considerable scholarly work, in part because their generic hybridity and metatextual reflexivity has been deemed high value (see, for example, Tornero 2013 and Palmer 2017).

The much-lauded essayistic documentary *Señorita extraviada* is a nonlinear, experimental, highly reflective meditation on power and religion, and, therefore, sits easily within the paradigms of prestige documentary film. Laura Podalsky's assessment succinctly sums up why this film is deemed high value and signals why others are deemed to fall short. For Podalsky, *Señorita extraviada* critiques the national and supranational causes of the murders by treating the murders as more than "a 'mere' crime traceable to specific culprits. The film situates itself as a response to globalization, understood as social trauma" (Podalsky 2011, 145). The "mere" speaks to a common discomfort with the use of genre cinema to tell these stories and the potential danger that blame for the murders can be ascribed to individual actions rather than structural failings.

In a similar vein, the more conventional documentary *Bajo Juárez: La ciudad devorando a sus hijas* centers on two primary figures, a mother seeking justice for her daughter, Lilia Alejandra García Andrade, who was kidnapped, assaulted, and murdered, and an eighteen-year-old young woman, Guadencia Valencia, from Veracruz in southeastern Mexico who has recently arrived in Juarez to find work. This focus provides ample opportunity to reveal some of the toll of living, working, and campaigning in Juarez as well as investigating those who are responsible through interviews with activists, the accused, journalists, investigators, police, and politicians intercut with archival footage predominantly from news outlets. Made over five years (2001–06) with the support of Mexican universities and cultural institutions, in the absence of a resolution and justice for many of the murdered and disappeared, *Bajo Juárez: La ciudad devorando a sus hijas* functions as a useful, albeit partial, primary source that provides contemporary context for the other texts under discussion.

El Traspatio conveys a realist version of the events using crime procedural conventions, with some shortcomings. The protagonist, Blanca Bravo (Ana de la Reguera), is a police officer who has been recently posted to Juarez. She attempts to solve the mystery of the women's deaths and unravel the corruption that has impeded justice running its course. By taking on the police perspective *El Traspatio* fails to address the systemic fault lines in the investigation of the murdered women in Juarez. Instead, it blames corrupt individuals. It employs the high-value aesthetics of social realist filmmaking by shooting in muted colors and putting the normally glamorous de la Reguera in dowdy clothing and grooming. Such aesthetic choices give it a sense of authenticity critiqued in *Bordertown* and *The Virgin of Juarez*. *Señorita extraviada*, *Bajo Juárez: La ciudad devorando a sus hijas*, and *El Traspatio* take different storytelling modes but are easily legitimated within the cultural field because of their adherence to conventional conceptions of taste.

In her deliberate signaling of the word "mere" in scare quotes when discussing films that fall short of the standard set by *Señorita extraviada*, Laura Podalsky appears to be making a reference to the quests undertaken by the protagonists of films such as *El Traspatio, Bordertown*, and *The Virgin of Juarez*. Within the constraints of a narrative feature film, *El Traspatio* has an awareness of the density of the history and politics it has to convey. Measured against their perceived inability to comprehend the nuances of the intersecting interests highlighted by Podalsky renders *Bordertown* and *The Virgin of Juarez* questionable according to standardized doxa of cultural value (see Bourdieu 2010, 238). Exploring how they fail to conform to these markers proves instructive in understanding the function of stars as tastemakers who can complicate and undermine an earnest attempt to raise consciousness and educate audiences about the femicides/feminicides.

Plot Overview: *Bordertown* and *The Virgin of Juarez*

Bordertown and *The Virgin of Juarez* have remarkably similar plots. In *Bordertown* Lauren (Jennifer Lopez) is a career-driven journalist employed by a prestigious Chicago-based newspaper who is commissioned to write about the women of Juarez. She is resistant at first, declaring that "no one gives a shit about Mexico." In a paratextual nod to the capacity that star presence has to draw attention to little-known issues, her editor (Martin Sheen) responds, "If you give a shit about it, they [the readers] will." Lauren goes to Mexico incentivized by a guaranteed promotion. She rekindles a friendship with a reporter in Mexico, Alfonso Diaz (Antonio Banderas), who helps her investigate the recent assault and attempted murder of a young woman, Eva (Maya Zapata). Eva was raped by two men, strangled, presumed dead, and buried. She emerges from the grave, returns home to her aunt, and, not trusting the police, they seek help from Diaz to find her aggressors. Lauren vows to help Eva in exchange for an exclusive on her story. She finds Eva shelter with an activist, Teresa Casillas (Sonia Braga), and investigates Eva's case. This leads Lauren to experience multiple facets of city life: she goes into the red light district; has a date with a suspect, one of the factory owners; attends an elaborate birthday party of the children of one of the city's elites; and goes undercover as a factory worker at one of the *maquiladoras* (factories) to investigate a suspected bus driver. There is a failed attempt to capture Eva's rapists. Diaz is assassinated at work because of his assistance on the case, reflecting the risks taken by Mexican journalists. Unconvinced by the chances of her assailants being arrested, Eva then tries to cross the Mexico-US border. She is deported and, on her return, she finds her neighborhood aflame and saves Lauren from an assault. The assailant falls and burns in the fire. Lauren accompanies Eva to the court to denounce her attackers. Eva returns to her small town in central Mexico. Lauren decides to leave her job in the US and takes over Diaz's job as editor of the newspaper in Juarez, committing herself to investigating the other murders. As a consequence of her encounter with this case, Lauren moves from avowed disinterested outsider to committed resident investigative journalist.

The Virgin of Juarez is more densely plotted. Karina Danes (Minnie Driver) is a freelance journalist and photographer who is affiliated to *This Week L.A.* (a type of Los Angeles-based alt-weekly). She goes to Juarez having decided to write a story about the murdered women. On arrival, she meets two activists, Father Herrera (Esai Morales) and Patrick Nunzio (Angus Macfayden). Through Father Herrera she meets with a mother of a disappeared woman (Marcia del Mar); Detective Lauro (Jacob Vargas), a police officer struggling to keep on top of his case load of femicides/feminicides and drug-related killings; and the special prosecutor (Ana Mercedes), who denies that there is a particular problem with violence against women in Juarez. These are all figures that find their equivalents in *Bajo Juárez: La ciudad devorando a sus hijas.*

Karina comes across an unusual case of a young woman, Mariela (Ana Claudia Talancón), who was raped, struck by a blunt instrument, buried, only to emerge from her grave seriously traumatized, but alive. Mariela has physical injuries including severe trauma to the palms of her hands. Her hands bleed while she is in the hospital. When this happens those who are present at her bedside all believe that her wounds are stigmata. These include Father Herrera; Sister Padilla (Indra Zuno), a nun who is also a nurse; and a hospital attendant and father of a disappeared woman, Isidro (Jorge Cervera Jr.). Stigmata are marks or bleeding interpreted by members of the Catholic Church as matching the crucifixion wounds of Jesus Christ and are ascribed mystical significance. Mariela has a false memory of seeing an apparition of the Virgin Mary in the desert and of speaking to her, which leads to Mariela becoming the leader of an underground cult on both sides of the border. Inspired by her mysticism, her followers pursue men from a wanted poster Karina has stolen from the police station that unwittingly ends up in Mariela's possession. Inspired by Mariela, Isidro leads this vigilante justice against those named in the poster in Juarez. As a result, Mariela becomes vulnerable to attack and goes into hiding protected by Father Herrera's brother, Gio (Noel Guglielmi), a gang leader in Los Angeles. Over the radio she broadcasts her message demanding justice through love, prayer, and action, and holds regular meetings with her followers who believe her bleeding hands to be a mystical sign. Karina interviews Mariela in Los Angeles and convinces her to meet with Nunzio, who claims to act as a neutral go-between for the Church and the factory owners. They are fearful of Mariela's power.

Unbeknownst to Karina and Mariela the FBI are pursuing Mariela for the murders her followers have committed. Mariela meets with Nunzio. Initially, he is wearing a wire so that the FBI can listen to their conversation. He soon turns this off once it is clear that Mariela realizes via flashbacks that he was her assailant. He begs for forgiveness. She forgives him despite recovering her memory and the trauma of the attack. Nunzio attempts to embrace her and because she is bleeding, he gets covered in her blood. Gio sees the blood and shoots Nunzio. On hearing gunshots the FBI agents start shooting into the warehouse where the meeting is taking place. The gang members shoot back. Karina arrives on the scene as the building starts to go up in flames and witnesses Mariela walking into the flames and disappearing. It is unclear whether she has died or, somehow, escaped. In the next shot her voice can be heard broadcasting her message of resistance while we see another young woman step off a bus in Juarez. This voice may be live, a supernatural transformation, or a recording. Karina calls Lauro and appears to believe in Mariela's mystical powers. She says, in Spanish, "está viva" (she is alive). Karina gets her scoop on this story, which she can now sell at a high price to a prestigious publication. Karina's journey appears to be a spiritual one with no clear social or political outcome beyond her personal growth and greater success as a journalist.

Both films have brutal assaults, attempted murders, burials, and resurrections. The plots end with fires that lead to forms of redemption and recovery that are differently realized. They employ horror film tropes, a genre with a strong tradition of rape-revenge narratives and potential for subjectivity for the victim-survivors, although this is diluted, as I explore in this chapter. The shifts in attention away from the victims in *Bordertown* and *The Virgin of Juarez* bring the focus back on the stars while indicating through voiceovers that these are films about the murdered and disappeared women of Juarez. This leads to confused signaling of whose lives are grievable.

Femicides/Feminicides: Facts and Theories

As mentioned in the introductory chapter, details and facts about the femicides/feminicides in Juarez are difficult to fully ascertain. Theories abound about who is responsible for the assaults and murders. This is due to the fact that the police investigations have been variously paltry, botched, or nonexistent (see Fregoso 2003; Villamil 2011; Vulliamy 2011; and Driver 2015). Families, activists, and their supporters have carried out their own investigations and tried to push for convictions and demand better policing. Some have had success, but most are left with unsatisfactory conclusions. In 2009, a case was brought, without any successful convictions, against thirty-six named civil servants for human rights abuses as a result of their behavior toward victims' families and supporters (Villamil 2011, 12). In the face of national and international pressure, including a 2003 report by Amnesty International (Villamil 2011, 12), in 2012 special officers were brought in to establish a center to investigate the crimes in Juarez. This led to the review of some convictions. The most notorious of these were the 2003 case brought against the supposed serial killer Latif Sharif Sharif, nicknamed "the Egyptian," and accusations against two bus drivers in 2005, who were allegedly part of a larger gang, Los Choferos (The Drivers) (Villamil 2011, 11). The cases against these men were weak. Among the many problems with these allegations were that the forensic material was found to be false, evidence was scant, and the two bus drivers' confessions were obtained through torture and, therefore, deemed inadmissible in court (Villamil 2011, 11–12, and Vulliamy 2011, 168–71).

Bordertown explores the possibility that Sharif Sharif could be to blame for the attack on Eva but chooses to portray the assailant as a bus driver, a fixer for wealthy men, who is also a rapist and attempted murderer. This narrative thread is muddled with another theory, the collusion of the so-called Juniors, young men who have inherited wealth and influence, and, consequently, have evaded justice. The films do claim to be accurate and appeal to solidarity for the women in Juarez, but they are not documentaries. Therefore, they do have some license to fictionalize and dramatize the events. The choice of who is to blame for the rape and attempted murder of Eva in *Bordertown* works as a commentary on the working conditions of the women, alludes to a broader societal cause for their assaults and deaths, but avoids laying direct blame on the justice system. Unlike what has happened in reality, as detailed in the 2011 special issue on the murdered women of Juarez in the Mexican news magazine

Proceso, in *Bordertown* the justice system works. Once the accused is caught there is faith that justice will be served. Eva testifies against her aggressor and she also gets a form of rape revenge by hitting Lauren's aggressor in a dramatic denouement that mirrors her own attack, as I will discuss.

In addition to the absence of justice, a key point of contention is how victims have been blamed for their assaults and death (Driver 2015). As a consequence, there has been much emphasis by the victim's families to stress the purity of their relatives who have been murdered, by which I mean their conformity to an idea of womanhood that fits with Mexico's conservative gender values. This practice can be seen in the interviews with mothers in *Señorita extraviada* and *Bajo Juárez: La ciudad devorando a sus hijas*. In the latter film, the mother of Alejandra describes awards, achievements, and full engagement with school activities including basketball, chess, and poetry. I mention this neither to undermine this practice nor to criticize the families for their need to do so. It is understandable for the families to highlight the women's goodness in the context of victim blaming by investigators and officers of the law. In *Bajo Juárez: La ciudad devorando a sus hijas*, police assert that the women were sex workers and, as a consequence, brought their deaths upon themselves. Similarly, the government-appointed special investigator, María López Urbina, suggests that the fault lies with the parents for not imposing strict discipline and for letting their daughters out late at night. As well as highly moralizing and deeply troubling, a further flaw in their logic is that a majority of women have been abducted and killed in daytime while going through what would be considered the ordinary and conventional routines that are blameless even in a victim-blaming culture. In line with this tendency, the creation of unambiguously good victimhood is heavily emphasized in *Bordertown* and *The Virgin of Juarez*, both using religion and an affinity with traditional values as markers of purity. This functions to normalize the good/bad, virgin/whore victim dichotomy.

Star Status and Racialized Bodies

Women's bodies are central to the narrative and to how *Bordertown* and *The Virgin of Juarez* are read. Star status determines how the women's bodies are differently privileged. Jennifer Lopez has a significant career as a singer, actor, and star entrepreneur, while Minnie Driver is a performer with a solid, but less high-profile, career. Maya Zapata and Ana Claudia

Talancón are well-known film and television stars in Mexico, but little known outside of Spanish-language film and television. In *Bordertown*, Lopez/Lauren's Hispanic origin is integral to the plot, as is her need to reconnect with this heretofore suppressed part of her persona. Driver/Karina's whiteness and lack of understanding of what, to her, is a foreign culture is equally important to the narrative of *The Virgin of Juarez*. Driver (a British actress) often plays American women, and her whiteness is a key component of her star persona. Lopez (a US actress) moves between acting white and Hispanic, albeit not always seamlessly given her markedly Hispanic persona as a singer and star. In *Bordertown* and *The Virgin of Juarez*, while Zapata and Talancón's Mexicanness inscribes them as victims, which is facilely racialized, Lopez's and Driver's star texts are used as means of drawing attention to a terrible reality. Their racialized bodies are conflated with notions of taste that are imbricated into the narratives. Acting as the audience's proxies, Lopez and Driver negotiate Zapata's and Talancón's purported difference and otherness in frequently troubling ways. The distinct star status, valence, and influence of Lopez, Zapata, Driver, and Talancón has consequences for how they can be read as tastemakers.

Born in New York to Puerto Rican parents, Lopez started her career as a dancer, became an actor, but has had most financial and critical success with her singing career. Her debut single, "If You Had My Love," was released in May 1999 and had immediate critical and commercial success. She emerged at a time when other so-called Latin singers, such as Ricky Martin, were gaining momentum as crossover artists, that is, performers who not only appeal to their perceived market segment but have success in the mainstream. Her Hispanic-ness has been an important part of her personal brand as a singer as evidenced in the mix of Latin pop, dance, R&B, hip hop, rock, funk, house, and salsa her songs employ. As well as code-switching she frequently sings in Spanish, sometimes releasing songs in Spanish and English-language versions simultaneously.

Before this success as a singer, Lopez acted. Her first major film role was in Gregory Nava's ensemble multigenerational narrative *My Family* (1995), which was positively reviewed, followed by a starring role in the biopic of the crossover singer, *Selena* (1997), also by Nava. *Bordertown* is her third role in a film by Nava, a renowned Mexican American filmmaker whose work has focused on border narratives that use generic conventions. Therefore, Lopez's first roles align with her subsequent star persona as a singer. Her other acting roles are varied: from the markedly Hispanic Marisa Ventura in *Maid in Manhattan* (Wayne Wang, 2002),

Karen Sisco in *Out of Sight* (Steven Soderbergh, 1998), and Ramona in *Hustlers* (Lorene Scafaria, 2019), to the Anglo Zoe in *The Back-Up Plan* (Alan Poul, 2010) and Holly in *What to Expect When You're Expecting* (Kirk Jones, 2012). In each case, the character names act as an easy metonymic ethnic identifier, albeit one that is oftentimes challenged by Lopez's offscreen star and musical persona. Like many stars, Lopez has a production company, Nuyorican Films. *Bordertown* was the first film produced by the company, which suggests that she had a significant stake in the success of the film.

Performing alongside Lopez in *Bordertown*, Maya Zapata began acting as a child in small roles in Mexican and transnational arthouse films, getting her breakthrough starring role in *De la calle/Streeters* (Gerardo Tort, 2001), a social realist film about street children in Mexico City. Throughout her career, she has worked in Mexican film and television with an occasional role in US productions. One of her recent starring roles is as the *tejana* singer Selena in the Telemundo *telenovela* (a limited duration television series), *El secreto de Selena* (2018), based on the same character previously played by Lopez. While her television roles are typically melodramatic, Zapata's film career is marked by low-key realist performances. In interviews she identifies as someone who foregrounds the craft of acting. She mentions her occasional theater roles and states that she chooses roles carefully according to her personal criteria of value, eschewing roles that perpetuate negative and reductive representations of women as objects (see Brett 2015 and León 2016). She is also conscious of how an individual's phenotype determines acting opportunities in Mexico. This colorism means that while she has played the love interest and been given considerable agency in her roles, her black hair, dark skin, and brown eyes frequently lead to her being cast as a working-class character in film and television (Brett 2015). In *Bordertown* these same characteristics set her apart from Lopez and mean that she can be cast as an indigenous woman.

Dark haired, white-skinned Minnie Driver is British born, grew up in Barbados, and went to boarding school in England. Much of her career has been in Hollywood films. Her ancestry is European (English, Welsh, Italian, Irish, Scottish, German, and French). Therefore, her background falls along the spectrum of whiteness, as classified by Richard Dyer, what he calls a "category of maybe" (1997, 19). These are "people who may be let in to whiteness under particular historical circumstances"; "the Irish, Mexicans, Jews and people of mixed race provide striking instances: often excluded, sometimes indeed being assimilated into the category of whiteness, and at others treated as a 'buffer' between the white and the black or indigenous" (1997, 19). Curiously, then, if we broaden out Dyer's reference to Mexicans as part of the buffer category to read more broadly to mean Latin Americans of southern European descent, because of her Irish/Welsh/Italian origins Driver should be read to be as white or nonwhite as Lopez or Zapata. But, of course, this is not the case. Driver always plays white, sometimes plays British, on one occasion Irish (*Circle of Friends*, Pat O'Connor, 1995), but most usually her characters have US (white) accents. This is the case in *The Virgin of Juarez*. Driver has had a low-profile singing career, which has resulted in some collaborations with neo-folk and indie musicians and songwriters. Unlike Lopez, this has yielded little commercial or critical success. While she is credited with having seventy-nine acting roles in both television and film, few have been as lead actor. The majority of her roles have been in comedy or as a character actor. For example, she has made regular appearances in the US sitcom *Will and Grace* (1998–) as Karen Walker's (Megan Mullally) combative step-daughter, Lorraine Finster. *The Virgin of Juarez* is one of her rare dramatic leading roles.

Like Zapata, Ana Claudia Talancón has consistently worked in film and television. She has starred as a romantic lead in a number of successful Mexican films including as a young woman from a small village seduced by a priest in the record-breaking box office adaptation *El crimen del padre Amaro/The Crime of Father Amaro* (Carlos Carrera, 2002) and as the protagonist, Catalina, a young woman who became wealthy and powerful through marriage in another adaptation, *Arráncame la vida/Tear This Heart Out* (Roberto Sneider, 2008). She has producer credits on the Mexican remake of the Argentine *telenovela*, *Soy tu fan* (2010–12), in which she acted alongside Zapata. Talancón has also starred in transnational and US films and television series, most recently two border crossing narratives: the Telemundo series *El recluso* (2018–) and the film *American Curious* (Gabylu Lara, 2018). Her approach to acting is the result of her formation in *telenovelas* that require melodramatic performances and expressive responses privileged through close-ups at key affective moments. This is evident in *The Virgin of Juarez* as is her ability to convey character through stillness and interiority when required. Her first role in the US, in *Fast Food Nation* (Richard Linklater, 2006) as a migrant worker, reveals that she is read as clearly Mexican from a US perspective because of her skin, hair, and eye color. She has commented on this and the growing opportunities for Mexican actors in the US in a

2018 interview, saying, "creo que no hay forma de que no se den cuenta de que el mundo de hoy no es más Estados Unidos y puros güeritos de ojos azules" (it can no longer be ignored that the world is bigger than just the United States and blue-eyed blondes) (Agencia EFE 2018). This reveals Talancón's awareness of how she has been racially marked outside of Mexico and of the opportunities becoming available to her because of changes in casting. She has star status in Mexico because of her film and television work but is relatively unknown to Anglophone audiences. Like Zapata, she is cast in *The Virgin of Juarez* not as a star but as an actor who is recognizably Mexican for US audiences.

Star Texts: Embodied Subjectivity

Film star texts often map onto their public persona (Shingler 2012). Much is made in the popular press and fashion magazines about Lopez's curvaceous figure as a marker of her ethnicity, which is linked to excess. There is considerable emphasis, in particular, on the roundness of her buttocks. From the early days of her fame, Lopez has asserted considerable power over her star persona. She plays up to the attention given to her curves. Her physique has had an appeal for the largely white press, which have praised her body for characteristics most usually associated with the black body (see Molina Guzmán and Valdivia 2004). There is frequent allusion in the press to her buttocks using the words "asset" and "bootilicious" (Dijkstra 2013), and in the accompanying images of her now infamous over the shoulder pose where she stands at an oblique angle toward the cameras looking back at the photographer. The focus on Lopez's buttocks is a predecessor to what is written about Kim Kardashian and the ways Kardashian performs her white black body (see Sastre 2014 and Muñoz 2018). Just as Kardashian is deemed playful in her presentation of self, Lopez's Hispanic body is valorized for her controlled performance of racialized particularities that have a long history of being denigrated in US culture. For a woman so famous that she gets her own press nickname, "J-Lo," this play between whiteness and Latinness is complicated. To talk about a Hispanic body as if this were a single phenotype is absurd. It is more properly a "confusing proliferation of pluralities," as Suzanne Chávez-Silverman (2003, 216) describes it. But, repeatedly, Lopez's body is upheld as indicative of her Hispanic otherness. Her physiognomy is often read as an integral feature of her Latinness, which is very much part of her star text as a singer, while in her acting career she has often mixed acting as Latina and Anglo characters. Although she still poses on the red carpet showing her rear (see, for example, MTV Awards 2019), there have been changes in the focus from her bottom to her sculpted physique as she enters her fifth decade. Her social media accounts, in particular her regular posts on Instagram, attest to this. She is valorized for defying age expectations and, thanks to a carefully managed eating regime and long gym sessions, she has a contained body that still conforms to expectations of her raced body. That is, as along with having well-defined abs, she is still curvy.

In recent years, Driver's "private" star persona is that of a valiant single parent and an actor who is outspoken on issues affecting women in the film industry. In contrast with Lopez's complicated and shape-shifting body, much is made of Driver's taut, contained body, carefully sculpted and toned from the gym. This reading of her muscled abdomen as an expression of her self-control chimes with Dyer's discussion of the "white spirit." When, for example, the British tabloid newspaper the *Daily Mail* (Dadds 2013) describes Driver as having "slim pins and tall physique" and "rock hard abs and washboard stomach" they are extolling her ability to be, in Dyer's words, "both master and transcend the white body, while the non-white soul was [is still read to be, in the case of Lopez] a prey to the promptings and fallibilities of the body" (1997, 23). Of course, the word "master" reveals the extent to which there is another particularity: the male white body on which Dyer focuses his attention. How Driver is valorized, here, fits with his identification of the level of control for which she is praised. Dyer dedicated a chapter in *White: Essays on Race and Culture* to muscle films of the 1980s and how the toned male body was read in these. Assessments of Driver's body in the popular press slip between his descriptions and falls out of it, simultaneously. Her body is not the "hard, contoured body" of stars like Sylvester Stallone and Arnold Schwarzenegger, yet it is being praised for a similar containment, "a sense of separation and boundedness" (1997, 152) that Dyer identifies as being male, which "can resist being submerged into the horror of femininity and non-whiteness" (1997, 153). The photographs accompanying the *Daily Mail* (Dadds 2013) piece emphasize the femininity of her body, and the text judges it to be a "perfect bikini body." It also foregrounds her relationship with her son, thereby privileging her maternity. Through her physique and its containment, her body reads as white, but not unproblematically so. For the popular press she does not bear the excess, the thrilling otherness of Lopez's Latin physique. Driver's body is valorized as the outcome of discipline and training that is within the natural reach of her whiteness, while Lopez's is signaled as integral to her racial origins, albeit bearing its own exceptional markers. The fact that Lopez and how her body has been interpreted has been the subject of much academic interest (Chávez-Silverman 2003; Molina Guzmán and Valdivia 2004; Mendible 2007; and Burns-Ardolino 2009), but Driver has not is, in part, an indicator of the former's star status and profile, as well as the preoccupation and discomfort with how Lopez as a Latina has both exploited and been subject of much press attention.

As stars in Mexico, Zapata and Talancón have cultivated different star personas. As part of the television star system both Zapata and Talancón regularly appear in magazines dedicated to *telenovela* story lines and gossip about their personal lives as well as promotional interviews related to their film roles. In these interviews Zapata emphasizes her commitment to social change, the presentation of an entrepreneurial self through her investment in a restaurant, and the importance of being understood as an actor who makes considered decisions about the roles she takes. Talancón presents as a rounded individual who discusses work success in terms of a balance between a busy long-lasting career and engagement in charitable acts as well as her move into painting and sculpture. Her physical beauty is often the subject of press comment and is something she is comfortable foregrounding through modeling for a lingerie brand and photographic spreads for magazines such as *Gentleman's Quarterly* in Mexico. Race in Mexican stardom is an underexplored area, but has its own particularities because it takes the form of colorism. While Zapata is racially other in Mexico because of her dark hair, skin, and eye color, Talancón conforms to a certain idea of beauty and glamour in Mexico that privileges a Southern European phenotype because of her light brown skin, hair, and eye color. This means that in *Bordertown* Zapata can perform as an indigenous woman and Talancón can be a successful border crosser in *The Virgin of Juarez*.

Lopez, Zapata, Driver, and Talancón have differential levels of star status. Lopez is a transnational star with a considerable following in the US and across the Spanish-speaking market. Driver has a narrower level of fame and is known mostly for her character performances and television roles. Zapata's realist performance style in *Bordertown* fits with Lopez's performance, while in *The Virgin of Juarez* Talancón's tendency toward melodramatic and highly gestural performance matches that of Driver. Their casting is as actors with star appeal in Mexico that gives credence to the roles, but more so for their capacity to match the performance style of the star leads and to appear Mexican to a non-Mexican audience.

Valuing Lives through Clothes, Ornament, and Taste

Clothing determines how the body is valorized through associations with class and race and, in turn, how these categories intersect with questions of the valorization of the individual (Bourdieu 2010, 385). In film, clothes have a rich narrative function "in constructing and inflecting star images, and in producing meaning as a significant element" (Moseley 2005, 2). Clothing is foregrounded in *Bordertown* as an insight into Lauren's evolution as a character. At first, Lauren/Lopez wears a practical waist-length shirt and trousers that mark her as someone ready for field reporting. In her border crossing she has a consistent wardrobe as a marker of her difference from those around her, and her clothing is to be read as tasteful and measured. After delivering Eva to the safehouse owned by activist and campaigner Teresa, Lauren/Lopez starts to come to terms with her Mexican-ness and wears looser white calf-length tops, indicating a shift away from her career-driven self. In a further wardrobe change, when on a date with a factory owner, Lopez wears a figure-hugging short dress. This works to remind us of Lopez's star persona whose clothing choices are subject to much press commentary and is also used as shorthand for Lauren's sexual availability. This costume is about Lauren asserting power over her dinner date, a rich factory owner, in order to get information about an elite circle who are later revealed to be responsible of the murders. This power has considerable limitations because it is burdened with assumptions about men's inability to resist women's bodies. In a film that tackles violence against women, who have been accused of being misunderstood as sexually available because of their clothing, this is redolent with confused signifiers that the film appears unable to resolve.

Lopez's wardrobe, performances, music, lyrics, and public star persona are imbricated into a particular racialized discourse that suggests that Latinas are hypersexual. This is a system she both upholds and challenges. At her public appearances she asserts a glamorous persona through her clothing as well as providing a brief shorthand of her cultural capital and identity through her poses and comments to the awaiting press. Lopez's aesthetic choices offscreen often fall under the same terrain as a costume that has a storytelling function. The clothes "manipulate through tools such as silhouettes, color, nuances, design lines, or fabric textures" (Stutesman 2011, 22). The repeated press emphasis on the shape of her clothed body is, clearly, a question of race. It is an instance of fashion as translation, as described by Patrizia Calefato, where "fashion is a system that goes beyond the mere dimension of an individual's dressing habits: it is 'costume,' in other words a social institution that regulates and reproduces the clothed body" (Calefato 2010, 345). She proposes the term *cultural translation* to describe when "a subordinate culture [is] being forcedly transferred into a dominant culture and in the sense of a space of interaction" (2010, 345). Lopez's already existing star persona as cultural translator is employed in *Bordertown* where fashion is used to indicate shifts and changes in Lauren from Anglo to Mexican as a form of gradual assimilation and translation for the Anglo viewer. The display and concealment of her body is integral to her character's development and the tastemaking in the film. Lopez claims her excessive body, which is celebrated in high-status magazines. By deploying and subverting stereotypes to her own end Lopez has contributed to a rethinking of beauty in popular culture. Yet, when intersected with the normative assessments made about the victims in Juarez, Lopez's foregrounded othered body displaces theirs rather than bringing them into relief.

Figure 6. Lauren/Lopez as reporter.

I want to turn to the most densely significant wardrobe change. In a move to gather evidence against the driver of a factory bus, who is implicated in Eva's attempted murder, Lauren/Lopez dresses up as a factory worker and completes a shift at a *maquiladora*. Lauren describes herself as "bait" because she is in uniform, while Eva carefully oversees the disguise. Lauren's language and her wardrobe change simultaneously draws attention to the factory workers' vulnerability and disposability. On putting finishing touches to the look, Eva/Zapata says, "now, you look like me." This is a powerful message. The film broaches the differences between Lopez/Lauren and Zapata/Eva because it self-consciously deploys the "convenient fiction" of the Latina body, whereby the distance between Lopez and Zapata is a mere matter of clothing, whereas the distance between the presumed white audience and either actor is not reduced (Mendible 2007, 1). Their bodies are conflated in the dialogue and through the temporary disguise even though Lopez is an international star and Zapata is little known outside of Mexico.

Lopez's star persona both disrupts and reinforces normative perceptions of the victims. Her ability to slip in and out of the roles of *maqui-*

Figure 7. Lauren/Lopez as worker.

ladora worker from career-obsessed US-based journalist to seductress foreground these different forms of femininity as performative (pace Butler 2004) and, consequently, not fixed. Her changing wardrobe and feminine performativity also suggest that all women have these freedoms to adapt and deploy their femininity in ways that emphasize individual control, when the economic needs of the characters and the signification of Lopez's star text suggest otherwise. There is potential for these wardrobe changes to invite larger questions around women's bodies and, specifically, how the Latina body is read. If Zapata/Eva had similar wardrobe changes from worker to glamorous seductress, for example, this would push the narrative beyond a single performance to wider questions about racialized bodies. As a star reliant on a fluid series of selves, Lopez/Lauren's ability to shift is more a commentary on Lopez as performer and fundamentally fails to challenge the systemic ills underpinning the reality of the women's lives working in the *maquiladoras* in Juarez.

Lopez/Lauren's capacity to dress up in a *maquiladora* uniform is worth considering in light of the gendered experience of working in these factories that *Bordertown* only partly reveals. Tamar Diana Wilson (2003) analyzes the working conditions in *maquiladoras* and how they intersect with gendered relations along the border area. In the *maquiladoras* women's working lives are managed by a "benevolent patriarchy" that structures their work environment and interactions with management and fellow workers, whereby a form of femininity associated with "docility and self-acceptance of subordination" is privileged and rewarded (Wilson 2003, 64). Lauren/Lopez's wardrobe as the submissive worker in a uniform worn with care and accessorized with hoop earrings and hairpins are markers of working-class femininity and self-control. Such clothing is represented as the necessary invisibilizing armory of disguise all the while it normalizes a loss of individuality and the absolute obedience of the worker. The advocate and campaigner Esther Chávez Cano explains that integral to the reason why women are murdered in Juarez is because they "have no value. They are faceless" (Vulliamy 2011, 165). Lauren/Lopez's performance of physical submissiveness to the manager's hurried demands reinforces Eva as the "good" victim, because Lauren is modeling "good" behavior learned from Eva. *Bordertown* underscores this "goodness" and disposability through the ease with which Lopez/Lauren steps into the factory for a day's work with the right accessories and uniform, but with no practical training. As good victim and replicable worker, Zapata/Eva is cast as a type rather than imbuing her with subjectivity in contrast with the particularities of Lopez/Lauren, who can step in and out of these roles as required and has a narrative arc worthy of attention.

What is clear, then, is that the lexical tropes and popular press obsessions that surround Lopez are not just particular to her gender, they are also very specific to how she is read racially. Dyer concludes in his study on whiteness that there is pattern to be found in how "non-whiteness . . . is already peculiar, marked, exceptional: it is always, in relation to notions of the human in Western culture, particular and has no ordinariness" (1997, 222–23). Where white women can have their bodies unmarked by race, Lopez's body is read through it. Such a reading evokes Rosalind Galt's (2011, 97) suggestion that a focus on "ornament" can provide an understanding for those elements of mass culture that are dismissed and often misunderstood as lacking in meaning or value. For Galt, ornament

> is one word for the excessive investment in the cosmetic that classical aesthetics associates with the feminine. Like the woman, ornament is a supplement, secondary and may be surplus to masculine requirements. It likewise connotes the geopolitical outsider, the primitive whose absence regulates the central place of the European cultural order. In European aesthetics, non-Europeans and women are projected as loving ornament because these groups are viewed as a decorative supplement to that aesthetics. Thus the political quality of the ornament: it may be tolerated, but only if it knows its place. (2011, 97)

This is twofold for Lopez and Zapata in *Bordertown*. Zapata/Eva and Lopez/Lauren's hoop earrings and hairpin are modest examples of such ornament. There is a change in the value attached to the body as a result of clothing choices, which are linked to a complicated otherness. Lopez is an insider outsider, while Zapata's are naturalized because she is identified as a priori a worker, which is part of why the costume changes in *Bordertown* are both readable and confused. Nonetheless, they signal a form of tastemaking that attempts to revalorize and foreground low-value clothing.

Where Lopez as Lauren has multiple wardrobe changes in *Bordertown* to convey the evolution of her character, Driver as Karina in *The Virgin of Juarez* has a consistent low-key wardrobe of practical coordinates that convey her seriousness as a journalist. In *The Virgin of Juarez*, Talancón/Mariela is the one who changes her wardrobe. Unlike Lopez/Lauren's clothing changes, Talancón/Mariela's are not reliant on an awareness of her star persona. At the opening, on her arrival from Veracruz to Juarez, Talancón/Mariela is dressed in a modest, calf-length, flowery summer dress that evokes innocence. This changes to a T-shirt, skirt, and bib as a *maquiladora* worker, similar to that worn by Lopez/Lauren and Zapata/Eva in *Bordertown*. When Mariela is attacked, she has just changed into her calf-length white sleeveless night dress, underlining her purity and conveying the added horror of the assault as a violation of this coded "goodness." After surviving, she alternates between white robes and head pieces (bandages and nun-like veils) and guerrilla gang clothing (headband, tank top, with army shirt, combat pants, and boots). These are outfits that carry radically different meanings, and, in the absence of clearer interpretive frames, mask more than they reveal. As forms of Calefato's cultural translation, they fall into "stereotyped reasoning" (2010, 345), that is, mere shorthand for Mariela's othering, and, simultaneously, a projection of her assimilation into two distinct disciplinary communities: the Catholic Church and gang culture.

Through wearing clothing that is consistent, first, with the male gang members and, second, with the nun, Sister Padilla, Mariela/Talancón is clearly wearing distinct uniforms that are a "meaningful manifestation of how clothing can become for the body a regulatory apparatus that determines a closed system of correspondences between the external appearances and social order" (Calefato 2010, 348). In this vein, Mariela appears to have some power over the gun-toting gang members who are protecting her. In conversation with Karina, Mariela describes them as "warriors" on a mission to help women from Juarez and elsewhere in the world. Thereby, she acknowledges the gang's capacity for violence but claims that it is serving a communal good. Her donning of the white gown and veil convey purity of purpose. As this uniform is worn in her appearances in front of her spiritual followers, it could either be understood as clothing appropriate to spiritual practices or a fraudulent simulation intended to manipulate others. The wearing of these uniforms allows Mariela some opportunity to challenge the good/bad woman dichotomy, because she is both in one. She is the fragile cypher of spiritual hope and a subversive leader. Such rapid wardrobe changes have potential to build nuance and shift the attention to Mariela as agent of change. To a degree, this is the case not through her clothing but through the afterlife of her voice where she is given that power. This power is undermined because of her passivity at a key moment when she could have wrought revenge at the end of the film, and because, ultimately, Karina is the protagonist with clear agency.

Understanding Violence through Videographic Thinking

The challenge of looking at taste in film is that the traditional critical tools favor high-value elements, not absence of legitimacy. In order to find a new way into a close textual analysis of their value, I have made an audiovisual essay using Final Cut Pro X by manipulating, editing, and organizing the material so that the films could be effectively compared (Thornton 2020c). This involved cutting the sound and visuals to elicit an understanding of key scenes and sequences that have narrative similarities, but under such close scrutiny it was revealed that they have substantial differences. The chosen scenes were intercut and placed in split screen according to timings, visual contrasts or correspondences, and as a way of highlighting key variances. What follows are the outcomes of this experiment.

The three sequences included in the audiovisual essay because of their salience and similarities were the violent assault and attempted murders of the women; their emergence from the graves; and the fires that take place at the denouement of both films. Of the three, the first are the most unsettling. Rape and murder scenes have a history of gratuitous display in cinema and *Bordertown* is no exception (see Prince 1998; Projansky 2001; and Thornton 2013a). In it, we see two men rape Eva and delight in each other's pleasure at inflicting pain and violence. This is rape as a form of torture, a weapon whereby gang rape becomes a way for aggressors to become "consolidated . . . as a group" (Franco 2013, 15–16). Throughout Eva struggles to escape. There are frequent close-ups of her face as she screams and fights for air while one of her rapists, Domingo Esparza (Irineo Alvarez), strangles her. For the most part the sequence is shot tightly, intercutting her face in close-up with Esparza's hand around her neck and shots of the two men's faces, Esparza's as he assaults Eva and another unnamed man's as he watches and smiles. There are two significant wide shots: one that makes it clear that Esparza is the one physically assailing Eva and another where he appears to have finished and bites her breast. This gesture links his actions to a pattern of harm inflicted on many of the murdered women of Juarez, many of whom were found with bite marks.

To disrupt the point of view, there are canted angles and quick cuts, and the scene is shot in sepia tones, ending with a fade to white. These techniques are only partially successful. The shots of Eva are from above, that is, from the perpetrators' points of view, while the assailants are shot from oblique angles or from the side. This means that the point of view that dominates this sequence is either that of one of the perpetrators on-screen or of another unaccounted for assailant. Visually, we are included in their circle. In this rape-murder scene we are given the perpetrators' point of view. The victim, in turn, is denied a point of view. To do this is to give the perpetrators more agency and to deny Eva any. There could be radical storytelling potential in us occupying the perpetrator position if it were followed through in the narrative in ways that would implicate us in this violence and, hence, in a critique of this violence. Given that the film does suggest that transnational capitalism is a culprit in these murders, this could be a rich seam in the script. But *Bordertown* does not pursue it, instead taking a conventional crime genre problem-solving approach. As a result, its privileging of the perpetrator point of view is deeply flawed. For this reason and informed by a similar ethical approach taken by Liz Greene (2018) in her "Do It for Van Gogh" video essay, where she layered scenes from *Blue Velvet* (David Lynch, 1986), in my audiovisual experiment I cut the perpetrator point of view shots in these rape scenes and replaced them with a black screen and the words "Eve/Mariela/Lauren is raped," as appropriate. As I edited the material I realized the extent to which the original films reproduced the perpetrators' point of view. Instead, to give a sense of comparative duration and to privilege the victims' experiences, I retained the audio, thus displacing the perpetrators' point of view.

Bordertown is not alone in foregrounding the perpetrator's perspective. Marianne Hirsch (2003 and 2014; also see Hirsch and Spitzer 2008) has written extensively about the problem of perpetrator images and the perpetrator point of view. She focuses on the photograph as memory text and its implications for those trying to locate knowledge through the "attenuated indexicality" of approximate reconstructions of past atrocities (Hirsch and Spitzer 2008, 139). For Hirsch, there is "an uncomfortably tainted position we always occupy when we view perpetrator images" (2003, 34). When the images are photographs taken by a perpetrator it is burdened by the acts of violence perpetrated on the subject. This does not map precisely onto the point of view of *Bordertown*, insofar as neither the director, Nava, nor his crew are implicated in or sympathize with the horrific acts of violence against women in Juarez; however, through the structuring of this scene, they are inviting us to take up the perpetrators' point of view over that of the victim. As a consequence, *Bordertown* denies us "connectivity" with the victim that could provide us with insight and solidarity and her with agency (Hirsch 2014, 334). *The Virgin of Juarez* avoids this pitfall of occupying the perpetrator point of view in the rape scene; instead, it falls into a different trap by inviting us to empathize with the rapist's inner turmoil.

In *The Virgin of Juarez* Mariela recalls her assault when she agrees to meet Patrick Nunzio in his capacity as a campaigner on behalf of the disappeared women. Their meeting takes place in the final act of the film in the covert church in East Los Angeles where her followers regularly gather to see her perform miracles. Her supposed visions and epiphany in the desert have resulted in her becoming a symbol of hope on both sides of the border and an inspiration for some to become vigilantes hunting down assailants. Moments into their meeting Mariela stumbles and appears to enter a waking trance as she remembers her assault, burial, and resurrection by Nunzio. It is told in a series of hard cuts. As a flashback to her trauma and to invite identification with her, normally it would be from her point of view. Instead, the sequence is shot from a third-person point of view and starts with Nunzio uncovering his face. This reveal is a narrative surprise and references the scene earlier in the film when a figure arrives to her room, head bowed with his hand covering his face. In the flashback, the camera dwells on his smiling face looking at Mariela as he assaults her. The camera moves behind her head while he continues to take up most of the frame. His domination of the frame in this way underscores his power over her. This clear message foregrounding his responsibility for the violence in this sequence is undermined by his apparent vulnerability in what follows. In the next shot he is standing up with his hand over his face, again. This time he has an expression of remorse and she is cowering on the mattress against the wall. But the remorse doesn't seem to last, for this is followed by a montage sequence in which he grabs her, she struggles against him, he drags her outside, and then they are in his truck. Next, she is on the floor of the passenger side as he bangs on his steering wheel in frustration. In what could only be read as victim blaming, her resistance is portrayed as a catalyst for his subsequent actions. They drive into wasteland, she jumps out of the truck, he stops it, chases after her, and captures her. He straddles her and punches her repeatedly, then he goes to his truck and grabs a shovel. In the next cut we see her body in the ground. For this entire sequence—from the moment he drags her to the truck to the shot of her being buried in a shallow grave—we see only his face. Hers is either in shadow or covered by her hair. He occupies most of the visual space in close and medium shots while her screams dominate the soundscape. This gives her an incomplete presence until she is in the grave (see Greene 2009). From a medium shot of her in the grave she recovers consciousness, and this is followed by further struggle. The next cut is to a wide shot of her attempting to escape while he tries to contain her.

Through this extended flashback, Mariela's false memory of walking in the desert, seeing a light that she was convinced was an apparition of the Virgin Mary, and hearing a voice that she understood bore a message from God is reconfigured. She recovers the real memory of the assault, attempted murder, and subsequent resurrection, and comes to realize that the light she saw was not the Virgin Mary but was from a car and the voice was that of someone rescuing her. Significantly, the flashback reveals her wounds, which have been a source of others' belief in her sanctity, are injuries caused when Nunzio tried to stab her as she attempted to escape from her grave and she defended herself with her hands. These revelations shatter her worldview and she is no longer able to hold on to the belief that she has divine powers. Nunzio kneels before her and begs for forgiveness, which she grants him. Her wounds reopen when she pushes him away as he seeks to embrace her. It is not clear what the value of her forgiveness is, as the dramatic denouement is ambivalent as to her survival and the final message of the film. It is likely impelled by her Christian faith, but the way it is delivered lacks dramatic force.

Resurrection and Rebirth

Both resurrection scenes are disconcerting and, conventionally, should render the women powerful. The more ghostly, eerie, yet naturalistic style of *Bordertown*'s grave sequence may evoke the horror film motif and yet it simultaneously plays it down by using a very muted blue tone and not giving Eva any power as a consequence of her rebirth. From her shallow grave Eva pushes her face out first and then raises her hand. This is shown in a midshot that then cuts to a wide shot of Eva walking at sunrise across an expanse of open space. This and the soaring musical annotation in the nondiegetic score gives it a further epic tone. In contrast, in *The Virgin of Juarez* the lighting and makeup appear to reference zombie films. Mariela emerges from her grave with the zombie film conceit of indeterminate dirt on her face. When the lighting changes, it becomes clear that it is blood, thus alluding to the blood and flesh zombies have around their mouths as flesh eaters. Mariela also moves slowly and bewilderingly toward the light. By implication she is undead. The scene is part of a flashback, hence the initial bleached-out colors that make it hard to distinguish the substance around her mouth.

It is not clear where Mariela's recovered memory leaves her followers. Shortly after Gio shoots Nunzio, the FBI agents who had orchestrated the meeting respond and start a shootout with the gang members, killing many of them. A ricocheting bullet knocks over one of the many candles in the church and starts a fire. As the shooting continues Karina tries to enter the building through the back to rescue Mariela. Instead of leaving, Mariela walks away from safety and into a backroom of the building. Karina is blocked from rescuing her by a minor explosion and Mariela appears to deliberately self-immolate. This is a relatively short, highly ambiguous, yet significant scene that suggests at rebirth through fire.

The Virgin of Juarez ends with Karina calling the Mexican detective, Lauro, in charge of the case to tell him that Mariela is dead. From her upbeat tone Karina appears to suggest that Mariela's spirit persists despite her death. This belief is reinforced by the next scene. In direct parallel with the opening scene of the film, which follows Mariela's arrival in Juarez and assault shortly after alighting from the bus, another young woman experiences the same harassment, except this unnamed woman is kidnapped and taken away in a white van. Amid this narrative repetition, Mariela can be heard in a voiceover calling for justice. As a voiceover Mariela's voice is detached from her body as an *acousmêtre* (Chion 1999), consistent with horror conceits given the parallels with her own story that her spirit might be about to inhabit the young woman being kidnapped. For Michel Chion, the *acousmêtre* is a voice that is not attached to a body and thereby is "invested with magical powers" that are "usually malevolent, occasionally tutelary" (Chion 1999, 23). However, Mariela's voice does not have the mysterious source required of Chion's *acousmêtre* and the film has not sufficiently rooted itself in horror, therefore, there is no further hint at transposition, haunting, or rebirth. Mariela has been broadcasting her spiritually based message of resistance via radio. So, this voiceover could simply be a rebroadcast of one of her recordings. The partial horror film citations and the muddled ending weaken the potential power of the message of *The Virgin of Juarez*. The meaning of this ending can be found through analysis of the fire scene in *Bordertown*.

Fire, Revenge, and Justice in *Bordertown*

The extended fire sequence in *Bordertown* is a form of revenge wrought against Lauren's assailant by Eva. It is worth considering because the film has a resolution denied survivors and families and appears to be deliberately fantastical. Lauren arrives at Eva's house in an informal settlement trying to ascertain whether Eva will turn up to testify the following morning. Lauren finds Eva's house abandoned save for the hairpin she wore as a factory worker. Lauren is attacked from behind just as someone has accidentally started a fire by illegally connecting their home to the electricity source. The fire soon spreads throughout the neighborhood of mostly wooden homes. The assailant, Aris Rodríguez (Rene Rivera), continues his assault on Lauren, pulling at her clothes, partially strangling her, and positioning her to rape her in ways that match Eva's assault. This sequence is densely burdened with meanings that are both allusive and ambiguous. Videographic criticism facilitated an understanding of the details of a sequence made up of multiple cuts. In a series of cross-cuts from inside the shack to outside, where neighbors are trying to save themselves, to flashbacks of Eva's assault, Lauren's traumatic childhood memories, and a montage of other victims screaming, Eva arrives on the scene. A shot that is repeated in the rapid edit is of the neighborhood shrine aflame, yet the statue of the Virgin Mary within it remains intact. The statue appears to be an allusion to Eva's spirituality and, both through repetition in this sequence and its ordering just before Eva hears Lauren's screams, it suggests that the Virgin Mary intercedes on Lauren's behalf. On finding Lauren in danger, Eva picks up a fallen plank and hits Aris over the head twice. The second time he falls into the fire unconscious and is burned to death. The fire-vengeance could be a metatexual citation of *Carrie* (Brian de Palma, 1976) and the well-known prom sequence where Carrie uses her supernatural powers to burn down the school. In *Bordertown*, there is a hint of rebirth to this moment in the fire and a sense of it taking place in a time and space outside of Lauren's frustrated attempts to solve the crimes. Eva has just been deported after a failed attempt to cross the Mexico-US border and her house in Juarez is now in ashes, therefore she must return to her family and community to live in rural central Mexico. As befits her more complex characterization, Lauren gets more agency in her ending.

The graphic match between the assaults is made evident through a flashback to Eva's assault, rendered confusing by being told through

Lauren's, not Eva's, perspective. In the closing sequence of the film Lauren in voiceover states that she has moved to Juarez to become a journalist in order to dedicate herself to telling the truth and, consequently, attaining justice for the families. These dual forms of justice are presented as the first win of many. Franco's (2013) critique, cited at the introduction to this chapter, speaks to a problem with this film: by aligning itself closely to genre expectations the story has closure where reality has none. *Bordertown* fails its "witnessing function" that it purports to produce through paratextual elements, narrative concerns, and voiceover, which should be "designed to summon politically, morally and socially engaged publics" (Torchin 2012, 3). Instead, this horror-fantasy closure to Eva's story leaves the viewer with a satisfactory resolution and little impetus to act, which is a problem when the film claims to demand change. Videographic criticism reveals that *Bordertown* repeats the tropes of the authorities of the good/bad victim and sidelines the victim's narrative in favor of a more powerful protagonist, which is deeply troubling, especially when the film claims to be a tool for advocacy.

Hybrid Horror and the Horror of Sexual Assault

In this context, it is important to understand the interpolation of the clothing and bodies of Lopez, Zapata, Talancón, and Driver and their star personas in a reading of the text, but it is also crucial to consider how *Bordertown* and *The Virgin of Juarez* draw on horror motifs. There are remarkable similarities in the plotlines of the two films. In both there are two women who are brutally raped, savagely beaten, and buried in shallow graves. Taking place at different points of the narratives and given different screen time, the audiovisual experiment facilitated close textual analysis. The women emerge from their graves in a trope that is familiar from horror films, raising an open palm after having scratched their way out in order to seek revenge. In *Bordertown* and *The Virgin of Juarez* revenge is meted out with the aid of others—that is, they find their way to people who will protect them. The films have some of the characteristics of rape revenge and that genre's ethical "ambivalence toward revenge" (Henry 2014, 25). Despite the visual parallels with horror films, neither Eva nor Mariela are the avenging angels, nor are they sinister monstrous beings familiar to that genre. Both films employ these tropes incompletely and unsatisfactorily.

Although purportedly originating in the film *Deliverance* (John Boorman, 1972), the most well-known visual reference for the hand emerging from the grave is *Carrie* (Brian de Palma, 1976), a film frequently criticized for its depiction of teenage-hood and nascent sexuality as something to be feared (Greven 2011, 91–115). *Bordertown*'s and *The Virgin of Juarez*'s borrowing of the *Carrie* trope evoke horror. Placed differently, the resurrection scenes have distinctive potency. In *Bordertown* the resurrection and Eva's subsequent secondary role in the narrative defuses its potential to unsettle audiences because the survivor has no lasting power. In *The Virgin of Juarez* the capacity of Mariela's emergence from the grave to disrupt is diluted by the overdetermined action and performances of the scene in which it is revealed as a flashback. In both films the women are granted only partial agency over their resurrections and for their subsequent actions.

Horror is a genre that has been assessed as both reactionary and progressive (Grant 2007 and Wood 2018). The zombie subgenre, which both of these films reference, often tackles issues of race in ways that challenge dominant imaginings of the other, both placing them center stage and addressing normative fears. Victoria McCollum's (2016, 2019) recent and forthcoming assessments of horror during both the George W. Bush and Donald Trump presidencies signals that "horror repeatedly emerges as a counternarrative in response to such turbulent political climates" (2019, n.p.). Drawing on this reading of progressive horror the two women emerge from the dead as a form of haunting that has potential as a radical challenge to the status quo. Eva/Zapata's and Mariela/Talancón's Mexican bodies are to be understood as other, doubly so in the case of Eva because she is allied to an indigeneity that exoticizes her to the protagonist-reporter. However, theirs is not a horror film rebirth, which would give them greater power and agency, it is a return from a presumed death and trauma from which they must be saved by the more powerful Karina and Lauren, respectively. Eva and Mariela give indications that they have had some approximation to death that leaves them considerably altered, and has strengthened their link to a spirit world, but it diminishes Eva and makes Mariela a folk hero with uncertain control over her followers.

Mariela and Eva are monstrous women in these films. They take on elements of what Carol Clover calls the "female victim-hero" (Clover 2015, 4). In her discussion of Brian de Palma's *Carrie*, Clover identifies the vengeful fire and the subsequent resurrection as the moment when

Carrie (Sissy Spacek) "becomes a kind of monstrous hero—hero insofar as she has risen against and defeated the forces of monstrosity, monster insofar as she has herself become excessive, demonic" (2015, 4). Unlike Carrie, who enacts her own revenge, Eva and Mariela need the journalist advocates and others to act as the heroes. Eva in *Bordertown* is more passive and vulnerable in this regard. To a large degree this is because Lopez's star status overshadows the narrative center. In *The Virgin of Juarez* Mariela's power resides in her false memory, which results in her becoming an iconic heroic spokesperson and spiritual inspiration for acts of vengeance. Her power is ambiguous yet consistent with gendered horror representations, because it emerges from her body's excesses. She bleeds from wounds in her hands, which are read by her followers as religious in nature. At first, the blood arises involuntarily and produces pain, evidenced by her screaming. Later, she seems to control her bleeding when she appears in front of her believers and covers their religious artifacts (bibles, medals, rosary beads, and so forth) in her blood on demand. Her archetypically feminine passivity and bodily excess—an inability to shoot Nunzio, fainting, trance-like state, and uncontrolled bleeding—result in Nunzio's death when Gio, her guardian and the gang leader, comes in to protect her. Gio's action is a response to Mariela's inaction. Gio shoots Nunzio because Nunzio looks deranged and is covered in Mariela's blood. This is evidence of how gendered roles have been strictly codified in horror, where "the perceived nature of the function generates the characters that will represent it, mobile heroism wanting male representatives, and passive dank spaces wanting female ones" (Clover 2015, 13). Mariela is a mix of passivity and excess, which requires a male protector and a female interlocutor in Karina.

As Franco (2013), Sayak Valencia (2018), and Oswaldo Zavala (2018) have argued, there is an ethics to the representation of violent crimes that have yet to attain justice. This does not mean attending to the precise details of a specific case or choosing realism as the primary form of representation. It does mean that there has to be a careful alignment with the broad touchstones of reality, which these films attempt to do. However, to premise a film on the possibility of justice, where its absence is integral to the struggles of victims' families and activists, is to ignore one of the central issues at stake. The imperatives of the conventional rape-revenge genre usually lead to closure. Its absence in reality led the directors to opt for horror because it allows space for open-ended terrors to persist. What these films required was not less attendance to the requirements of genre, they needed fuller commitment to a genre that better fits the horrific crimes and to be centered on what the absence of justice means to families and the broader society. To fail to do so led to them falling into a quagmire of uncertain identification.

By exploring theories that have broad coverage in the press, *Bordertown* and *The Virgin of Juarez* are films with an eye to realism. They open and close with sequences and text that contextualize the narratives in documented fact and emphasize their truth, thereby they claim to be inspired by true events. The mix of truth and fiction is always the prerogative of a filmmaker, yet such framing can be troubling when tropes of genre fiction are employed (such as horror and rape revenge) without more diligent recourse to genre imperatives.

Conclusion

This is a chapter about failure within limited legitimating paradigms, that is, what constitutes a productive failure and what can be learned from it. There are two central failures in these films. First, the incomplete deployment of horror tropes as a means of conveying the real-life horror of women being murdered. The victims become imbued with extraordinary powers through their capacity to survive, but this is diffused rather than fully embraced. The second failure is linked to star casting because it determines whose story is given import. The decision to overburden the stars as protagonists means that their personas determine any reading of the films and their presence sidelines the agency of the victim-characters. Where horror tropes could have given the victim-characters power, star casting and the ways their narratives arcs dominate take it away.

Bordertown and *The Virgin of Juarez* are important to study because of what they tell us about taste, stardom, and genre. The repetitions and variations of these two films allow for and even encourage comparison. Videographic criticism facilitates close textual analysis and an examination of the distinct techniques and aesthetic choices employed by *Bordertown* and *The Virgin of Juarez* to convey similar narrative arcs. The videographic experiments revealed perpetrator points of view shifting to heroic escapes and differently realized justice. One of the key revelations was how little audiovisual space the two stars occupy in these central scenes, and yet they have a centrifugal force in the narratives that dominate the frame of reference. The use of two actors with very distinct star personas is highly meaningful, not least because of how the narratives exploit Lopez/Lauren's affinity to Zapata/Eva in *Bordertown* and emphasizes Driver/Karina's ignorance of Talancón/Mariela in *The Virgin of Juarez*. Their star texts act as a subtext in both films.

Lopez has sufficient cultural capital to have contributed to a redefinition of women's bodies on the red carpet. This tastemaking spills over into how her film roles are read. She is still read as excessive—"too cute and too J-Lo." How Driver is valorized is symptomatic of how she is read as a white actor who carefully contains and sculpts her body. Yet this containment does not guarantee success. Both Zapata's and Talancón's stardom is not centered in these narratives. Instead, they are stand-ins for racialized victimhood that lacks agency and requires saving.

Lopez's racial identification and racialized body operates in dialogue with the multilayered discourses that circulates around the dead women of Juarez. She moves from one of "us" to one of "them" through clothes and wardrobe as well as physical movements and temperament. Meanwhile, Driver's body operates as a polyvalent signifier, that is, as a figure of identification for the assumed audience; as a sexual being, albeit one who is controlled; and as a white person among nonwhite people, with all the meanings such a(n invisible) racial marker might signify. It would be too much to say that Driver/Karina's whiteness and lack of understanding of the cultural context and the subjects of her article is to blame for the shifting identificatory positions of the film. There are more substantial issues at play with actors who have star personas. They bring with them the baggage of their star texts and the requirement that their star bodies will be aesthetically foregrounded. Driver and Lopez do not occupy the same realm of celebrity and stardom, yet the resulting films are similar. Therefore, stardom cannot be blamed for any failings of the films. To do so is to legitimate higher order actors and dismiss those whose stardom affects how their performances are read. The lack of complete identification with the victims, or of knowing them as fully rounded characters beyond a conformity to a check box identificatory set of characteristics, is because the films could not imbue the women with the potency to unsettle that a full commitment to the imperatives of horror would have made possible.

Location, crew, narrative focus, and star presence can foreground the transnational. With variously US-based, British, and Australian casts and crews set at the border between the US and Mexico, *Bordertown* and *The Virgin of Juarez* are transnational films about violence that has root causes across national borders, which take place in a specific locale. Although they received distribution in Mexico and have well-known Mexican actors in key roles, it is clear that both films are intended for non-Mexican audiences. *Bordertown* and *The Virgin of Juarez* aimed to draw international attention to the killing of women taking place in Mexico, which determined the aesthetic and generic approaches. With transnational stars—Jennifer Lopez and Minnie Driver—as the protagonists, their outsider status is foregrounded, functioning as the identificatory position, and allowing them to act as cultural interpreters for the audience. *Bordertown* and *The Virgin of Juarez* are operating within an established stratified developed/underdeveloped North American–South American imaginary, as discussed by John Patrick Leary (2016, 13), where the US projects onto Mexico and Latin America a "space that is 'ours' from that which is 'theirs,' and relatedly, of producing forms of knowledge that enforce the relations between the one and the other." Thus, the films have to navigate an assumed "us" who are from the developed US and are invited to empathize and understand "them," the erstwhile underdeveloped Mexicans. When the audience is not viewing from this geographic or relational position, there are always further complications that the texts do not readily facilitate.

Eva and Mariela are vulnerable, seriously injured, and in need of protection. In *Bordertown* this protection comes in the form of Lauren. In *The Virgin of Juarez* a cult-like Catholic religious group take over the care of Mariela, believing her to have special powers. Driver's journalist character Karina grapples but never quite gets a grip on what to her are the bizarre beliefs of the Mexican and Mexican Americans who remain mysterious to her. Similarly, despite her Hispanic roots, Lauren is troubled by Eva's indigenous cosmovision, having been told by Teresa that Eva cannot differentiate between what's real and imagined because "she comes from an Indian culture." This nonspecific "Indian culture" flattens out the differences between traditions and practices across indigenous peoples in Mexico and reduces Eva to an unknowable other whose primary function is to impel Lauren to rediscover her origins as a result of this encounter.

In these ways, the victims—real and imagined—are other to both Lauren and Karina. This is particularly marked for Karina because she is to be read as Anglo and, therefore, outside of the signifying codes that are to be understood to be native to Mexico until the very end of the film when she witnesses Mariela walking into the flames. The film suggests that her journalistic rational mind requires proof unlike the mystical Mexican and Mexican American believers among Mariela's followers. As a consequence, Karina is able to write the perfect article that becomes subject to a bidding war among magazine editors. In *The Virgin of Juarez*, personal career success is a central narrative concern. Earlier in the film Karina's work was treated with jaded indifference by Eve (Joanna Cassidy), her editor on *This Week L.A.*, who had dismissed her pitch for a story about the murdered women as passé. The women's stories have no currency, little novelty, are not grievable, and, therefore, not worth the newspaper's attention until Karina finds a new angle. In a form of metatextual commentary, Karina's success in publishing her article is because the story is more than just another story about an ungrievable dead woman from Juarez of the sort that her editor rejects, but one that has brought supernatural elements and local (Los Angeles) interest. This detail shows awareness by the filmmakers of the exigencies of the attention economy, which they apply to their own narrative.

While the number of women murdered in Mexico in recent years has been substantial and there is much about the absence of justice for their deaths that is unique to Mexico, it is hardly the only place where gender violence is a serious issue deserving of critical cinematic representation. Therefore, the lessons in failure learned from these films have potential to inform other contexts. The tastemaking explored in this book brings the threat of death and the experience of embodied violence into relief. This is clear in *Bordertown* and *The Virgin of Juarez*. Drawing on body genres that are associated with excess, these films try to convince us of the agency of their subjects and fail to do so. In part, this is the result of the decision to employ a hodgepodge of genres without a full commitment to any; it is also because of the use of stars whose polyvalent racialized bodies confuse and detract from the purported message of the films. As narratives focused on assault and murder starring well-known actors, bodies are at the center of these films and, following Linda Williams's (1991) assessment of the body genre, invite embodied audience reaction. They are instances of how bodies have distinct meanings that ascribe them with various levels of subjectivity, grievability, othering, and objectification, sometimes simultaneously. A resistance to indulge the impulses associated with bad taste leads to failure. The films' attempt to give agency to their subjects via partial use of the tropes of horror and rape revenge fails because the excess is neither excessive enough nor fully committed to genre conventions. This chapter explores what this failure can suggest about tastemaking and suggests that there is potential to embrace excess in the representation of violence. I propose that even when a film fails, we can find ethical acts of tastemaking behind failure through an understanding of excess as it is attached to gender, race, and genre. Chapter 5 continues to examine stardom and its intersection with celebrity as a marker of tastemaking. In this instance, the focus is on television.

Chapter Five

Curating Cruelty and Criminality
The Radical Mediation of Kate del Castillo

Kate del Castillo has built a considerable career in Mexican film and television. Previously little-known outside of Spanish-language television, she is now recognized for two interconnected reasons. The first is her starring role as Teresa Mendoza in *La reina del sur* (2011–), a transnational television series about the rise to power of a female drug dealer. Originally airing on network television, it is now streaming on Netflix and has broken audience figures in Mexico and Spain. The second is that, on the back of that role, she facilitated an interview between the US actor Sean Penn and a criminal on the run, Joaquín "El Chapo" Guzmán Loera, for *Rolling Stone* magazine (Penn 2016). As a result, del Castillo has gained star status from the television series and notoriety akin to celebrity for the encounter between Hollywood and criminality. Initially, her career trajectory was representative of patterns in Mexican television, but it has evolved distinctly in the ways she performs and presents her on-screen and offscreen persona. In an unusual move, she went to Los Angeles at the peak of her career to effectively start anew and try to break into film and television in the US with variable success all the while becoming a star entrepreneur as a founder of a tequila company and a film producer. As someone whose star-celebrity persona illuminates wider patterns of the public/private self, illustrates a highly individual pathway, and who is associated with a popular form frequently ascribed low value, she further extends tastemaking.

This chapter draws on Richard Grusin's development of the concept "radical mediation" (2015). He makes the case for elevating mediation from being a "secondary concept or category" to the "experiential immediacy of mediation" (Grusin 2015, 130). Rather than plot out the differences between media and their consumption, he suggests that radical mediation can serve to appreciate the ways "all connections involve modulation, translation, or transformation, not just linkings" (Grusin 2015, 138). Grusin does not provide examples of radical mediation in his analysis, but del Castillo fits as an exemplar because of how she sits within a complex, interrelated network of mediated practices. Taking del Castillo as a node and *La reina del sur* as a focal point in order to understand interrelated worlds of form, genres, style, performance, and the embodied self, I will provide a way into articulating del Castillo as a tastemaker. This chapter considers how *La reina del sur* functions within and beyond the usual scope of drug narratives and, therefore, operates as tastemaking television. I will extend this to consider del Castillo's star-celebrity persona as a tastemaker.

La reina del sur has had multiple versions and is a truly transnational product. Originating in a popular Mexican song, adapted to a bestselling novel by a Spanish author, and then reversioned back into a song, the television series is coproduced by US, Colombian, and Spanish TV companies and is set in Mexico, Gibraltar, the US, and Spain and its enclaves in North Africa. By placing the narrative at multiple liminal sites, the narrative reinscribes how borders are conceived. The shift from the national to the global is reflective of developments in the television industry that encourage transnational storytelling and radically reconfigures responsibility, agency, and exceptionalism for violent action.

La reina del sur locates sites of difference and sameness within the protagonist, Teresa, through del Castillo's performance and presence. Teresa's evolution into a drug trafficker functions as a way of working through the current violence in Mexico in a transnational context, thereby making the drug war less just Mexico's problem and more of a global issue. Gender is at the fore in the series in unconventional ways. Where the narratives set on the borderland discussed in chapter 4 emphasize Mexican women's vulnerability, *La reina del sur* follows how Teresa attains power. She is fearful for her life, not because she is a woman, but because of her association with drug dealers. At first, this is because her boyfriend is a smuggler, and then because she herself becomes a powerful trafficker. How violence is enacted upon her is particular to her being a woman, but del Castillo as Teresa complicates this. She performs powerful vulnerability when she encounters violence. That is, she has an ability to navigate and excel amid a dangerous milieu yet is always conscious of her vulnerability to gendered violence.

Unlike other television stars, del Castillo does not easily fit into clear binary concepts of beauty and physical performativity evident in other Mexican television stars. Physically lean and gym fit, she slips between high glamour at public events and casual unisex, albeit form-fitting, clothing in her downtime and in many of her roles, including as Teresa in *La reina del sur*. Del Castillo's fluid presentation and nonstandard gender performance is reflective of wider shifts in television roles for women. Taking her role as Teresa as a focal point allows space to consider this gender performance and the limited doxa attributed to even successful Mexican television series, in particular those set in the illegal drug trade.

At a metatextual and theoretical level I want to reflect on a radical mediation through language that surrounds the works and worlds I am analyzing. Many scholars (for example, Benavides 2008; Vásquez Mejías 2016; Palacio and Romero Santos 2017) use "narco" as an unproblematic term. Such language choice merits reflection. I have dealt with the question of "narco" as a predicate or prefix for literary and audiovisual culture in the introduction to this book. While it is useful shorthand, it is worth noting the analyses of two distinct authors on the notion of using "narco" when describing these cultural outputs. Oswaldo Zavala (2018, loc 1252) finds *La reina del sur* (both novel and television series) to blame for a type of misdirection whereby the drug-related violence is something that crosses borders and, consequently, no single nation can be made responsible, and Sayak Valencia (2018, 235–37) has little regard for the representation of violence on television and games. Zavala's (2018) assertion is consistent with his thesis that specificity is important because Mexico needs to address the sociopolitical problems that have resulted in horrific violence and brutal deaths. Valencia's (2018) argument against mediatized violence suggests that all forms necessarily glorify violence and direct attention away from looking at its root causes in the current stage of what she calls "gore" capitalism. Rather than argue against Zavala (2018) and Valencia (2018), I bring up their disavowal of narco culture to suggest that they have more in common than it first appears. Narco is a slippery prefix or label for much of the cultural outputs depicting the drug trade (in Mexico and elsewhere) as well as the performance of certain forms of consumption and propaganda by those benefitting financially from criminality (Campbell 2014). *La reina del sur*, like many of these cultural outputs, is focused on the trade and is not concerned with taking drugs, nor with addiction or its consequences. As a signifier narco is in danger of emptying out and collapsing into successful brands, books, and television series across multiple networks and versions, whose most recent version, *Narcos: Mexico* (Mexico/US, Netflix, 2018–), sustains the mode and tone of previous versions by glorifying and delighting in the trade without entering into critiques of its causes and consequences. Where possible, I opt out of using "narco" and tend to adopt more cumbersome circumlocutions to acknowledge this and foreground the problem with the language currently in circulation.

In chapter 3 I proposed thick adaptation as a new mode of analytical approach when considering two film versions of *Los de abajo*, a novel that, in turn, had its own unstable origins. In this chapter, I propose a similarly multilayered approach to a television series that is the product of multiple sources and has spawned its own subsequent versions. This approach simultaneously refutes a canonical hierarchy in the analysis or a singular final version at the same time as it uses the *telenovela* version as a primary entry point in a radical mediation between texts and their creators.

The Telenovela: Origins and Evolution

The telenovela is a mode of serialized storytelling usually with a defined running length. It is popular throughout Latin America, Russia, Eastern and Southern Europe, the US, China, and, most recently, Africa (Contreras 2006 and Palacio and Romero Santos 2017). Telenovelas are often denigrated for their excessive characters, nonrealistic narratives, exposition through dialogue, and Manichean outlook. This overlooks key components integral to the subversive potential of the melodramatic mode it draws upon, such as class critique, the privileging of women's (often domestic) narratives, and the capacity to confront social stratification.

Carlos Contreras (2006) provides a brief history of the Latin American telenovela from its foundations in serialized radio dramas in the 1930s, arguing that the telenovela benefitted from the movement of skilled cast and crew from cinema to television just as the Golden Age of cinema was waning in the 1950s. This success was consolidated in the 1960s and 1970s and Mexico became one of the major "hubs" of telenovela production alongside Brazil, Venezuela, and, more recently, south Florida in the US (Contreras 2006, 38). Telenovelas have been efficiently run productions made lucrative through worldwide syndication. Because of the continual need for new talent, many of Mexico's most famous actors have launched their careers in telenovelas and have consistently worked across both television and film. Examples range from Silvia Pinal and Diego Luna to Gael García Bernal and Salma Hayek. Therefore, it is a route to success for an actor as well as a lifelong lucrative and high-profile career for many. In Mexico there is not as clear a line between high/low roles for actors as there has been in places such as the US where much of the current academic paradigm for assessing performances and suppositions about quality television are posited.

Although often low cost, high-value telenovelas have become more commonplace since the 1990s. *La reina del sur* is representative of this shift toward high-cost, high-value telenovelas aiming for large viewing figures, increased global distribution, and, since the 2000s, an afterlife in DVD sales, and, more recently, streaming. It reached a record-breaking 16.6 million total viewers and averaged 4.2 million viewers per week on its initial run on Telemundo, and has been purchased for distribution by the Netflix streaming services, which have a growing range of non-English-language television series available for the Anglophone market (*Marketing Weekly News* 2011; Netflix 2018; and Hecht 2019). After the success of the Netflix original *Club de Cuervos* (2015–19), the streaming service has subsequently bought other telenovelas for distribution, primarily Mexican and Spanish, as well as producing telenovelas, including *Ingobernable* (2017–18), also starring del Castillo.

In addition, Palacio and Romero Santos (2017, 151) note that *La reina del sur* is a breakthrough in a new female-led subgenre, the "narco (tele) novela," which followed on from successful Colombian telenovelas, *Las muñecas de la mafia* (The Mafia Girls) (2009), *Sin tetas no hay paraíso* (Without Tits There's No Heaven) (2006), and the Argentine *Mujeres asesinas* (Female Assassins) (2005–08). What makes *La reina del sur* distinct from these earlier series is that Telemundo has taken a different approach to other networks, as analyzed by Ainhoa Vásquez Mejías (2016). Where in the abovementioned telenovelas, women are punished for becoming active agents (Vásquez Mejías 2016, 214–15), this is not the case for the protagonists in *La reina del sur, Camelia la texana* (2014), and *Dueños del paraíso* (2015), suggesting a different approach by the Telemundo network. These Telemundo series have female characters with considerable agency who have distinctive features from male-centered narratives about drug traffickers. The plot-driven narratives draw on melodrama's concern with their emotional trajectories. The female characters are not motivated by ostentatious spending, use violence as a necessary means rather than an end, and are criminals with a clear sense of social justice and emotional intelligence (Vásquez Mejías 2016, 223–27). *La reina del sur* is part of a complex ecosystem of television that has emerged in recent years and has taken the telenovela in new directions via coproductions by smaller television networks and, more recently, funding from the growing streaming services.

Territorial Travels: Multiple Versions and Media Landscapes

As previously mentioned, *La reina del sur* has had multiple versions: a *narcocorrido* (song) adapted into a novel adapted back to a narcocorrido, and a multiversion television series. I will touch on each of these versions as iterations of radical mediation before carrying out an analysis of the 2011 television series. The original source text for *La reina del sur* is "Contrabando y Traición" (Contraband and Betrayal), a narcocorrido by the popular, award-winning *norteño* group Los Tigres del Norte, who recorded the song in 1972 (see González Luna 2013 and Jaramillo 2014). Narcocorridos are folk ballads centered on antiheroes involved in drug trafficking. They often use highly encoded language and "mixed messages about the consequence of involvement in trafficking" (Edberg 2011, 75). Usually fact-based "anthems celebrating drug traffickers or chronicling events and the way of life of people in the narco-world," "La reina del sur" narcocorrido is fictional (Campbell 2014, 70). Focused on the character Camelia, this song was also the inspiration for the low-budget 1977 film *Contrabando y Traición* by Arturo Martínez and, in turn, the telenovela *Camelia la texana* in 2014. There are gendered particularities to the narcocorrido that are another nodal point in this tastemaking framework. Until recently, female characters have not been serious subjects of television series set in the drug trade, but women are "historically privileged by narcocorridos" (Jaramillo 2014, 1597; see also González Luna 2013). Therefore, one of the existing versions that is among the source texts for *La reina del sur* draws on conventional representations of women that the telenovela challenges. The musical versions have continued. The publication of the 2002 book prompted Los Tigres del Norte to record another updated narcocorrido called "La Reina del Sur," which was highly successful. This version has been covered by another group as I detail later.

La reina del sur has been multiply mediated and has crossed geographic boundaries. With a focus on the Spanish cultural production history, Manuel Palacio and Rubén Romero Santos (2017) provide a useful overview of some of the versions from the perspective of the 2011 telenovela. They include a brief synopsis of the career of the novel's author, Arturo Pérez Reverte, across fiction, film, and television. Pérez Reverte is worth pausing on because he is a renowned and outspoken figure in Spanish public life and someone who presents as an arbiter of value. Primarily known as a writer of thrillers, several of which have been adapted for film and television, he has also worked as a screenwriter (Palacio and Romero Santos 2017, 146). Like many Spanish novelists, he is a public intellectual. He frequently contributes opinion pieces to national newspapers; is a presenter on the public television station, Televisión Española; and is a regular on social media where he often courts controversy by expressing scathing criticisms of cultural issues and enters into lively spats with fellow writers in order to court media exposure (Palacio and Romero Santos 2017, 146). He is a member of the Real Academia Española (Spanish Royal Academy), an elite group of authors and academics who oversee the rules and grammar of Spanish language, a clear measure of national and institutional esteem. He is positioned at the center of Spanish intellectual life as well as contributing to framing questions of prestige within the language and culture. These associations suggest that the novel is the product of someone at the peak of a prestigious career.

Like *Los de abajo,* discussed in chapter 3, *La reina del sur* is a novel that has divided opinion on its cultural worth while simultaneously figuring as a text that has granted some prestige status to its author. Taste and tastemaking are central to how both novels have been consumed. Formally more innovative than most of his output, with a keen ear for the accents and specificities of the language spoken by its cast of multinational characters, for Palacio and Romero Santos *La reina del sur* was a key novel in Pérez Reverte's career linking it to his admission into the Royal Spanish Academy in 2003 (2017, 147). Hugo Benavides is hyperbolic in his assessment of the novel, describing it as a "provocative reassessment of the narco-genre" and designating the character, Teresa, as a "literary achievement of continental and generational proportions" (Benavides 2008, 152). Others, such as Zavala (2018), have been more critical, suggesting that *La reina del sur* is indicative of a generic approach to novel writing that feeds a marketplace hungry for exploitative drug narratives. Irrespective of these qualitative assessments, it is clear that Pérez Reverte's reputation benefited from the publication of the novel. In part, this is because the novel is focused on a male protagonist.

The novel has a journalist as protagonist-narrator who uses investigative reporting and interviews with key personnel to write about Teresa, foregrounding how unusual it is for a woman to become a prominent figure in the drug trade. The narrator creatively fills in material that he is unable to fully source. The novel draws on the conventions of documentary fiction, albeit fictionalized and using crime thriller conceits, making it the work of an author proficient at working across genres. While adept in form and style, with metafictional notes on the limitations of journalistic truth, it is curtailed by its perspective. The narrator is a Spanish man who is intrigued and fascinated by Teresa as an exotic and attractive other. He has no self-awareness of his situatedness and the narrative does not invite the reader to read against this narrow perspective. From this source text a more expansive female-centered world was created in the telenovela version.

The opening credits of each episode have the cover of Los Tigres del Norte's second narcocorrido "La Reina del Sur" by Los Cuates de Sinaloa, a group that Deborah Jaramillo describes as deeply embedded in the drug trade (2014, 1596). That is, they are more closely aligned to the violence and its celebration. For Jaramillo, "the recording of the song represents, in a cultural sense, the mainstreaming of a maligned subgenre," a necessary shift away from its primary close association with the horrors of the drug trade (2014, 1596). Jaramillo's interpretation gives a sense of the cultural capital of the telenovela form in popular culture. The elevation of the narcocorrido to the soundtrack of a quality telenovela also works for the appeal and sense of authenticity of the telenovela. The telenovela co-opts the genre's popularity and morbid association with criminality and becomes integral to del Castillo as tastemaker. This is radical mediation as tastemaking working horizontally across popular forms and adapting their attendant features. Although popular, this reversioning means that the song moves from marginal outsider status to becoming a significant node in the radical mediation of the drug trafficker.

There is a fluidity to the narcocorrido that opens up the possibility of reversioning. None of the lyrics of these versions of Camelia/Teresa's stories map precisely onto one another. They are self-consciously different. Narcocorridos can pick up a thread and alter or enhance the preexisting version, making them multilayered metatexts that can stand alone but nod to those who understand their codes, characters, and motifs. The version played over the opening credits of the series provides some broad-brush sense of Teresa as myth and hints of her life story, but not the precise details of her trajectory. Therefore, "when the narcocorrido and telenovela meet we are confronted with a hybrid that constructs a third meaning" (Jaramillo 2014, 1596). Given the popularity of these versions, it is likely that some members of the audience have prior knowledge of the narcocorrido. In addition, there is an expectation that the audience will be familiar with the cultural codes of the narcocorrido and, as intelligent readers and listeners of the intertextuality between the telenovela and narcocorrido, are capable of listening against its literal narrative. This assessment underscores one of the many ways of building on its source text, the narcocorrido, and *La reina del sur* is another illustration of a sophisticated thick adaptation discussed in chapter 3, this time with a reversioning that bears comparison with high-value television.

The novel was originally slated to be a film in Spanish and, later, in English, but neither got financial backing (Palacio and Romero Santos 2017, 147–48). A confluence of shifts in the transnational media landscape favored its development into a telenovela. In 2010, the private Spanish television channel, Antena 3, signed an agreement with Telemundo—a network founded in Puerto Rico, headquartered in Miami, and owned by the US network, NBC Universal—in order to compete in the growing Spanish-language television marketplace in the US (Jaramillo 2014, 1595). The intention was to create multiple versions of *La reina del sur* following the commercial success of the multiple versions of *Yo soy Betty, la fea/ Ugly Betty* (RCN Televisión, 1999–2001) (Palacio and Romero Santos 2017, 149). There has been a less successful, but nonetheless enduring, English-language version, *The Queen of the South* (2016–19). It stars the Brazilian Alice Braga as Teresa, a Mexican. Where the action in the Spanish-language version moves between Mexico, North Africa, the US, and Spain and involves transnational cartels, the English-language version is more firmly located in the North-South axis of the US and is a more conventional US crime drama. Scott Rosenbaum, M. A. Fortin, and Joshua John Miller are the showrunners, all of whom have written for US-based genre (horror, crime, and comedy) film and television. In their version, there is little sensitivity to cultural nuance and characters speak in English even when Spanish would be more realistic. As adaptation, it has thinned out much of what is innovative and, unlike the 2011 version, it does not bear the markers of quality television, evident in the Spanish-language version, as I will discuss.

To add to the multiplicity of versions and the effect this has on reception and quality, there is a peculiarity in formatting in the 2011 versions of *La reina del sur* on either side of the Atlantic. In Spain, *La reina del sur* was released in an edited form as a thirteen-episode series, while in the Americas it was shown as a sixty-four-episode telenovela. Critical of the Spanish version, Pérez Reverte described it as "una bazofia" (garbage), preferring the longer version released in the Americas (Palacio and Romero Santos 2017, 151). There is potential for comparison, elsewhere, between the English- and Spanish-language versions, but due to lack of space, my focus is on the version released in the Americas. This story of versions tells of the primacy given the novel form, whereby the author gets invited to join a prestigious national organization, while the other versions are denigrated because of their association with criminality (the narcocorridos) or melodrama (the telenovela). At the same time, the narcocorrido's use in the telenovela elevates it to a higher value plane. Such assessments provide a sense of the multinodal radical mediation and tastemaking of all of these forms and genres and their narrative sophistication.

The Telenovela Narrative: Quality and Complexity

The new high-quality telenovela is building on previously successful high-budget telenovelas. But *La reina del sur* also bears comparison with developments in US television and the emergence of what Jason Mittell calls "complex television" (2015). In his book of the same name, Mittell details the emergence of complex television as the consequence of industry and cultural shifts that include a changing media landscape where network television has been supplanted by pay-per-view cable and streaming services accompanied by online fora and social media, which provide space for audience engagement. This means that "the serial text itself is less of a linear storytelling object than a sprawling library of narrative content that might be consumed via a wide range of practices, sequences, fragments, moments, choices, and repetitions" (Mittell 2015, 7). This description fits with Grusin's (2015) radical mediation. Both Teresa as character and del Castillo's celebrity/star persona are key features of this multinodal radical mediation of narrative content as her story and its development plays out online and offline with direct linkages to the telenovela narrative.

Rethinking the telenovela provides an opportunity to consider assumptions about quality and taste. The telenovela is a form that is usually denigrated, and yet some of the characteristics Mittell identifies as integral to complex television are also integral to telenovelas. His is a detailed analysis of a situated evolution in US television that lends itself to comparison with the telenovela. Evidently, there have been different developments across the US and Latin American marketplaces, but it's worth examining a few of the shared narrative patterns, because complex television is a designation of quality that is considered absent in the telenovela. Narrative complexity is a marker of complex television, which is an identifiable feature integral to the telenovela. Expectations of the viewing patterns of telenovelas mean that the audience tends to be consistent and is expected to keep up with the plot twists and turns, whereas the long-running soap operas and low-value US sitcoms on network television do not rely on such consistency, which has led to risk-averse decision-making by US networks. This approach to television production in the US changed with the advent of cable television with its higher budgets and more selective and consistent audience post-1990s (Mittell 2015, 30–34). Whereas telenovelas have always had to satisfy audience expectations across multiple nation spaces, so they have long pushed the boundaries of expectations in order to compete in a crowded marketplace. Therefore, integral to the telenovela form are complexities and innovative practices only recently adopted by US television.

Another key characteristic of complex television is the development of the antihero. Audience engagement with complex television allows for an antihero narrative arc with a necessarily emergent character transformation. The "gradual shift of morality, attitudes, and sense of self that manifests itself in altered actions and long-term repercussions" can be found in the antihero "who is our primary point of ongoing narrative alignment but whose behaviour and beliefs provoke ambiguous, conflicted or negative moral allegiance" (Mittell 2015, 141–43). The telenovela has long adopted the antihero. Teresa's character arc follows this trajectory. The identifying position of the series is with Teresa. The plot developments hinge on her successes and failures in the drug trade and in love. As has been previously noted by Jaramillo (2014), a useful point of comparison is Walter White (Bryan Cranston) in *Breaking Bad* (2008–13). He starts as a conventional, even boring, teacher who, due to an extraordinary set of circumstances, becomes a methamphetamine cook and later dealer. His trajectory is from a legitimate profession to an illegitimate business. The series follows his emotional and moral evolution from apparently a simple, loyal, and loving father and husband to murderous criminal. His story is at the center, just as Teresa's is in *La reina del sur*. Like Walter, Teresa's attainment of power is achieved through a series of compromises of ever-increasing seriousness. This does not necessarily legitimize the decisions to kill and inflict trauma on others, but reveals how an individual gets to that point.

As another marker of prestige (albeit one I have nuanced in chapter 3), many telenovelas are adaptations. Like complex television (Mittell 2015, 22), they have been compared to literary fiction because of their densely layered character development, fully realized story world, unexpected events, and frequently playing with temporality, "using suspense to keep the interest of the viewers who follow the romantic escapades of characters, defying social injustice in their quest for a traditional happy ending" (Contreras 2006, 37). *La reina del sur*, as one of multiple versions, draws on all of these elements. Therefore, to draw a clear line between one of the source texts, even one with literary credentials, would be false, especially when each has variable prior markers of value. *La reina del sur* is a product of a dense series of radical mediations that are, in turn, reflections of cultural value, prestige, and tastemaking. As a consequence, it sets out a challenge to singular culturally situated celebrations of value and is a text that invites a rethinking of how the telenovela should be valued.

There is a shift in *La reina del sur* in its reversioning from the novel that is integral to thick adaptation and the sort of emphasis on the antihero common to complex television. The mode of storytelling in *La reina del sur*, where the camera takes on the narrator function, contrasts with the original source novel, which tells the story from the perspective of a journalist narrator. Thus, the telenovela places del Castillo/Teresa at its center. The novel's narrator struggles to find information on Teresa and consistently foregrounds the ways in which his research comes to unsatisfactory dead ends. In the novel the journalist provides an account of his research, which alternates with chapters from the novel he is writing. This metafictional technique suggests the unknowable nature of the drug world and distances the reader from Teresa. In contrast, in the series we have direct access to Teresa's lived experience and are invited to identify with her struggles and decisions. Like *Breaking Bad*, *La reina del sur* sets up a morally complex identificatory position for the viewer and demands some reflection on our own implication in this global illegal drug market. Clearly, then, *La reina del sur* carries many of the markers of value and quality ascribed to complex television.

Its use of the melodramatic mode, which privileges affect, with the excessive elements of Mexican telenovelas mark it as feminine with the attendant tendency to denigrate the female viewer. Complex television as a category has tended to be ascribed to male-centered narratives. Therefore, it is telling of how gender is a factor in the assessment of television that a shift from the novel as high-value work with its male narrator to a female-centered telenovela renders *La reina del sur* low value.

Narrative Thread, Powerful Vulnerability, and the Melodramatic Mode

As is to be expected in a sixty-four-episode telenovela, there are multiple plots and subplots in *La reina del sur*. Notwithstanding, I want to provide a broad overview of the narrative thread to orient the reader. The protagonist, Teresa Mendoza (Kate del Castillo), starts out as a young street trader in Culiácan, Sinaloa, in northern Mexico specializing in currency exchange, who falls in love with a pilot for a drug gang, El Güero Dávila (Rafael Amaya). He is killed by Epifanio Vargas (Humberto Zurita), head of a drug cartel for whom El Güero formerly worked, and the gang pursues Teresa, suspecting that she has inside knowledge. Teresa flees Mexico and goes to Melilla via Texas and Madrid and becomes a bar manager at a brothel, Yamila, managed by Dris Larbi (Nacho Fresneda). There she befriends the prostitutes, in particular Fátima Mansur (Mónica Estarreado). Her math skills are frequently useful and it is made clear that they are part of the reason she is kept as a manager and is not encouraged into sex work at Yamila. She falls in love with Santiago Fisterra (Iván Sánchez), a boat pilot who trafficks illegal cigarettes, marijuana, and (reluctantly) people between Melilla and Gibraltar. He is killed in a high-speed chase with the police, and she takes over his route. Teresa becomes successful, again, because of her unique talents, but is caught and imprisoned. While in prison she befriends a wealthy Spanish lesbian, Pati O'Farrell (Cristina Urgel), a heroin smuggler. On release from prison, they go into business and Teresa gets involved with Russian dealers trading drugs via Mexico, Colombia, and North Africa. They come into conflict with a Turkish cartel, with terrible consequences.

The series is an account of Teresa's evolution from streetwise worker on the lower rungs of the black market to head or "queen" of a large drug smuggling operation. In picaresque fashion her trajectory is a move through a multilevel industry and explores the vulnerabilities and power that she and others have at these different levels. Consistent with female-centered telenovelas, *La reina del sur* provides insights into the emotional toll of the violence inflicted on the characters and the deaths resulting from the high-stake risks of the business. It is also concerned with the complex dealings, which involve collusion by many layers of the legal system as well as by those who operate outside the law.

Romance and relationships with others are central to the narrative. *La reina del sur* fits with Ana María López's (1995) and Hugo Benavides's (2008) assessment that melodrama is a primary mode of Latin American telenovelas. It is a mode that draws on a particularly Mexican inflection that is given low status as a women-centered genre. Adriana Estill (2001, 173) suggests that a "playful and excessive" use of melodrama is typical of Mexican telenovelas. Excess and emotion are markers of femininity that are frequently dismissed, as I have discussed in relation to female stars in chapter 4. Darlene Sadlier (2009) signals the differences between the US/Hollywood melodrama and that of Mexico. Where the former is primarily and almost exclusively domestic the latter includes "historical epics in which family life is viewed in relation to larger national issues" (2009, 3). As Jesús Martín-Barbero (1987, 66) states, the Latin American telenovela melodrama "cotidianiza el entorno social y da cuenta de sus transformaciones, concilia el tiempo histórico de los grandes eventos" (renders everyday and normal events of great social and historical import), thereby making such events comprehensible in affective and relational terms. Suited to tackling an issue of global concern, Sadlier (2009, 15) suggests that it brings "groups who have lacked social power into communities of emotional solidarity and strength."

In the case of *La reina del sur* Teresa's community is made up of friends and allies working within or on the periphery of the drug trade, an industry given epic significance because of its global reach. Melodrama allows *La reina del sur* to move beyond a simple Manichean binary of good and evil to make space for greater density and thickness in the relationships between those in the illegal drug market and the communities in which they operate. Melodrama serves as a way into creating an affective community between the characters, the many dilemmas and problems they face, and the audience. It is also a reason why *La reina del sur* can fall outside of the usual assessments of quality.

Therefore, integral to the telenovela form is affect. The emotional world of the characters is tied to everyday concerns and desires (for love, friendship, and community building) and to the traumatic consequences of the illegal drug trade. Both are fully explored and deployed in the narrative. Teresa repeatedly suffers the loss of friends and lovers as a direct consequence of the nature of what is involved in trafficking. There are also other traumas faced by those who are on the losing side of stringent border controls. In particular, this is explored in the subplot involving moving Fatima's son from Morocco to Spain. Having no legal residency papers in Spain, disenfranchised as a woman in Morocco (this is accounted for in a troubling way to be a consequence of it being a Muslim country), marginalized as a prostitute working in a form of indentured labor, Fatima is shown to have to take considerable risks to cross the land border between the Spanish territory of Melilla to recover her son from her small village in northern Morocco. The child can be taken to Spain only through a combination of Teresa tapping into her unique access to the local head of a drug and people trafficking gang, her border-crossing skills as a Mexican (this is foregrounded through dialogue), Fatima's local knowledge, and their ability to access a network of empathetic individuals,. The narrative emphasizes the exceptionalism, both of this scenario and of Teresa's skills, while also highlighting the emotional pain resulting from hard borders. Therefore, *La reina del sur* reveals the affective consequences of the inequality of access to movement across borders all the while conforming to the generic conventions, which demand emotional release through satisfying resolutions of the plot. This is not to say that all plot lines result in positive outcomes, but that a sufficient number do to prevent the narrative from being relentlessly dark. Traumas are explored. There are instances such as Fatima's reunion with her son that provide emotional catharsis followed by other events with terrible outcomes. It is a telenovela that fully exposes the multiple layers of the drug trade and its consequences on the individuals involved and explores tangential personal experiences of marginalized subjectivity in a global marketplace.

La reina del sur shows the impact the drug trade has on an affective level and how it implicates many more than those directly involved in its buying and selling, thereby conforming to López's assessment of the telenovela as a mode that "ceaselessly offers its audience dramas of recognition and re-cognition by locating social and political issues in personal and familial terms and thus making sense of an increasingly complex world" (1995, 258). It brings large and complex issues into the living rooms of the television viewer. Extending this analysis and building on Martín-Barbero's work, Omar Rincón (2009, n.p.) suggests that telenovelas act as a form of news media that helps to interpret the complex world of drug distribution and violence, "La telenovela es una esfera pública para pensarnos como sociedad y es el modelo narrativo para comprender la política en América Latina" (the telenovela is a public forum to help us imagine ourselves as a society and it is the narrative model that provides a means of understanding Latin American politics). Earlier analysis of drug narratives emphasized their regionality or distinct national character. For example, Benavides suggests that "narco-dramas reflect a distinct regional, North Mexican culture, particularly of the border states" (2008, 3), whose function is both as a "coping mechanism" (2008, 5) and to "exoticise these communities to create a media image that is then reprocessed for export, making the people's marginality the key element in the telenovela's production" (2008, 5). The novel's Spanish narrator and the discoveries he describes encourage this examination of the Mexican protagonist as other.

In contrast, *La reina del sur* uses the telenovela form to provide recognition (or re-cognition, pace Lopez 1995) of the horrific violence of the so-called drug war that has dominated Mexican politics and public life in the last twenty years. There is potential to watch this series as a Mexican with a deep understanding of the events related to the violence enacted as a consequence of drug trafficking and find it to be a reframing of geopolitical responsibilities through the global perspective. That is, Mexico clearly bears responsibility and is the locale for some of the trade, but it is a trade with a wider reach. It is also possible to watch it with little knowledge and not to facilely slip into an easy reading of the drug trade as something that happens elsewhere at a distant remove. Unlike the othering of the novel, integral to the telenovela is a relational response and understanding suggested by López (1995) and Rincón (2009). *La reina del sur* is a challenge to the recurrent tendency in narratives of the drug trade to tell it at a remove and therefore other those involved as inherently violent. Foregrounding the move of people, goods, and violence across borders is an act of ethical tastemaking because it clearly shows it as a global trade with powerful global actors.

Drug Trafficking and the Local-Global Marketplace

The narrative of the telenovela is global, reflecting how the drug trade operates across borders and territories. Just as the English-language version taps into a long history of locating the source of violence and criminality south of the Mexico-US border, *La reina del sur*'s global perspective is an act of tastemaking that happens for strategic and economic reasons. Discussing globalization and cultural objects, Anny Brooksbank Jones (2007, 10) asserts that they are simultaneously products of the local and, through distribution and consumption patterns, become "re-embedded and reterritorialized in new contexts." A precis of the funding and locations used gives a sense of the transnational nature of the telenovela. *La reina del sur* was produced by Telemundo Studios and RTI Producciones by the Colombian Patricio Wills. The scriptwriters, Roberto Stopello, Valentina Párraga, and Juan Marcos Blanco, have worked on Colombian and Venezuelan telenovelas. It was shot in Colombia, Mexico, the US, Spain (Madrid, Malaga, Melilla), and Gibraltar, all of which are made evident in the narrative. With a large budget of $600,000 per episode (Palacio and Romero Santos 2017, 149–50), *La reina del sur* is a high-value telenovela that pivots between being highly situated and self-consciously global. The global perspective goes beyond a check box requirement of locations and actors; it takes a sophisticated approach to the issues and tensions that arise from the drug trade. People and locations are imbued with dense layers of meaning that serve as a commentary on power and access to spaces.

Characters have variable access to global movement, which reveals much about inequality and the structural violence inherent in the current form of capitalism. The focus on the drug trade allows for a dramatized (and frequently dramatic) exploration of the interdependence of nations, the global scale of the trade, and the skilled and unskilled workforce required for its success. El Güero is integral to his gang and becomes a target for murder because of his unique skill set, that is, he is able to fly small planes loaded with drugs and to land on small airstrips. Santiago is repeatedly said to be the most skilled at piloting the fast boats (*pateras*) used to bring drugs and people across the narrow strait between northern Africa and Spain. Teresa's success is down to her multiple intellectual and physical skills as boat pilot, her rapid mental arithmetic, street know-how, feminine charms carefully and tactically deployed, and her strategic sense. *La reina del sur* is an instance of how the drug trade exemplifies "globalisation [which is] driven dominantly by economic priorities with consequences that condition cultural imaginaries and have material cultural effects" (Brooksbank Jones 2007, 15). The drug trade is shown to be a highly meritocratic and complex network, albeit an extremely violent and brutal one.

Teresa is a contemporary global *pícara* (female picaresque character), and, as befits established picaresque convention, she moves up and across multiple different social strata of the nation spaces she inhabits (see Anadón Pérez 2005). I use the term *global* loosely, here, because although it "has no unitary definition" (Brooksbank Jones 2007, 4), it is useful when discussing *La reina del sur*. The locations used or referenced in the telenovela are very much defined as part of distinct nation spaces and marked by linguistic and cultural identifiers that cause miscommunications, clashes, and some onscreen humor. Maintaining these cultural distinctions is an unusual move in a high-cost telenovela where, usually, differences are flattened out (Contreras 2006, 40). For example, when Teresa arrives in Madrid she finds it difficult to understand the local Spanish accent and lexis. As her journeying continues, she puzzles over maps, looks askance upon cultural practices that limit women's freedom of movement in Morocco, is subject of other characters teasing about her proclivity for tequila, and so on. In *La reina del sur*, globalization has not smoothed out differences, but has created opportunities for encounters and shared experiences for those who can afford to access them.

Figure 8. Teresa/del Castillo finding her way.

Therefore, the global is both integral to everyday experience and in constant tension with the local. The characters are never more of their place of origin than when they are outside of it. Teresa is defined by her Mexican-ness, when in Spain, Fatima by her Moroccan origins, and even on a subnational level, Santiago by his Galician-ness. There are other details that can be noted in character nicknames, which reveal race-based social stratification. Teresa moves from being Prietita (little dark skinned one)—an affectionate nickname given to her by El Güero (blonde guy), when she is in Mexico—to being erroneously described as *sudaca*, an insulting term for South Americans in Spain, to eventually self-describing as *la mexicana*. Prietita and El Güero are identifiers of ethnic and class differences within Mexico, a country highly stratified by race and colorism. Her darkness is read as Mexican in Spain, a country with its own troubled history of reading racial characteristics. Therefore, the affective impact and engagement with markers of difference are made evident just as the impact of the intention of those employing them. Multilayered, nuanced, and highly self-reflective negotiation of difference is integral to the tastemaking of *La reina del sur*.

Teresa's Mexican nationality is a key identifier in the telenovela and, alongside the skills she learned on the streets of Culiacán, the perception of what this means to the multinational individuals she encounters is essential to her success as a drug trafficker. In his analysis of the novel, Benavides suggests that this is tied to "the nostalgia of exile, [which] serves to buttress her social capital in symbolically lucrative ways" (2008, 154). It is his contention that assumptions are made that because she is Mexican she has insider knowledge of the drug trade. This is more marked in the novel as the inevitable affiliation to a lost land, but is enacted differently in the telenovela. While the (mis)perception of the inevitability of her involvement serves her well and she exploits it, it does not tell the full story. Although correct in this instance, it is made obvious that not all Mexicans have connections to the drug trade. This attitude challenges a single story of the horrors of the drug trade played out on global television news that is further reinforced by attitudes toward Mexican migrants in the US, a prejudice Teresa exploits. In this way, *La reina del sur* tackles stereotyped thinking that even complex television can reproduce.

Teresa's relationship with El Güero meant that she had a growing connection with the trade, but as his companion and because of the gendered assumptions made about women in the trade in Mexico, she was not initially taken seriously by others as an active agent in their enterprise under his chain of command. Mexican traffickers are not alone in their prejudices. There are numerous set pieces throughout the series where others' preconceptions about women's capacity to engage in the drug business are shown up in their interactions. When she moves to Spain, being Mexican elides some of these suppositions. Vásquez Mejías (2016, 221) notes Teresa's insistence throughout the series that she should be called "la mexicana" (the Mexican), whereas others try and persist with the title of "La reina del sur." Vásquez Mejías (2016, 221) describes this insistence on making her a queen and denying her self-identification to be a form of epistemic violence that attempts to trivialize Teresa as a powerful agent. It mythicizes her and allies her with the inglorious history of misrepresenting women as objects or of othering them in telenovelas set in the drug trade, whereby women are frequently represented as acquisitions because of their sexual allure, as faithful long-suffering wives, or as innocent bystanders (Rincón 2009 and Vásquez Mejías 2016). Teresa consistently counters this violence and self-describes through the use of a gendered national moniker, *la mexicana*, becoming powerful enough to insist upon it and to assert equivalency with the Spanish, Russian, and Turkish dealers with whom she is conducting business. This is further evidence of how the series foregrounds the constant navigation of local and particular to be found amid a global trade.

The practicalities of movement are integral to the narrative. Money and power facilitate transit. Lack of access to these by those who could be labeled as marginal subjects is vividly portrayed. It makes the trade in drugs and its violent consequences a global issue, rather than one that troubles one particular nation space. Globalization is about the movement of people and goods, but, as the series makes clear, it is heavily regulated by states and nonstate actors, and both produces and is the product of significant violence and injustices. The consistent challenges to prejudices—against Mexicans, women, migrants—are forms of ethical tastemaking.

The second series has been released in 2019 as nations are becoming even more boundaried because political parties have proposed even greater physical barriers; it is clear that the idea of the nation has considerable force. When the focus of a film or television series is centered on events of national significance, it reinforces its national specificity. Conversely, film and television continue to be transnational in scope, aspiring to the widest possible audiences. This is differentiated according to genre, aesthetics, style, and channels of distribution whether via physical media (film stock, video, DVD) or digital streaming. Each one of these has a specific economics and its own barriers that can be difficult to fully unpack.

The North-South position is complicated in this series when the South is elsewhere. Taking into account funding, its multiple locations, and international cast and crew, *La reina del sur* (2011–) is clearly transnational and shifts the primary focus from the US-Mexico axis to Mexico-Europe–North Africa. As a telenovela with multiple sources—songs and novel—and specific genre expectations, it draws on these in line with television taste expectations in each territory and extends them to become a tastemaker. Within the transnational, there is also work that is repackaged or edited, or both, subject to its territorial distribution, which complicates its reception. On its initial run, the television series was differently distributed in the Americas and Spain. Such decisions are about audience expectations and channels of distribution. Extending this to how it has been bought for distribution by the streaming service Netflix further complicates how this series is viewed. Sitting alongside other successful narratives focused on the drug trade, such as *Narcos* (2015–17) and *Narcos: Mexico* (2018–), it becomes another intervention into a geopolitical narrative that crosses nations and has transnational appeal. Where the original intended audience had been established markets for Spanish/Colombian/Mexican telenovelas, the viewers of the series have been expanded and extended through streaming to territories, such as northern Europe, that are new markets. Such unanticipated success complicates and blurs the expectations of intentioned audiences and supposes reframing when considering the second series funded and distributed by Netflix.

Recalibrating Responsibility for the Global Drug Trade

The intersection of the local and the global results in a shift from a narrow focus on a singular cause or individual at the root of illegal drug trafficking to a wide-ranging look at the complexity of the multiple economic interests involved. Chris Hables Gray (1997, 30–31) suggests that the Cold War did not end; instead, it evolved to become the Drug War. The particularities of the drug war and its origins are complicated and located in specifically US politics of international relations as well as local conditions in Mexico that facilitated its development (Vulliamy 2011; Watt and Zepeda 2012; and Valencia 2018). What is redolent, here, is not where the drug war originated, but that it can be understood as global and that it should be read as a transnational conflict with multiple state and nonstate actors that have political and economic interests, variously, in its existence or destruction.

It is worth considering the context in which this series was aired in Mexico in 2011. Death and violence as a result of the drug trade was at a terrible peak, with the death toll in the tens of thousands and graphic stories abounding of the horrific nature of many of these (Mendoza and Navarro 2011). International news coverage of Mexico almost exclusively reported these deaths to the exclusion of other stories. This is reflective of the scale of the violence and is an issue of the types of stories that get international attention. It also makes the events exclusively Mexico's problem that require a response from the nation-state, rather than a more complicated nexus of local factors and global trade. Through revealing the multiple nodes, hot spots, interdependencies, and flows in the drugs trade, *La reina del sur* demands a wider vision and implicates all nation-states through the extension of the countries involved, thus showing it to be a truly global market in scope. The telenovela is unusual in its retention of the local inflections in language and accent and in repeatedly highlighting regional or national affiliation. It is a deliberate reinscription of the discursive practices and narrative framing that is evidence of how this series acts as a tastemaker. Intersecting with this is how del Castillo's style of gender performativity unsettles conventional gendered scripts and adds to the radical mediation of tastemaking.

Foregrounding the individual experiences and the practicalities of the local-global trade in drugs is a recalibration of where responsibility lies for violence. Although called *La reina del sur* Teresa consistently challenges the notion that she is a central figure, thus upending a facile conclusion that she is the sole originator or organizer of the trade. The multiple other characters competing for dominance or a place within the trade, as well as the narrative trajectory, operate to further undermine any sense that there is one singular powerful individual who is responsible. She is not a female version of the archetypal male drug lord, as he is frequently framed, because *La reina del sur* clearly asserts that such a primary figure is mere myth.

Violence, War, and Gendered Scripts

Del Castillo/Teresa's gender is integral to how she is valorized and should be understood as a tastemaker. Traversing this are preconceptions about women and violence. Neil Whitehead has suggested that media representations, even in fictional forms, can determine and provide "violent scripts and fantasies of masculinity" (2004, 16) that may "not cause people to kill, but it certainly suggests the poetics by which killing can be made meaningful to an audience" (2004, 19). It is important to reflect on the gendered script that is being created in this series and what it means for the local and global audiences. As a tastemaker del Castillo has to occupy a role normally scripted for a man, thus recodifying how women perform violent roles.

Conflicts and violent criminality have highly codified gendered relations where men have all the power, albeit differentially, and women are objects of exchange, booty of war, or victims of deliberate violence or collateral damage in violent exchanges (see *Cockburn 2001, 20–21). They are not perceived as actors in such contexts. That Teresa occupies a position of power normally identified as masculine is worthy of reflection. There is an implicit allusion to the real-life so-called *Reina del Pacífico*, Sandra Ávila Beltrán, in the title of the series (see Scherer García 2008). Unlike Ávila Beltrán, who is attached to a specific locale (Baja California in northwestern Mexico), Teresa's geographic alignment is more situational. The "sur" (south) in the series is never clarified and repeatedly disregarded by Teresa. It refers to multiple sites: the North African enclaves where she begins her business, the south of Spain, and Mexico as a nation located in the global south, suggesting that the title should resonate with reality, but not be taken as an account of it (see Benavides 2008, 158). Teresa must carefully navigate her way in what is frequently clearly marked as a male world. Even if the audience did not already read her as exceptional, at various points in the narrative characters draw attention to how unusual it is for a woman to be a major actor in this illegal market.

How Teresa/del Castillo's gender is to be read visually and narratively is carefully negotiated and troubled by how women are codified in war, the terrible acts of violence committed against women in northern Mexico (discussed in chapter 4), and how women's bodies are objectified on-screen. This means that *La reina del sur* repeatedly and self-consciously addresses these anxieties around a woman in this role in ways that are not easily resolved. Teresa is physically fit, skilled with firearms, mathematically adept, and learns mechanics and piloting easily. These are all abilities more usually (and erroneously) marked as masculine. Additionally, the casting of del Castillo is worthy of note. She is a woman with well-defined muscles from gym workouts, conforming to Richard Dyer's (1997, 152) notion of the "hard, contoured body" discussed in chapter 4, which contrasts with the softer appearance of many of the other actresses in the series. This toned body is dwelt upon through frequent lingering close-ups, but is also dressed in ways that emphasize an easily codified femininity: high-heeled shoes, tight jeans, and low-cut tops, or she is shown in various stages of undress. If these are not evidence enough of her femininity—by this, read cisgendered—the camera emphasizes her attractiveness to most of the male characters by focusing on their gaze, and the dialogue reminds us at regular intervals that she is desirable to men as well as the occasional woman. On the face of it, this preoccupation with how she conforms to a particular type of femininity and a repeated assertion that she is straight is curious. However, in representations of war or conflict, this need to establish rigid gender binaries is a familiar trope and one that is similarly foregrounded, because "in warfare, . . . the instruments with which the body is abused in order to break the spirit tend to be gender differentiated and, in the case of women, to be sexualised" (Cockburn 2001, 22). Additionally, del Castillo has performed queer roles, as Cleotilde, a lesbian in *Without Men* (Gabriela Tagliavini, 2011), and as a transgendered woman, Mousey, in *Cell K-11* (Jules Stewart, 2012). Her body is one that is easily troubled (pace Butler 2004), and her casting complicates how her character is read.

Her celebrity image involves a foregrounding of this body—in bikinis on the beach, in tight and revealing clothing at media events—but she does not share her gym sessions or workouts, as other celebrities such as Jennifer Lopez do. This suggests an anxiety around how she could be misread as not conforming to archetypal femininity because she is in a role that is normally associated with men. Discussing the portrayal of Teresa in the novel and the strengths and limitations that this gender transgression poses, Benavides finds that it conveys the "patriarchal structure" of the drug trade that Teresa is required to navigate, "always knowing it to be a culturally created scenario that does not respond to her organic understanding of herself or the world" (2008, 159). Benavides is addressing the challenge faced by Teresa in navigating sexism and the suppositions attached to her allure. Filtered through the journalist narrator, the novel invites the reader to join in this gaze. In the telenovela, her gender is subject to commentary. She plays with perceptions about her body, addresses its objectification where it is not welcome, and uses her attractiveness to manipulate potentially violent adversaries. In this way, she is navigating a sexist world with the tools and skills she has while the narrative draws attention to the necessity to do so. As telenovela it navigates Teresa's response to the unwanted advances in a more sophisticated fashion than the novel through the shift from male narrator to del Castillo/Teresa's performance of powerful vulnerability. The telenovela does not normalize sexism, as the novel does, it serves to challenge it. Read through the history of gendered representation of violence on-screen, del Castillo as Teresa draws on her star/celebrity persona where her body is that of a soft hard woman, moving between downplaying her hardness in favor of her softness all the while showing herself capable of the multiple skilled activities her physicality enables her to do. As tastemaking, the telenovela explores the affective and physical toll it takes to be a powerful woman. In turn, there are assumptions made about del Castillo as performer that have had real life consequences, which are linked to questions of taste.

Kate del Castillo Is Connected: Stardom, Celebrity, Social Media, and Drug Narratives

Kate del Castillo is a successful star, whose father, Eric del Castillo, is a well-established actor in theater, film, and, more latterly, in television. He had the lead role in the 1976 version of *Los de abajo* considered in chapter 3. This fact is not meant to overshadow her qualities; instead, it places her alongside other members of renowned families in Mexican film and television, most notably the producer-director Ripstein and the actor-director Bracho lineages. The status ascribed to Mexican television and the melodramatic roles del Castillo has performed on film have ensured that her star text is most often assigned a lesser value. This is reinforced in the recent film roles she has taken as mother and wife, respectively, in Patricia Riggen's *Bajo la misma luna* (2008) and *Los 33* (2015), both of which tend toward television-style melodrama that is considered of low value. In contrast, she has attained celebrity akin to notoriety as a result of being involved in a recent high-profile incident, the interview of the drug lord Joaquín "El Chapo" Guzmán Loera by US actor Sean Penn, accusations of criminal wrongdoing brought against her by Mexican authorities, and her ownership of these events in the documentary *The Day I Met El Chapo: The Kate del Castillo Story* (Carlos Armella, 2017) (see Vertiz De La Fuente 2018).

Given her public implication in the drug trade and in order to understand how del Castillo acts as polyvalent signifier in *La reina del sur*, it is useful to consider how we define her celebrity and stardom in relation to taste and value. As a film and television actor in Mexico she is a star according to conventional definitions, because she has attained fame through her performances on-screen and the attendant promotion of her offscreen persona (see Dyer 1998 and Shingler 2012). At the same time, she became famous in the US as a result of the interview with El Chapo. This is a form of celebrity resulting from becoming well known. Robert van Krieken defines celebrity as "a quality or status characterized by a capacity to attract attention, generating some 'surplus value' or benefit derived from the fact of being well known (highly visible) in itself in at least one public arena. It can be either positive or negative, including notoriety" (van Krieken 2012, 10). Celebrity is often differentiated from stardom as "a set of circulated strategies and practices" (Marwick and boyd 2011, 140). That is, celebrity is a being, not a doing. As a celebrity, an individual is assumed to be rewarded for inherent qualities rather than for their skills. Celebrity is a significant force within contemporary culture and influences how narrative media is consumed.

Often dismissed for the apparent lack of skill involved in its production and acquisition, celebrity merits a rethink. For Lee Barron, "celebrity culture . . . represents a potent intersection point for many of the social factors that dominate twenty-first-century societies within national and international contexts" (2015, 3). The power of celebrities in media and politics makes this a prescient comment (Klein 2017). Celebrity needs more precise definitions where the individual acquires and maintains attention through a variety of means that intersect with other skills and talents. I propose that Del Castillo should be understood as a celebrity-star tastemaker—a label that is deliberately active. Del Castillo's reinscription of both celebrity and stardom is worthy of analysis, because she is at the interstices of both, as a star in Mexico (and those territories where *La reina del sur* has been consumed) and as a celebrity in the US, and requires a reevaluation of how questions of taste and value are attached to screen performances and notoriety.

La reina del sur is significant in this story of stardom and celebrity because it was the reported reason El Chapo felt he could relate to del Castillo. Mittell proposes the term *alignment* in his analysis of complex television fandom, which proves useful in describing El Chapo's response to Teresa/del Castillo, that is, "the connections viewers feel with characters both within the storyworld and parasocially outside it" (2015, 129). Patricia Riggen's interpretation of El Chapo's fan approach to del Castillo echoes this understanding of alignment, "when you meet an actor, you think you know that person really well" (quoted in Draper 2016). El Chapo's decision to engage with del Castillo is reflective of a pattern of consumption and reading that has been noted across cultural production related to drug trafficking, as noted by scholars and writers, such as Rincón (2009), Vulliamy (2011), Franco (2013), Valencia (2018), and Zavala (2018), and is the reason why many of these authors make high demands on the realism and morality of representations of the drug trade.

The interaction between El Chapo and del Castillo has been well documented, but I want to pause briefly on the significance of the interaction and what it says about celebrity, stardom, and fame in representations of the drug trade. Del Castillo initiated interaction with El Chapo through a long series of tweets on January 9 in which she expressed dismay at the state of present-day governments and mentions him by name:

> Hoy creo más en el Chapo Guzmán que en los gobiernos que me esconden verdades aunque sean dolorosas, quienes esconden la cura para el cáncer, el sida, etc. para su propio beneficio y riqueza.
>
> SR. CHAPO, NO ESTARIA PADRE QUE EMPEZARA A TRAFICAR CON EL BIEN? (Uppercase in original, *Quién 2012)
>
> (Today I believe more in El Chapo Guzmán than I do in the governments that hide truths from me, even if they are painful, who hide the cures for cancer, AIDS, etc., for their own benefit. Mr Chapo, wouldn't it be cool if you started trafficking with the good?) (Draper 2016, lowercase in translation)

This extract is the most quoted section from what has been described as a letter in tweet form that includes expressions of her belief system (including religious, familial, marriage, and so forth); call outs to friends; mention of her favorite music; rejection of negativity; and proposal of selected affirmations. This apparent stream of consciousness tweet subsequently led to an exchange of correspondence and a meeting between del Castillo, Penn, and El Chapo in October 2014 in Mexico while he was on the run, having escaped from jail (Draper 2016). Penn had initiated the meeting ostensibly to discuss possible film rights to El Chapo's life story. Subsequently, it was clear that Penn (2016) had been commissioned to write an article about this meeting for *Rolling Stone*. The article sparked some controversy. In another instance of multiple versions and reversioning, Robert Draper

(2016) has written an account of the *Rolling Stone* article by Penn and the consequences for del Castillo for the *New Yorker* and, in turn, del Castillo has produced the aforementioned documentary in response to the fallout. Falling into high/low value judgments, Draper (2016) portrays Penn as someone joining this trip in a professional capacity. I do not have space for a full analysis of his participation in this incident (see Zavala 2018, loc 1795–1889), but a salient feature that emerges of Penn's persona in the article and the documentary is as an activist-journalist and film star. These are privileged over del Castillo's low-value status for Draper (2016), as she is framed primarily as a television actor with an emphasis on how little known she is in the US, and consequently of lesser interest and value.

Sometimes quoting her friends and family, Draper (2016) uses nouns and adjectives to describe del Castillo such as "innocence," "naïveté," and "impulsive" because of her description of a drug lord as someone who can fight for the underdog. Draper (2016) ignores the reality as it is lived for many, that this image attached to El Chapo is a quality that del Castillo is cognizant of and which resonates more broadly because it is integral to the narco-narrative. As Benavides in his study of telenovelas and narco-dramas suggests, the "films portray narcos (drug dealers) as ambivalent subjects who, although involved in the illegal drug trade, maintain strong social and personal commitment to their local communities, family members, and friends" (2008, 15). He describes territories in northern Mexico where the drug trade has long been normalized in some communities that are alienated from the official, legal systems of governance and power. Del Castillo's 2012 tweet reflects this opinion, demonstrating that she is versed in the discursive practices and tropes of this culture.

Del Castillo's social media presence and popularity are directly linked to *La reina del sur*. The networks, Telemundo and Antena 3, led a strong social media campaign alongside the release of the series, which meant that *La reina del sur* led to a social media bump for those attached to it, in particular del Castillo. Del Castillo has gained 2.8 million Twitter followers and also maintains a lively presence on Instagram (Palacio and Romero Santos 2017, 150–51). Her persona on social media is reflective of how recent developments have led to a "fragmented media landscape," meaning that instead of "a highly controlled and regulated institutional model" of star-celebrity management there is a shift to a "practice [that] involves ongoing maintenance of a fan base, performed intimacy, authenticity and access, and construction of a consumable persona" (Marwick and boyd 2011, 139–40). Drawing on Erving Goffman's (1990) analogy of "front stage" and "back stage" for an individual's public and private self, they propose this as carefully managed access to the performed self. As a consequence, Twitter has become a way to access the "backstage" where "there is no singular formula for celebrity practice; it consists of a set of learned techniques that are leveraged differently by individuals" (Marwick and boyd 2011, 144). Del Castillo's decision to directly address a dangerous and notorious individual within the drug trade is part of the performance of her backstage self online and blurs the line between her persona as the star of dramas set in the drug trade and builds a celebrity self aligned to this world. Through how her tweet has been read by El Chapo and others, the difference between the character, Teresa, and del Castillo's backstage self has been collapsed. As a consequence, El Chapo's act is about performing his fandom through inviting her and Penn to his safe house to interview him. This is an unusual, but telling, version of access and availability to celebrity facilitated by social media. It is also an enactment of authenticity and a form of "micro-celebrity," as theorized by Alice E. Marwick (2013).

Marwick (2013) discusses the self, authenticity, micro-celebrity, and self-branding on social media, as a high-value mode of entering the global economy since the mid-2000s. Originating in a particularly Northern Californian "ideal of entrepreneurship expanded beyond the technology into other aspects of life, including our most personal understandings of selfhood, relationships, and the body" (Marwick 2013, 4), it is inherently unequal, "intrinsically focused on individuals," and privileges rich white male experiences (Marwick 2013, 7). Its "broadcasting ability has transformed social status, encouraging people to prioritize attention and visibility" (Marwick 2013, 10). This has led to a new form of celebrity, the micro-celebrity that redefines what constitutes the online self and its relationship to the offline self. Marwick explains that "becoming a micro-celebrity requires creating a persona, producing content, and strategically appealing to online fans by being 'authentic'" (2013, 114). Authenticity is a notion that is difficult to define in screen performances. The same can be said for authenticity in an online persona. This "slipperiness is part of what makes it useful: it can satisfy many objectives, and can be interpreted widely" (Marwick 2013, 121) because it "is not an absolute quality, but a social judgement that is always made in distinction to something else" (Marwick 2013, 119). Del Castillo is adept at performing her authentic backstage self online and offline, which is something she has brought to her on-screen character, Teresa. Her celebrity self is akin to micro-celebrity, if celebrity has been understood as "something someone is," micro-celebrity "is something someone does" (Marwick 2013, 115). This makes micro-celebrity a consequence of doing, like stardom, rather than the mere generation of surplus value often ascribed to celebrity. Del Castillo's stardom comes from the roles she plays, but her micro-celebrity comes from the actions (or doing) attached to facilitating the interview between Penn and El Chapo.

Penn emerged from the interview and the attendant publicity with his persona as film star–activist intact. His place in the hierarchy of value attached to film stardom is part of this, as too is his gender. Del Castillo had considerable fallout from the encounter with El Chapo, as she makes clear in an interview with Colomba Vértiz de la Fuente (2018) and in *The Day I Met El Chapo: The Kate del Castillo Story*. Some of this was online, but she was also pursued by the Mexican government and falsely accused of money laundering, finding herself unable to return to Mexico for two years. Her nationality was a factor in this decision, but so too was the persona she has crafted on-screen and through her social media. She had become aligned with her characters and the low status attached to television acting as lacking in technique and craft. Her acting is assessed as a being not a doing, and the consequence has been that she is framed as a lower value celebrity rather than high-value actor and star.

The intersections of being and doing that were involved in this encounter reveal a form of exchange that is particular to social media, but also to older forms of fandom and star interactions. As well as Penn as star and del Castillo as celebrity, El Chapo is a fan and, also, a micro-celebrity. Without getting too deep into his role in trafficking nor the multiple layers attached to his criminal persona, El Chapo is a celebrity following van Krieken's (2012) definition, because he is notorious and his appeal to Penn and Castillo has generated surplus value. Picking up Marwick's definitions, El Chapo's fame also falls into the category of micro-celebrity because it involves doing and authenticity. In the multilevel illegal drug trade with its many competing groups and an ever-changing roster of individuals, El Chapo has proven a useful constant for media coverage that avoids careful reporting and analysis. As Zavala argues, "la celebridad global de capos como Joaquín 'El Chapo' Guzmán se debe en gran medida a la imposibilidad de pensar políticamente el fenómeno" (the global celebrity afforded capos like Joaquín 'El Chapo' Guzmán is the result of an inability to think politically about the phenomenon) (2018, loc 1643). While *La reina del sur* helps comprehend the drug trade and resituates it beyond

Mexico for its audiences, conversely, El Chapo serves as a focal point and, sometimes, distraction from the root causes and complexity of the issue.

This incident and the consequences for del Castillo are a form of radical mediation, with del Castillo and her role in *La reina del sur* as the central axis of the narrative. It has created a new version of the narrative with commentators and even the Mexican government, either willfully or unwittingly misreading del Castillo as closely aligned to her telenovela character. This speaks to assumptions about taste and value attached to television performances and to how del Castillo has created a character in Teresa Mendoza that has formed taste because of its apparent authenticity.

Conclusion

Del Castillo and the many versions of *La reina del sur* are nodes in radically mediated tastemaking. These are thick adaptations of selfhood and text. High quality, complex, and multilayered, *La reina del sur* required a nuanced performance that was misread as being (involved in the trade) rather than doing (her performance) and led to legal difficulties and physical risk for del Castillo. Upending conventional forms of self-presentation in Mexico and Spanish-language telenovelas and situated in the interface between celebrity and star, del Castillo provides an opportunity to foreground and challenge fixed hierarchies of value. *La reina del sur* as telenovela and del Castillo's star/celebrity persona provide a means of comprehending the local and global illegal drug trade and a possible way into avoiding simple good/bad polarities. In a low valued form, these are high-value tastemakers.

Tastemaking inhabits a space where low prestige productions (the telenovela) intersect with low valued fame (celebrity). Considering *La reina del sur* and del Castillo as tastemakers complicates the potential othering of Teresa (and Mexico) and invites comparisons with complex television. *La reina del sur* sits within the television landscape as a telenovela requiring contextual understanding because it is both typical of Mexican narratives of the drug trade and highly atypical. It is a female-centered narrative about a woman impelled into becoming involved in the international drug trade by incidents in the first episode. Her trajectory is dramatic and relational whereby she is involved in criminality out of necessity not out of greed or a quest for power. Her success in the drug trade is not presented as a move from good to evil, as is the case with Walter White in *Breaking*

Bad, for example, whereby at first he seems to happen upon drug production and dealing out of economic necessity only to reveal himself as clearly reveling in the power and riches that this successful venture has brought to his otherwise uneventful life. Teresa's move from working on the street as a vendor in Mexico to becoming a key player in the drug trade with global reach is motivated by happenstance, external factors, and her particular talents. Both Teresa and Walter attain power through their guile and unique skill set. Despite the many commonalities in these series, how taste and hierarchies of value are gendered and attached to specific genres determine that *Breaking Bad* is lauded as complex television and has launched Bryan Cranston's career as a Hollywood star, while *La reina del sur* is used as evidence that del Castillo is merely performing a self.

When the telenovela places its narrative within an ongoing conflict and makes it both spectacle and, through melodrama, focalizes on the individual experiences of violence, it makes it comprehensible. Such attention to Teresa's story and the people she engages with from all strata of society confronts the complex infrastructure and complicity involved in sustaining a criminal trade. It gets behind the mythification of a singular powerful individual and invites reflection on the wider consequences and the transnational nature of the illegal drug trade. In *La reina del sur* the violence is spectacular but not cathartic or desirable. True to its melodramatic mode, affect and relationships are what drive the narrative, which facilitates a new way into understanding the specific individual experiences and consequences of a transnational trade.

If we take on the approaches of Martín-Barbero (1987), López (1995), Estill (2001), and Rincón (2009) to the telenovela as a form of news media and community building that enables a deeper and affective understanding of difficult to comprehend sociopolitical issues, then *La reina del sur* is tastemaking as a storytelling tool using nonconventional stories on a global scale. The shift between the highly situated local and the global makes those involved responsible and the multilevel, multinational practices of the trade easier to grasp. Much naturalization of Mexico as inherently violent facilitates a geopolitical conflict (the "war on drugs") and feeds into prejudicial attitudes toward Mexican migrants in the US. *La reina del sur* works to counter these false preconceptions.

Typically on-screen, Mexico is the source and locale for much of the violence related to drugs in a booming industry of cultural production. The attendant features of these series are violence, criminality, and the illegal drug trade. Set and released against the backdrop of the violence associated with this trade in Mexico, and despite the key character being Mexican, the narrative of the first series of *La reina del sur* mostly takes place elsewhere. In a shift from such tired representations, as the most expensive and highest-earning television series in the Spanish-speaking market, *La reina del sur* relocates the violence to signal its inherently transnational nature. The multiple locations are integral to the tastemaking nature of the series. The consequence is that it thereby renders the violence an outcome of a global trade and, implicitly, challenges the facile correlation between Mexico and violence.

La reina del sur is largely a picaresque journey through the often violent drug trade. It is alive with references to cultural differences, but it seeks ways to reconcile these, not to elide them, and to find commonalities and unity. Given the context in which it was made and released and the afterlife it has had in its reversioning as narcocorrido and telenovela, that it frames this within the drug trade through the sympathetic portrayal of a female drug dealer is a significant move. Through del Castillo's offscreen persona it provides spaces for a rethink of form and celebrity-star tastemaking.

Conclusion

Ethical Reflections on Legitimation and Taste

The case studies in *Tastemakers and Tastemaking: Mexico and Curated Screen Violence* are centered on Mexico, violence, and gender. Violence has a terrible clarifying nature. It brings into relief alliances, affinities, solidarities, and enmity. Inherently excessive because of the spectacle of violence (on-screen or in actuality), violence elicits powerful emotional responses and can result in a traumatic aftermath. Violence is not tasteful, but its representation can be assessed subject to the ways that tastemaking has been codified and tastemakers have accrued cultural capital. The focus of this book has been unpacking where the fault lines lie and where the presuppositions about taste persist. While there is potential for application in other contexts, locales, and communities of creators, Mexico as a nexus of tastemaking and tastemakers has local and transnational significance.

Mexico has a long history of the representation of violence, resulting in a considerable range and variety of audiovisual material that requires close analysis. The impossibility of any individual examining all of this creative output, and a tendency for scholars to apply narrow doxa, which legitimate a relatively small selection, has allowed questions of taste to predominate. Looking at audiovisual material and its production through the perspective of tastemaking opens up the possibility of reaching a broader understanding of a fuller range of screen violence. Focusing on individuals as tastemakers and their relationship to a wider field of production is a way to comprehend how taste manifests itself through national and international value systems.

These case studies reveal that taste judgements are made because of underpinning assumptions about gender and race. When a film is dismissed because the star is too much herself (e.g., "too J-Lo"), it reveals that women's bodies, how they ornament themselves, and how they are racialized becomes a category of value overshadowing the other features of their work. This is why looking at films that are classed as failures and considering where they fall short functions as a way into understanding how taste operates in relation to films starring women and about women's devalued lives. In distinct ways, del Castillo, Jennifer Lopez, Maya Zapata, Ana Claudia Talancón, and Minnie Driver are either agents as tastemakers or can be considered within tastemaking practices because the narratives they are associated with are judged on the basis of their gendered star personas, which, in turn, are linked to their racialized bodies and how these are clothed.

None of us are immune to falling into practices of assessing work based on our taste formations. Even Pierre Bourdieu (2010), whose work has been fundamental in theorizing taste, has been prone to classification and judgments grounded in notions of value. In his work, Bourdieu uses a mix of nouns that carry historical baggage of definitional investigation, such as beauty, which he explores in depth, alongside others that are less well defined academically, and, consequently, less serious, such as "ugly," "lower," "coarse," "venal," "servile," and "vulgar" (Bourdieu 2010, xxx). All of these words carry moral weight. This demonstrates that even while attempting to go against the grain and challenge conventional doxa, Bourdieu is curtailed by his own taste formation. While trying to dismantle the high/low, good/bad, popular/elite dyads he sets up other assumptions about popular culture as lacking in depth and without its own encoding. That Bourdieu is hidebound by his own taste formation is not to undermine his position. Instead, it illustrates how, by illuminating the ways "good" or "bad" taste can be read and misread, tastemaking can extend his work and proves a useful way of understanding what work is valued. Tastemaking can allow us to address how we can be subject to our own cultural formation and open the door to looking at culture beyond a narrow canon. Tastemaking as an approach proposes that work does not need to meet certain prescribed aesthetic criteria but may involve using modes that are frequently assessed as low value, such as horror or the *telenovela*.

Examining tastemakers allows a perspective on patterns and anomalies. As I examine in chapter 2, Amat Escalante, like many of his male peers, employs the aesthetics and techniques of prestige film, thus facilitating his inclusion in festival programs. Combining the shocking with the banal, he invites reflection on the mediatization of violence and the multilayered socioeconomic structures that support its persistence. As discussed in chapter 1, when programming his cycle, Nelson Carro rewards Mexican filmmakers who take this approach and yet places such films alongside less conventional international films to invite reflection on the nature of the commemoration of violent conflicts. Thinking of Escalante and Carro as being engaged in tastemaking practice facilitates an understanding of violence on-screen, its circulation, and signification. Tastemaking is a means of getting beyond ranking representations of violence and of considering the work as imbricated in a multilayered nodal system that lies within and without national borders.

There are ethical considerations to screen violence and tastemaking that have wider implications and that, in recent times, have had considerable political consequences. Curators and creatives must make choices conscious of facile assumptions about Mexicans' relationship with violence and the use that has been made of this by politicians in the US. *Tastemakers and Tastemaking: Mexico and Curated Screen Violence* speaks to these concerns whereby Mexico and Mexicans are portrayed as inherently violent by outsiders, particularly in US film and television. To return to a much-lauded exemplar of quality, discussed in chapter 5, the complex television series *Breaking Bad*'s representation of Mexicans is worth some reflection. While it is ultimately about the moral decline of Walter White as he pursues power through drug dealing, his poor behavior is frequently contrasted with the horrors of Mexicans involved in the drug trade. His behavior is logical and strategic, whereas the Mexican characters are preoccupied with destroying the enemy through extreme violence. A clear example can be found in "Negro y Azul" (season 2, episode 7) when a major Mexican drug dealer turned informer, Tortuga (Danny Trejo), is decapitated and his head is glued to a tortoise. The tortoise and head combination then explodes and kills several El Paso police officers, both sending a message to the police and as evidence of extreme sadistic violence by the Mexican gang. In its representation of Mexicans, *Breaking Bad* rarely gets beyond the assumption that Mexicans are inherently violent. With the exception of Gus (Giancarlo Esposito), as one of the few Latino characters who is fleshed out, none are presented as intellectual equals to Walter. In a series that is otherwise nuanced, cleverly plotted, and highly referential, the Mexican characters are still just scapegoats or cyphers. While Walter and other white characters are given multidimensional characterization, Tortuga and many other Mexican characters are ascribed singular characteristics, lack agency, and are not grievable.

In such ways, there has been a normalization in US film and television of Mexico as a place of violence filled with individuals who have the capacity for horrific criminality. This has been exacerbated by the forty-fifth president of the US and his talk of the need to build walls to keep out imaginary rapists and criminals, but the rhetoric has deep roots in US cultural history. The conditions for fear and hatred preexisted any recent statements, and there are myriad examples of dehumanized individuals whose only agency resides in violent impulses to be found throughout the otherized representations of Mexicans in US culture.

In this context, Valencia's (2018) and Zavala's (2018) requirements for realism and accuracy, discussed in the introduction to this book, have greater urgency than they would in times of stability. In the absence of press reporting, tastemakers carry considerable power and responsibility through the stories they tell and curate. Taking into account the mediascape and the economic, political, and social context, the ethical approaches emphasized by Sobchack (1984), Sontag (2003), and Butler (2009) should be understood as urgent and integral to assessments of tastemaking. Such demands for ethics can be confused with fixed ideas around high value or prestige productions. There is a need to rethink narrow conceptions of taste, especially when value is attached to work on the basis of the accrual of cultural capital because it means that work that would otherwise merit investigation is ignored. Taking tastemaking as a significant act and focusing on the tastemaker as a node elides notions of value, thus repositioning the discussion.

The ingrained practice of misrepresentation has real-life consequences when it reinforces prejudices and endangers lives. It leads to critical unease that can flag taste and value as markers for inaccurate representations of violence in Mexico, which are not productive or easily defined. Critical demands for realism in creative culture can be explained by the lack of accurate reporting. In part, this is because, with fewer journalists and reduced revenue, there is a decline in news journalism at a global level. This means that coverage of news, such as the violence related to the drug trade in Mexico, is paltry, reduced to sound bites and feeding into preexisting stereotypes. Lack of reporting is also a result of Mexican government collusion and obfuscation whereby facts and details are difficult to access (Campbell 2014, 64–70, and Hootsen 2018). Additionally, reporting on the violence is dangerous. Repeatedly since 2006, Mexico is ranked as one of the most dangerous places in the world to be a journalist for reasons directly related to the recent violence (Hootsen 2018).

It would be tempting to stay away from an analysis of violence in Mexican culture in case it is read as reiterating or celebrating violence, or both. Instead, *Tastemakers and Tastemaking: Mexico and Curated Screen Violence* is premised on the fact that, while violence happens everywhere, Mexico has an imaginative pull and has been a major producer of film and television, thus making it a focal point for the analysis of violence on-screen. Examining creative work and those who create or curate it as tastemakers opens up new readings of texts and repositions whose work and lives are valued.

Folded into my exploration of taste and value is who gets to decide whose story is worthy of attention as tastemaking practice. Sometimes this is a necessary exercise in sifting through a large archive, as Carro did for the commemorations in the Cineteca that legitimizes a specific field of production. This is not a neutral task. As a tastemaker he upholds certain stories and overlooks others with their attendant aesthetic or generic approaches. Tastemakers are curators with sometimes stark choices. A choice can have an ethical consideration when it has consequences on deciding whose lives are grievable, such as the stories of the women in Juarez or the hanging bodies who are victims of the drug trade.

With ethical considerations in mind, assessing the case studies through tastemaking and tastemakers has produced multiple ethical dilemmas. While researching and writing this book I had to confront these dilemmas and consider what it might mean in the analysis of the work. Integral to understanding a tastemaker is to draw on their public/private persona as it is encoded and performed in relation to their work. Therefore, when I encountered hints and rumors of directors' and actors' experiences of creative work it affected readings about their agency as tastemakers. In this regard, there are two incidents of note related to the case studies in this text.

The first is considered in chapter 3 and clearly has been a factor in how Servando González's version of *Los de abajo* (1976) has been ignored. His work for the Mexican government filming the students at Tlatelolco in 1968 resulted in his work being excluded and poses a question about whose work merits investigation and who gets to be discussed. It is clear that aesthetics and merit are not reasons for inclusion; instead, who is legitimated is the result of gatekeeping. Taste attached to a work is clearly more than its inherent value. Tastemaking provides space to analyze such work. To consider someone who has been deemed complicit in this way can be taken into account when looking at it as part of a wider tastemaking practice. Rather than elide misgivings it produces them as part of the reading. This framing places the film in the context of its production and as a contribution to multiple versions of the same narrative.

As González's film demonstrates, legitimation is not easily acquired. The two versions of *Los de abajo* (1939 and 1976) considered in chapter

3 reveal how it is determined by circumstance and scholarly decisions rather than salient aesthetic features. In this case, the novel as source text acquired legitimacy as a result of a public academic exchange. My side-by-side videographic experiments reveal the extent to which the pacing and performances expressed both filmmakers' ambivalences and understanding of the consequences of Revolutionary violence in distinct ways that reflect historical conditions. The opening and closing sequences of both film versions of *Los de abajo* are of similar duration, but their different aesthetic approaches reveal much about their creators and the context they were working in, and they enable a close reading of screen violence. In my videographic experiments, point of view and agency are issues that arise in relation to audiovisual violence. Dismissing the 1939 version as mere filming by rote from the industrial period, or the 1976 film as the product of a director implicated in government actions, overlooks what reversioning can tell us and how it can extend adaptation theory and how tastemaking evolves. These unstable texts, when considered as nodes of tastemaking, make good entry points for reflections on tastemakers and justify looking at the work of figures such as González.

Although what caused González to fall out of favor is clear-cut and easy to track, there are other questions that are more challenging to unpack due to the nature of the power structures of the film and television industry and because some of the information lies in the realm of secrecy and rumor. The second incident is concerned with speculation related to Kate del Castillo's decision to leave her successful career with the Televisa network (the largest multimedia corporation in the Spanish-speaking world) and move to Los Angeles to work in the film industry. A male contributor to the documentary *The Day I Met El Chapo: The Kate del Castillo Story* (Carlos Armella, 2017) suggests that she wanted to escape the atmosphere of casual and persistent sexual harassment facilitated by the network. This was told as if it were an open secret, much like many similar revelations that emerged from the #metoo movement. There were additional theories for her departure posited by other interviewees including personal ambition, a desire to try out different roles, and that she was seeking out a change of scene. If problems with harassment are true, del Castillo was forced into choosing to tolerate it or leave Televisa, thereby take a risk and start over elsewhere. Although her move proved successful for her television career, having to make this decision resonates with a dilemma that I have had to confront throughout this project, a dilemma that underpins what gets critical attention.

How del Castillo is valorized—as a woman, as a television actor, as a Mexican in the US—all signal how tastemaking practices intersect with gender, race, and related suppositions about genre and quality. The value ascribed to her work is lesser for all of these reasons, while the sexism that enables harassment is present in how her work is assessed. Despite a long and considered refutation of taste dyads (e.g., good/bad, high/low), we are still at a place of ignoring or dismissing women-centered dramas for female audiences. Del Castillo's popularity and high profile in a form that is still marked as low value have meant that she is misread or given little critical attention. Being a key performer in an ever-evolving form and a celebrity-star with a high profile make her representative of a significant moment in the development of the *telenovela* and indicative of how actors must navigate a public/private self. Viewing her as a tastemaker reconfigures the discussion around del Castillo by stepping away from misconstrued notions of value. Her contribution to tastemaking makes her work significant irrespective of the value attributed to it or to her as a performer.

The #metoo activist movements and stories have opened up questions around why women have not been listened to when they have suggested that there are serious problems with the behavior of specific individuals and why harassment and assault is often the sort of open secret alluded to in the del Castillo documentary. Some of this links to taste underpinned by who and what is valued. Part of the responsibility of assessing work by tastemakers involves taking into account these challenging aspects of their public/private persona. Tastemaking facilitates a gendered consciousness and shifts the discussion away from false binaries and to a more refined discussion of the work and its creators.

Del Castillo's and González's stories are linked as individuals whose work has been ignored because they fall beyond the legitimating paradigms of gatekeepers. They reveal much about the hold a narrow conceptualization of taste has on film and television culture. While researching this book these are but some of the challenging discoveries of the sort that made me pause and consider how to continue to pursue certain lines of enquiry. Tastemaking practices require such ethical reflections and determine whose work has been upheld and ignored.

Gender determines how work is valorized. As a male filmmaker, Escalante can be a countertastemaker working inside and outside the legitimating paradigms of tastemaking. Excess is something that Escalante employs in his films but in ways that are legitimized by festivals and cultural gatekeepers. In part, this is because he mixes high-value aesthetics with low-value approaches in ways that conform to cultural doxa. *Los bastardos* and *Heli* are hyperrealist explorations of male workers employed to inflict pain or death that consider the traumatic consequences of these acts on the victims, their families, and the perpetrators. The decision to deploy arthouse aesthetics pushes the films into the realm of high-value tastemaking practices that have left reviewers ambivalent because of the hyperrealist violence, but it has resulted in prizes at prestigious festivals. They are films that sit in a hinterland of taste. Videographic criticism made it possible to consider the techniques and aesthetics of the slow cinema he uses in order to reflect on bodies in pain and the form of male labor involved in acts of violence.

While they have had different receptions than Escalante's films, *Bordertown* and *The Virgin of Juarez* also deployed excess. They pick up tropes of horror and employ star actors whose presence was criticized for overwhelming the narrative concern. They draw on generic conventions and, simultaneously, put forward a challenge to the medium's capacity to tell the women's stories. To get beyond these gender and genre-based criticisms, a mixed methodological approach proved fruitful in uncovering the stars as tastemakers. Through videographic experiments I found that in *Bordertown* and *The Virgin of Juarez* the inconsistencies of the films are not their excessive elements, but the slippery points of view of the assaults and attempted murders that privilege the perpetrator. In experiments for chapter 4, I had to reflect deeply on the ethical possibility of reproducing rape scenes that were deeply flawed because they were heavily weighted to the perpetrators' points of view, which, in turn, presented itself as the key issue in these films. To resolve this and not elide the problems in the source material I had to seek creative solutions. As tastemakers, the stars have considerable valence and importance that can serve to publicize issues. Conversely, this same presence did not escape participating in a long and flawed history of privileging the perpetrator in the representation of rape on-screen.

The tastemakers examined in this book focus on Mexico as the origin and inspiration for their work, because they are all engaging with significant moments and events in the nation's history. At the same time they draw on external influences and, sometimes, are specifically targeting external audiences. This awareness underpins the work and means that it operates in dialogue with wider global industries and conditions. The tastemaking is framed by a discrete situatedness within a nation-state and by a clear awareness of elsewhere either as source of inspiration, primary creative locale, or marketplace for their work. As a consequence, this book is informed by both national cinema and television studies and by its strong relationship with the international and the transnational.

Reconceptualizing the approach to analyzing screen violence as the activity of tastemaking implicitly challenges tired categories that are overdetermined by binary regimes of high/low taste. Through focusing on violence, with all its serious associations with death, life, politics, and national and community identities, I address why taste as a category works as a way of discovering new readings. Instead of evaluating how work conforms to assessments of value, there is a need to look inside, at, and beyond the frame to understand how taste is made, formed, and enacted. That is, there is a need to understand tastemaking and the tastemakers as thickly realized and informed by the context in which they pursue their creative and curatorial acts.

The case studies chosen are of tastemakers engaged in tastemaking practices because taste continues to concern cultural production and its curation. While assessments of taste can get caught up in the merits of a text or work, tastemaking considers the wider context and demands that tastemakers be held accountable for the choices they make. Looking at violence allows disquiet to creep in, because violence is not tasteful, and yet assessments of taste are made about its representation. To understand this is to comprehend a clarifying form of tastemaking and assess tastemakers who are aware of this history.

Despite frequent challenges, conceptualizations of taste have remained fixed. Therefore, *Tastemakers and Tastemaking: Mexico and Curated Screen Violence* proposes new approaches and methodologies demonstrating those that facilitate an understanding of tastemakers and their tastemaking practices. Looking at tastemaking requires a thorough analysis of text and context and yields fruitful results that are contingent, situated, and potentially transferable to other texts and contexts. This book argues that curation, prestige filmmaking, adaptation, stardom, and celebrity-stardom are acts of tastemaking.

Filmography

Ackerman, Chantal, dir. *Jeanne Dielman 23, Quai du Commerce, 1080 Bruxelles.* 1979; Belgium and France: Paradise Films and Unité Trois.
Alzaraki, Gary, and Michael Lam, dirs. *Club de Cuervos.* 2015–19; Mexico: Alzaraki Films and Netflix.
Armella, Carlos, dir. *The Day I Met El Chapo: The Kate del Castillo Story.* 2017; US: 25/7 Productions and Netflix.
Baiz, Andrés, Amat Escalante, Alonso Ruizpalacios, and Josef Kubota Wladyka, dirs. *Narcos: Mexico.* 2018–; Mexico and US: Gaumont International Television and Netflix.
Baiz, Andrés, Josef Kubota Wladyka, Fernando Coimbra, Gerardo Naranjo, Guillermo Navarro, José Padilha, and Gabriel Ripstein, dirs. *Narcos.* 2015–17; US, Colombia, and Mexico: Dynamo, Gaumont International Television, and Netflix.
Beatty, Warren, dir. *Reds.* 1981; US: Barclays Mercantile Industrial Finance and JRS Productions.
Benning, James, dir. *Landscape Suicide.* 1989; US: filmmuseum 68.
Benning, James, dir. *Los.* 2000; US: filmmuseum 68.
Beristáin, Natalia, and Alejandro Aimetta, dirs. *El secreto de Selena/Selena's Secret.* 2018; Mexico: BTF Media.
Berman, Sabina, and Isabelle Tardán, dirs. *Entre Pancho Villa y una mujer desnuda.* 1995; Mexico: Televicine S.A. de C.V. and Televisa S.A. de C.V.
Bolaños, José, dir. *La soldadera/The Female Soldier.* 1966; Mexico: Producciones marte and Productora de Técnicos Cinematográficos del Sindicato de Trabajadores de la Producción Cinematográfica.
Boorman, John, dir. *Deliverance.* 1972; US: Warner Bros. and Elmer Enterprises.
Bracho, Julio, dir. *La sombra del caudillo/The Shadow of the Caudillo.* 1960; Mexico: Sindicato de Trabajadores de la Producción Cinematográfica.
Bracho, Julio, dir. *La virgen que forjó una patria/The Virgin Who Founded a Nation.* 1942; Mexico: Films Mundiales.

Buñuel, Luis, dir. *Los olvidados/The Young and the Damned*. 1950; Mexico: Ultramar Films.
Burrows, James, dir. *Will and Grace*. 1998–; US: KoMut Entertainment, Three Princesses and a P, NBC Studios, and NBC Universal Television.
Carrera, Carlos, dir. *El crimen del padre Amaro/The Crime of Father Amaro*. 2002; Colombia, Spain, Argentina, and France: Alameda Films, FOPROCINE, IMCINE, Wanda Films, and Ibermedia.
Carrera, Carlos, dir. *El Traspatio/Backyard*. 2009; Mexico: Tardan/Berman, FOPROCINE, Coppel, and Argos Comunicación.
Chenillo, Mariana, Álvaro Hernández, and Gerardo Naranjo, dirs. *Soy tu fan/I'm Your Fan*. 2010–12; Mexico: Canana Films.
Coninx, Stijn, dir. *Daens*. 1992; Belgium, France, and Netherlands: Dérives Productions, Favourite Films, and Shooting Star Filmcompany BV.
Coppola, Sophia, dir. *Somewhere*. 2010; US, UK, Italy, and Japan: Focus Features, Pathé Distribution, and Medusa Films.
Cruz, Mauricio, and Walter Doehner, dirs. *La reina del sur/The Queen of the South*. 2011–19; US, Spain, Colombia, and Mexico: AG Studios, Antena 3 Televisión, RTI Televisión, and Telemundo Studios.
Cuarón, Alfonso, dir. *Roma*. 2018; US and Mexico: Esperanto Filmoj, Participant, and Pimienta Films.
Cuarón, Alfonso, dir. *Y tú mama también/And Your Mother Too*. 2001; Mexico: Anhelo producciones, Besame Mucho Pictures, and Producciones Anhelo.
de Fuentes, Fernando, dir. *Allá en el Rancho Grande/Out on the Big Ranch*. 1936; Mexico: Bustamente y Fuentes.
de Fuentes, Fernando, dir. *El compadre Mendoza/Godfather Mendoza*. 1933; Mexico: Interamericana Films.
de Fuentes, Fernando, dir. *¡Vámonos con Pancho Villa!/Let's Go with Pancho Villa*. 1936; Mexico: Cinematografica Latino Americana S.A.
de Palma, Brian, dir. *Carrie*. 1976; US: Redbank Films.
Dobson, Kevin James, dir. *The Virgin of Juarez*. 2006; US: Las Mujeres LLC.
Eisenstein, Sergei, dir. *Bronenosets Potemkin/Battleship Potempkin*. 1925; USSR: Goskino and Mosfilm.
Eisenstein, Sergei, dir. *Oktyabar/October*. 1927; USSR: Sovkino.
Escalante, Amat, dir. *Heli*. 2013; Mexico, Netherlands, Germany, and France: Mantarraya Producciones, Tres Tunas, CONACULTA, and FOPROCINE.
Escalante, Amat, dir. *La region salvaje/The Untamed*. 2016; Mexico, France, Denmark, Germany, Norway, and Switzerland: Mantarraya Producciones, Tres Tunas, IMCINE, and FOPROCINE
Escalante, Amat, dir. *Los bastardos*. 2008; Mexico, France, and US: Mantarraya Producciones, Tres Tunas, and FOPROCINE.
Escalante, Amat, dir. *Sangre*. 2005; Mexico, France: Mantarraya Producciones, Tres Tunas, and No Dream Cinema.

Estrada, Luis, dir. *El infierno/The Narco*. 2010; Mexico: Bandidos Films, IMCINE, FOPROCINE, Estudios Churubusco Azteca S.A., and FONCA.
Fernández, Emilio, dir. *Enamorada/A Woman in Love*. 1946; Mexico: Panamerican Films S.A.
Fernández, Emilio, dir. *Flor silvestre/Wildflower*. 1943; Mexico: Films Mundiales.
Fernández, Emilio, dir. *Víctimas del pecado/Victims of Sin*. 1950; Mexico: Cinematográfica Calderón S.A.
Fernández Violante, Marcela, dir. *Cananea*. 1977; Mexico: CONACINE.
Fernández Violante, Marcela, dir. *De todos modos Juan te llamas/General's Daughter/Whatever You Do It's No Good*. 1975; Mexico: Dirección de Difusión Cultural de la UNAM and Universidad Nacional Autónoma de México (UNAM).
Gilligan, Vince, dir. *Breaking Bad*. 2008–13; US: High Bridge Productions, Gran Via Productions, Sony Pictures Television, and AMC.
González, Servando, dir. *Expo 59*. 1959; Mexico: Government of Mexico.
González, Servando, dir. *Los de abajo/The Underdogs*. 1976; Mexico: CONACINE.
Gout, Albert, dir. *Aventurera*. 1949; Mexico: Cinematográfica Calderón S.A.
Haneke, Michael, dir. *Funny Games*. 1997; Austria: Wega Films.
Hernández Gómez, Guillermo, and Mario de Lara, dirs. *La Adelita*. 1937; Mexico: Iracheta y Elvira.
Hool, Lance, dir. *One Man's Hero*. 1999; US: Arco Films S.L., Hool/Macdonald Productions, and Silver Lion Films.
Ivory, James, dir. *A Room with a View*. 1985; UK: Merchant Ivory Productions.
Jones, Kirk, dir. *What to Expect When You're Expecting*. 2012; US: Lionsgate, Phoenix Pictures, and What to Expect Productions.
Kazan, Elia, dir. *¡Viva Zapata!* 1952; US: Twentieth Century Fox.
Kieślowski, Krzysztof, dir. *La double vie de Véronique/The Double Life of Véronique*. 1991; France, Poland, and Norway: Sidéral Produtions and Le Studio Canal+.
Landeta, Matilde, dir. *La negra angustias/Black Angustias*. 1949; Mexico: Tacma.
Lara, Gabylu, dir. *American Curious*. 2018; Mexico: Traziende Films.
Leduc, Paul, dir. *Reed, México insurgente/Reed, Insurgent Mexico*. 1972; Mexico: Ollín y Asociados.
Lilienthal, Peter, dir. *Hauptlehrer Hofer/Schoolmaster Hofer*. 1975; West Germany: Film Fernsehen Autoren Team GmbH and Westdeutscher Rundfunk.
Linklater, Richard, dir. *Fast Food Nation*. 2006; UK and USA: Fox Searchlight Pictures, HanWay Films, and BBC Films.
Lynch, David, dir. *Blue Velvet*. 1986; US: De Laurentiis Entertainment Group.
Lynch, David, dir. *Inland Empire*. 2006; France, Poland, and US: StudioCanal, Funacja Kultury, and Inland Empire Productions.
Martínez, Arturo, dir. *Contrabando y Traición/Contraband and Betrayal*. 1977; Mexico: Hermanos Benítez and Producciones Potosí S.A.
Masao, Adachi, dir. *AKA, Serial Killer*. 1969; Japan: Kōji Wakamatsu.

Nava, Gregory, dir. *Bordertown*. 2006; US and Mexico: Möbius Entertainment, El Norte Productions, Nuyorican Productions, and Mosaic Media Group.
Nava, Gregory, dir. *My Family*. 1995; US: American Playhouse, American Zoetrope, Majestic Films International, and Newcomb Productions.
Nava, Gregory, dir. *Selena*. 1997; US: Q Productions and Esparza/Katz Productions.
O'Connor, Pat, dir. *Circle of Friends*. 1995; Ireland, US, and UK: Price Entertainment. Lantana, Bórd Scannán na hÉireann/Irish Film Board, and the Rank Organisation.
Ordoñez, Rodrigo, Hilario Peña, and Marcelo Tobar, dirs. *Camelia la texana/ Camelia the Texan*. 2014; Mexico: Argos Comunicación.
Peckinpah, Sam, dir. *The Ballad of Cable Hogue*. 1970; US: Eaves Movie Ranch and Warner Bros.
Peckinpah, Sam, dir. *The Wild Bunch*. 1969; US: Warner Brothers/Seven Arts.
Pineda Barnet, Enrique, dir. *La bella del Alhambra/The Beauty of the Alhambra*. 1989; Cuba and Spain: Instituto Cubano del Arte e Industrias Cinematográficos and Televisión Española.
Portillo, Lourdes, dir. *Señorita extraviada/Missing Young Woman*. 2001; US: Women Make Movies.
Poul, Alan, dir. *The Back-Up Plan*. 2010; US: CBS Films and Escape Artists.
Restrepo, Luis Alberto, dir. *Las muñecas de la mafia/The Mafia Girls*. 2009; Colombia: Caracol Televisión.
Restrepo, Luis Alberto, dir. *Sin tetas no hay paraíso/Without Tits There's No Heaven*. 2006; Colombia: Caracol Televisión.
Reygadas, Carlos, dir. *Batalla en el cielo/Battle in Heaven*. 2005; Mexico, France, Belgium, and Germany: No Dream Cinema, Mantarraya Producciones, Arte France Cinéma, ZDF/Arte, Hubert Bals Fund, IMCINE, and Universidad de Guadalajara.
Reygadas, Carlos, dir. *Nuestro tiempo/Our Time*. 2018; Mexico: Eficine, FOPROCINE, No Dream Cinema, Mantarraya Producciones, and ZDF/Arte.
Ribeiro Ferreira, Marío, dir. *Yo soy Betty, la fea/Ugly Betty*. 1999–2001; Colombia: RCN Televisión.
Rodríguez, Ismael, dir. *La Cucaracha/The Soldiers of Pancho Villa*. 1958; Mexico: Películas Rodríguez.
Rodríguez, Ismael, dir. *Nosotros los pobres/We the Poor*. 1947; Mexico: Producciones Rodríguez Hermanos.
Rosas, Enrique, dir. *El automóvil gris/The Gray Automobile*. 1919; Mexico: Azteca Films and Rosas y Cía.
Sánchez, Alejandra, and José Antonio Cordero, dirs. *Bajo Juárez: La ciudad devorando a sus hijas/ Down in Juarez: The City That Devours Its Daughters*. 2006; Mexico: FOPROCINE, IMCINE, Pepa Films, and UNAM.
Sánchez, Eduardo, et al., dirs. *The Queen of the South*. 2016–19; US, Spain, Malta, and Mexico: Frequency Films, Latina Pictures, and USA Television Network.
Scafaria, Lorene, dir. *Hustlers*. 2019; US: Gloria Sanchez Productions, Nuyorican Productions, and STX Films.

Scorsese, Martin, dir. *The Age of Innocence*. 1993; US: Columbia Pictures and Cappa Production.
Scorsese, Martin, dir. *Gangs of New York*. 2002; US and Italy: Initial Entertainment Group and Alberto Grimaldi Productions.
Sevilla, Marcela, Mariano Ardanaz, Alfonso Pineda Ulloa, and Jorge Colón, dirs. *El recluso/The Inmate*. 2018–; Mexico: Animal de Luz Films.
Sneider, Roberto, dir. *Arráncame la vida/Tear This Heart Out*. 2008; Mexico: Altavista Films and La Banda Films.
Soderbergh, Steven, dir. *Out of Sight*. 1998; US: Universal Films and Jersey Films.
Sollima, Stefano, dir. *Sicario 2: Soldado*. 2018; US, Mexico: Columbia Pictures, Black Label Media, and Thunder Road Pictures.
Stewart Hunter, Samuel, and Pitibol Ybarra, dirs. *Ingobernable/Ungovernable*. 2017–18; Mexico: Netflix, AG Studios, and Argos Producciones.
Stewart, Jules, dir. *Cell-K11*. 2012; US: Libertine Films.
Suarez, María Fernanda, Carlos García Agraz, Álvaro Curiel, Chavas Cartas, and Pepe Castro, dirs. *Mujeres asesinas/Female Assassins*. 2005–08; Mexico: Mediamates S.A. de C.V.
Taboada, Carlos Enrique, dir. *La guerra santa/The Holy War*. 1977; Mexico: Conacite Uno.
Taboada Tabone, Francesco, dir. *Los últimos zapatistas, héroes olvidados/The Last Zapatistas, Forgotten Heroes*. 2002; Mexico: Fondo Estatal Para la Cultura y las Artes de Morelos and Universidad Autonoma del Estado de Morelos.
Tagliavini, Gabriela, dir. *Without Men*. 2011; US: Indalo Productions, Venus Films, and Vini Films.
Tort, Gerardo, dir. *De la calle/Streeters*. 2001; Mexico: IMCINE, Tiempo y Tono Films, and Zimat Consultores.
Toscano, Carmen, dir. *Memorias de un mexicano/Memories of a Mexican*. 1950; Mexico: Archivo Salvador Toscano.
Trapero, Pablo, dir. *Carancho*. 2010; Argentina, Chile, France, and South Korea: Finecut, Matanza Cine, Patagonik Film Group, and L90 Producciones.
Urueta, Chano, dir. *Los de abajo/The Underdogs*. 1939; Mexico: Nueva América, Producciones Amanecer.
Urueta, Chano, dir. *Si Adelita se fuera con otro/If Adelita Went with Another*. 1948; Mexico: Diana Films.
Van Sant, Gus, dir. *Milk*. 2008; US: Focus Features and Axon Films.
Vilaplana, Lilo, Nicolás Di Blasi, Leonardo Galavis, and Víctor Huerta, dirs. *Dueños del paraíso/Owners of Paradise*. 2015; US and Mexico: Telemundo Studios, Miami, and TVN.
Villeneuve, Denis, dir. *Sicario*. 2015; US, Mexico, Hong Kong: Lionsgate, Black Label Media, and Thunder Road Pictures.
Wajda, Andrzej, dir. *Ziema obiecana/The Promised Land*. 1975; Poland: Sfinks.
Wang, Wayne, dir. *Maid in Manhattan*. 2002; US: Revolution Studios and Red Om Films.

Weerasethaku, Apichatpong, dir. *Loong Boonmee raleuk chat/Uncle Boonmee Who Can Recall His Past Lives*. 2010; Thailand, UK, France, Germany, Spain, and Netherlands: Kick the Machine, Illuminations Films, Anna Sanders Films, and the Match Factory.

References

Agencia EFE. 2018. "Ana Claudia Talancón: 'El mundo no es solo puros güeritos de ojos azules.'" *Agencia EFE*, September 8. https://www.efe.com/efe/america/mexico/ana-claudia-talancon-el-mundo-no-es-solo-puros-gueritos-de-ojos-azules/50000545-3743475.

Agencia el Universal. 2016. "Cineteca Nacional de Mexico, 42 anos de historia." *El Universal de México*, January 17. Infotrac Newsstand. http://link.galegroup.com/apps/doc/A440162277/STND?u=livuni&sid=STND&xid=f497c2e9.

Aguilar, Carlos. 2017. "Pleasure and Pain in Guanajuato: Amat Escalante's *The Untamed* Is an Unusual Sort of Creature Feature." *Movie Maker*, August 1. https://www.moviemaker.com/archives/interviews/tentacle-love-amat-escalante-on-creating-the-creature-in-the-untamed-and-filming-in-his-native-guanajuato/.

Albarrán-Torres, César. 2017. "Spectacles of Death: Body Horror, Affect and Visual Culture in the Mexican Narco Wars." *Senses of Cinema* 84 (September). http://sensesofcinema.com/2017/feature-articles/mexican-narco-wars/.

Álvarez López, Cristina. 2012. "Double Lives, Second Chances." Translated by Catherine Grant. *Frames Cinema Journal* 1 (July 2). http://framescinemajournal.com/article/double-lives-second-chances/.

Anadón Pérez, María José. 2005. "Pícaros: Propuesta didáctica para un curso de perfeccionamiento de español como lengua extranjera (La vida de Lazarillo de Tormes, la ciudad de los prodigios, la reina del sur, Ilona llega con la lluvia)." *Revista electrónica de didáctica del español como lengua extranjera* 4 (June). doi:https://dialnet.unirioja.es/servlet/articulo?codigo=1350175.

Anderson, Benedict. 1983. *Imagined Communities: Reflections on the Origin and Spread of Nationalism*. London: Verso.

Appiah, Kwame Anthony. 2000. "Thick Translation." In *The Translation Studies Reader*, edited by Lawrence Venuti. London: Routledge.

Arroyo Quiroz, Claudia. 2009. "La novela de la Revolución Mexicana y su adaptación al cine: El caso de *Los de abajo* de Mariano Azuela." *Casa del tiempo* 4, no. 30: 58–61.

Azuela, Mariano. 1992. *The Underdogs*. Translated by Frederick H. Fornoff. Pittsburgh: University of Pittsburgh Press.
Azuela, Mariano. 1997. *Los de abajo*. Introduction and edited by Marta Portal. Madrid: Catedra.
Azuela, Mariano. 2002. *The Underdogs*. Translated by Beth E. Jörgensen. London: Penguin Books.
Azuela, Mariano. 2006. *The Underdogs*. Translated and edited by Gustavo Pellón. Indianapolis: Hackett Publishing.
Azuela, Mariano. 2012. *The Underdogs*. Translated by E. Munguía Jr. Radford, VA: Wilder Publications.
Azuela, Mariano. 2015. *The Underdogs*. Translated by Ilan Stavans and Anna More, edited by Ilan Stavans. New York: Norton.
Bailey, David C. 1974. *¡Viva Cristo Rey! The Cristero Rebellion and the Church and State Conflict in Mexico*. Austin: University of Texas Press.
Baker, Courtney R. 2015. "Framed and Shamed: Looking at the Lynched Body." In *Humane Insight: Looking at Images of African American Suffering and Death*, 35–68. Champaign: University of Illinois Press.
Baker, Mona. 2006. *Translation and Conflict: A Narrative Account*. London: Routledge.
Balzer, David. 2015. *Curationism: How Curating Took Over the Art World and Everything Else*. London: Pluto Press.
Baron, Jaimie. 2014. *The Archive Effect: Found Footage and the Audiovisual Experience of History*. New York: Routledge.
Barron, Lee. 2015. *Celebrity Cultures: An Introduction*. Los Angeles: Sage.
Bautista, Berenice. 2016. "Amat Escalante: 'Quise abrir la Realidad.'" *AP English Worldstream*, October 24.
Bautista, Berenice. 2018. "A New Wave of Mexican Filmmakers Succeeds Internationally." *AP English Worldstream*, March 22.
Benjamin, Thomas. 2000. *La Revolución: Mexico's Great Revolution as Memory, Myth, and History*. Austin: University of Texas Press.
Benjamin, Walter. 2002. *Illuminations*. New York: Random House.
Bourdieu, Pierre. 1993. *The Field of Cultural Production: Essays on Art and Literature*. Cambridge: Polity Press.
Bourdieu, Pierre. 2010. *Distinction: A Social Critique of the Judgement of Taste*. Translated by Richard Nice. Abingdon: Routledge.
Brett, Camilla. 2015. "In the Footsteps of Frida Kahlo: How Is Life Changing for Mexico City's Women?" *Guardian*, November 9. https://www.theguardian.com/cities/2015/nov/09/frida-kahlo-how-life-changing-mexico-city-women.
Brewster, Claire. 2005. *Responding to Crisis in Contemporary Mexico: The Political Writings of Paz, Fuentes, Monsiváis, and Poniatowska*. Tucson: University of Arizona Press.
Brewster, Keith, ed. 2010. *Reflections on Mexico '68*. Malden: Blackwell.

Brooksbank Jones, Anny. 2007. *Visual Culture in Spain and Mexico*. Manchester: Manchester University Press.
Burns-Ardolino, Wendy A. 2009. "Jiggle in My Walk: The Iconic Power of the 'Big Butt' in American Pop Culture." In *The Fat Studies Reader*, edited by Esther D. Rothblum and Sondra Solovay. New York: New York University Press
Butler, Judith. 2004. *Undoing Gender*. New York: Routledge.
Butler, Judith. 2009. *Frames of War: When Is Life Grievable?* London: Seagull Books.
Calderón, Felipe. 2010. "Programa de Actividades del Bicentenario de la Independencia y Centenario de la Revolución." Presidencia Felipe Calderón Hinojosa. *YouTube*, February 10. Accessed June 3, 3019. https://www.youtube.com/watch?v=uzFM7xdM2yU&t=975s.
Calefato, Patrizia. 2010. "Fashion as Cultural Translation: Knowledge, Constrictions and Transgressions on/of the Female Body." *Social Semiotics* 20, no. 4: 343–55.
Campbell, Howard. 2014. "Narco-Propaganda in the Mexican 'Drug War': An Anthropological Perspective." *Latin American Perspectives* 41, no. 2 (March): 60–77.
Carro, Nelson. 2013. Website. https://www.nelsoncarro.com/. Accessed June 17, 2019.
Cartmell, Deborah, and Imelda Whelehan, eds. 2007. *Cambridge Companion to Literature on Screen*. Cambridge: Cambridge University Press.
Cepeda, Alice, and Kathryn M. Nowotny. 2014. "A Border Context of Violence: Mexican Female Sex Workers on the U.S.-Mexico Border." *Violence Against Women* 20, no. 12: 1506–31. doi:10.1177/1077801214557955.
Cervantes Porrúa, Israel. 2017. "El drama de Felipe Calderón en la guerra en contra del narcotráfico/Felipe Calderon's Drama in the War against Drug Trafficking." *Andamios*, no. 34: 305–28.
Chamberlain, Lori. 2002. "Gender Metaphorics in Translation." In *The Interpreting Studies Reader*, edited by Franz Pöchhacker and Miriam Shlessinger. London: Routledge.
Chanan, Michael. 2009. "The Space between Fiction and Documentary in Latin American Cinema: Notes toward a Genealogy." In *Visual Synergies in Fiction and Documentary Film from Latin America*, edited by Miriam Haddu and Joanna Page, 15–26. New York: Palgrave Macmillan.
Charney, Leo. 2001. "The Violence of a Perfect Moment." In *Violence and American Cinema*, edited by J. David Slocum, 47–62. New York: Routledge.
Chávez, Daniel. 2016. "Film Adaption and Transnational Cultures of Production: The Case of Guillermo Arriaga." *A Contracorriente* 13, no. 3: 127–56.
Chávez-Silverman, Suzanne. 2003. "Gendered Bodies and Borders in Contemporary Chican@ Performance and Literature." In *Velvet Barrios*, edited by Alicia Garcia de Alba. New York: Palgrave Macmillan.
Chion, Michel. 1999. *The Voice in Cinema*. Translated by Claudia Gorbman. New York: Colombia University Press.

Choi, Jinhee. 2006. "National Cinema, the Very Idea." In *Philosophy of Film and Motion Pictures: An Anthology*, edited by Noël Carroll and Jinhee Choi. Oxford: Blackwell.

Cineteca Nacional. "Información." Accessed June 17, 2019. https://www.cinetecanacional.net/controlador.php?opcion=contexto.

Clover, Carol. 2015. *Men, Women, and Chain Saws: Gender in the Modern Horror Film*. Princeton, NJ: Princeton University Press.

Contreras, Carlos. 2006. "The Telenovela Goes Worldwide." *MultiLingual* 17, no. 8 (December): 37–41.

Coulthard, Lisa. 2016. "Acoustic Disgust: Sound, Affest, and Cinematic Violence." In *The Palgrave Handbook of Sound Design and Music in Screen Media*, edited by Liz Greene and Danijela Kulezic-Wilson. London: Palgrave Macmillan.

Cousins, Mark. 2013. "Widescreen on Film Festivals (2006)/Film Festival Form: A Manifesto (2012)." In *The Film Festival Reader*, edited by Dina Iordanova. St Andrews, Scotland: St Andrews Film Studies.

Dadds, Kimberley. 2013. "Showing Off Her Minnie Bikini Body: Driver Reveals Her Washboard Stomach as She Runs along the Beach with Son Henry." *Daily Mail*, September 2. https://www.dailymail.co.uk/tvshowbiz/article-2408852/Minnie-Driver-reveals-washboard-stomach-runs-beach-son-Henry.html.

de la Vega Alfaro, Eduardo. 1999. "The Decline of the Golden Age and the Making of a Crisis." In *Mexico's Cinema: A Century of Film and Filmmakers*, edited by Joanne Hershfield and David R. Maciel, 165–92. Wilmington, DE: SR Books.

de Luca, Tiago, and Nuno Barradas Jorge. 2016. "Introduction: From Slow Cinema to Slow Cinemas." In *Slow Cinema*, edited by Tiago de Luca and Jorge Nuno Barradas, 1–21. Edinburgh: Edinburgh University Press.

Desmond, John M., and Peter Hawkes. 2006. *Adaptation: Studying Film and Literature*. New York: McGraw Hill.

De Valck, Marijke. 2016a. "Introduction: What Is a Film Festival? How to Study Festivals and Why You Should." In *Film Festivals: History, Theory, Method, Practice*, edited by Marijke de Valck, Brendan Kredell, and Skadi Loist, 1–11. London: Routledge.

De Valck, Marijke. 2016b. "Fostering Art, Adding Value, Cultivating Taste: Film Festivals as Sites of Cultural Legitimization." In *Film Festivals: History, Theory, Method, Practice*, edited by Marijke de Valck, Brendan Kredell, and Skadi Loist, 100–116. London: Routledge.

Díaz Arciniega, Víctor. 2010. *Mariano Azuela: Retrato de viva voz*. Mexico: Consejo Nacional para la Cultura y las Artes.

Dijkstra, Maaike. 2013. "It's the Return of J-Lo: Jennifer Lopez Brings Her Best Asset Back to the Red Carpet." *Grazia*, January 25. Accessed May 17, 2017. http://www.graziadaily.co.uk/fashion/news/its-the-return-of-j-lo-jennifer-lopez-brings-her-best-asset-back-to-the-red-carpet.

Dovey, Lindiwe. 2015. *Curating Africa in the Age of Film Festivals: Film Festivals, Time, Resistance.* London: Palgrave Macmillan.
Draper, Robert. 2016. "The Go-Between: The Mexican Actress Who Dazzled El Chapo." *New Yorker*, March 11. https://www.newyorker.com/magazine/2016/03/21/kate-del-castillo-sean-penn-and-el-chapo.
Driver, Alice. 2015. *More or Less Dead: Feminicide, Haunting, and the Ethics of Representation in Mexico.* Tucson: University of Arizona Press.
Dyer, Richard. 1997. *White: Essays on Race and Culture.* London: Routledge.
Dyer, Richard. 1998. *Stars.* London: British Film Institute.
Edberg, Mark C. 2011. "Narcocorridos: Narratives of a Cultural Persona and Power on the Border." In *Transnational Encounters: Music and Performance at the U.S.-Mexico Border*, edited by Alejandro L. Madrid, 67–82. New York: Oxford University Press.
Elliott, Kamilla. 2013. "Theorizing Adaptations/Adapting Theories." In *Adaptation Studies: New Challenges, New Directions*, edited by Jorgen Bruhn, Anne Gjelsvik, and Erik Frisvold Hanssen, 19–45. New York: Bloomsbury.
Escalante, Amat. 2012. "The Greatest Films of All Time 2012." *BFI*. https://www.bfi.org.uk/films-tv-people/sightandsoundpoll2012/voter/859.
Estill, Adriana. 2001. "The Mexican Telenovela and Its Foundational Fictions." In *Latin American Literature and Mass Media*, edited by Edmundo Paz-Soldan and Debra A. Castillo. New York: Garland Publishing.
Faden, Eric S. 2009. "A Manifesto for Critical Media." *Mediascape: UCLA's Journal of Cinema and Media Studies* (Fall). http://www.tft.ucla.edu/mediascape/Spring08_ManifestoForCriticalMedia.html.
Falicov, Tamara L. 2010. "Migrating from South to North: The Role of Film Festivals in Funding and Shaping Global South Film and Video." In *Locating Migrating Media*, edited by Greg Elmer, Charles H. Davis, Janine Marchessault, and John McCullough, 3–21. Lanham, MD: Lexington Books.
Falicov, Tamara L. 2013. "'Cine en Construcción'/'Films in Progress': How Spanish and Latin American Film-Makers Negotiate the Construction of a Globalized Art-House Aesthetic." *Transnational Cinemas* 4, no. 2: 253–71.
Falicov, Tamara L. 2016. "The 'Festival Film': Film Festival Funds as Cultural Intermediaries." In *Film Festivals: History, Theory, Method, Practice*, edited by Marijke de Valck, Brendan Kredell, and Skadi Loist, 209–29. London: Routledge.
Falicov, Tamara L. 2017. "Film Funding Opportunities for Latin American Filmmakers: A Case for Further North-South Collaboration in Training and Film Festival Initiatives." In *A Companion to Latin American Cinema*, edited by Maria M. Delgado, Stephen M. Hart, and Randal Johnson, 85–98. Chichester, UK: Wiley Blackwell.
Felperin, Leslie. 2007. "Bordertown." *Variety*, February 20, 15.

Figueroa, Gabriel. 2005. *Memorias*. Mexico City: Pértiga.
Film Festival Research. 2017. "Welcome." http://www.filmfestivalresearch.org/.
Fischer, Alex. 2013. *Sustainable Projections: Concepts in Film Festival Management*. St Andrews, Scotland: St Andrews Film Studies.
Franco, Jean. 2002. *The Decline and Fall of the Lettered City: Latin America in the Cold War*. Cambridge, MA: Harvard University Press.
Franco, Jean. 2013. *Cruel Modernity*. Durham, NC: Duke University Press.
Fregoso, Rosa Linda. 2003. *MeXicana Encounters*. Berkeley: University of California Press.
Fregoso, Rosa Linda, and Cynthia L. Bejarano. 2010. "Introduction: A Cartography of Feminicide in the Américas." In *Terrorizing Women: Feminicide in the Américas,* edited by Rosa Linda Fregoso and Cynthia L. Bejarano. Durham, NC: Duke University Press.
Frémaux, Thierry. 2019. "The Festival in 2019, Interview with Thierry Frémaux." Festival de Cannes. https://www.festival-cannes.com/en/qui-sommes-nous/festival-de-cannes-1.
Frow, John. 1995. *Cultural Studies and Cultural Value*. Oxford: Clarendon Press.
Galt, Rosalind. 2011. *Pretty: Film and the Decorative Image*. New York: Colombia University Press.
Galt, Rosalind, and Karl Schoonover. 2010. "Introduction: The Impurity of Art Cinema." In *Global Art Cinema: New Theories and Histories*, edited by Rosalind Galt and Karl Schoonover. Oxford: Oxford University Press.
Garbarino, James, Kathleen Kostelny, and Nancy Dubrow. 1991. *No Place to Be a Child: Growing Up in a War Zone*. Lexington, MA: Lexington Books.
García Canclini, Néstor. 1995. *Hybrid Cultures: Strategies for Entering and Leaving Modernity*. Translated by Christopher L. Chiappari and Silvia L. López. Minneapolis: University of Minnesota Press.
García, Gustavo, and Rafael Aviña. 1997. *Época de oro del cine mexicano*. Mexico: Clío.
García Riera, Emilio. 1992. *Historia documental del cine mexicano*. Vol. 2, 1938–42. Guadalajara: Universidad de Guadalajara.
García Riera, Emilio. 1994. *Historia documental del cine mexicano*. Vol. 15, 1970–71. Guadalajara: Universidad de Guadalajara.
García Riera, Emilio. 1995. "The Impact of Rancho Grande." In *Mexican Cinema*, edited by Paulo Antonio Paranaguá. Translated by Ana M. López. Mexico City: IMCINE; London: BFI.
Geraghty, Christine. 2008. *Now a Major Motion Picture: Film Adaptations of Literature and Drama*. Lanham, MD: Rowman and Littlefield.
Goffman, Erving. 1990. *The Presentation of Self in Everyday Life*. London: Penguin Books.
González Luna, Ana María. 2013. "Del corrido mexicano a la novela de tipo periodístico: 'La Reina del Sur' de Arturo Pérez Reverte." *Tintas: Quaderni*

Di Letterature Iberiche e Iberoamericane, no. 28–30: 161. doi:10.13130/ 2240-5437/3571.
Grant, Catherine. 2013. "Déjà-Viewing? Videographic Experiments in Intertextual Film Studies." *Mediascape: UCLA's Journal of Cinema and Media Studies* (Fall). http://www.tft.ucla.edu/mediascape/Winter2013_DejaViewing.html.
Grant, Catherine. 2016. "Beyond Tautology? Audio-Visual Film Criticism." *Film Criticism* 40, no. 1 (January): 1–4.
Grant, Keith Barry. 2007. *Film Genre: From Iconography to Ideology*. London: Wallflower.
Greene, Liz. 2009. "Speaking, Singing, Screaming: Controlling the Female Voice in American Cinema." *Soundtrack* 2, no. 1: 63–76.
Greene, Liz. 2018. "Do It for Van Gogh." NECSUS Spring, https://necsus-ejms. org/do-it-for-van-gogh/.
Greven, David. 2011. "Medusa in the Mirror: Brian de Palma's Carrie." In *Representations of Femininity in American Genre Cinema: The Woman's Film, Film Noir, and Modern Horror*, 91–115. New York: Palgrave Macmillan.
Grønstad, Asbjørn. 2016. "Slow Cinema and the Ethics of Duration." In *Slow Cinema*, edited by Tiago de Luca and Jorge Nuno Barradas, 273–84. Edinburgh: Edinburgh University Press.
Grusin, Richard. 2015. "Radical Mediation." *Critical Inquiry* 42 (Autumn): 124–48.
Guzmán, Martín Luis. 1979. *La sombra del caudillo*. Mexico City: Editorial Porrua.
Hables Gray, Chris. 1997. *Postmodern War: The New Politics of Conflict*. London: Routledge.
Hecht, John. 2019. "Netflix to Produce 50 Projects in Mexico." *Hollywood Reporter*, February 12. https://www.hollywoodreporter.com/news/netflix-produce-50-projects-mexico-1185950.
Henry, Claire. 2014. *Revisionist Rape-Revenge: Redefining a Film Genre*. London: Palgrave Macmillan.
Hermansson, Casie. 2015. "Flogging Fidelity: In Defense of the (Un)Dead Horse." *Adaptation* 8, no. 2: 147–60.
Herrera-Sobek, María. 1993. *The Mexican Corrido: A Feminist Analysis*. Bloomington: Indiana University Press.
Hind, Emily. 2019. *Dude Lit: Mexican Men Writing and Performing Competence, 1955–2012*. Tucson: University of Arizona Press.
Hirsch, Marianne. 2003. "Nazi Photographs in Post-Holocaust Art: Gender as an Idiom of Memorialization." In *Phototextualities: Intersections of Photography and Narrative*, edited by Alex Hughes and Andrea Noble, 19–40. Albuquerque: University of New Mexico Press.
Hirsch, Marianne. 2014. "Connective Histories in Vulnerable Times." *PMLA* 129, no. 3: 330–48.
Hirsch, Marianne, and Leo Spitzer. 2008. "'There Was Never a Camp Here': Searching for Vapniarka." In *Locating Memory: Photographic Acts*, edited by Annette

Kuhn and Kirsten Emiko McAllister, 135–54. New York: Berghahn Books.

Holliday, Ruth, and Tracey Potts. 2012. *Kitsch! Cultural Politics and Taste*. Manchester: Manchester University Press.

Hootsen, Jan-Albert. 2018. "In Mexico, 'Narcopolitics' Is a Deadly Mix for Journalists Covering Crime and Politics." Committee to Protect Journalists, December 19. https://cpj.org/blog/2018/12/in-mexico-narcopolitics-is-a-deadly-mix-for-journa.php.

Ibarra, Jesús. 2006. *Los Bracho: Tres generaciones de cine mexicano*. Mexico City: Universidad Nacional Autónoma de México.

Iordanova, Dina. 2016. "Foreword: The Film Festival and Film Culture's Transnational Essence." In *Film Festivals: History, Theory, Method, Practice*, edited by Marijke de Valck, Brendan Kredell, and Skadi Loist, xi–xvii. London: Routledge.

Jaramillo, Deborah L. 2014. "Narcocorridos and Newbie Drug Dealers: The Changing Image of the Mexican Narco on US Television." *Ethnic & Racial Studies* 37, no. 9 (September): 1587–1604. doi:10.1080/01419870.2012.758862.

Joseph, Gilbert M., Anne Rubenstein, and Eric Zolov, eds. 2001. *Fragments of a Golden Age: The Politics of Culture in Mexico since 1940*. Durham, NC: Duke University Press.

Keathley, Christian, and Jason Mittell. 2016. "Teaching and Learning the Tools of Videographic Criticism." In *The Videographic Essay: Criticism in Sound and Image*, edited by Christian Keathley and Jason Mittell, 3–23. Montreal: Caboose.

Kennedy-Karpat, Colleen, and Eric Sandberg. 2017. "Adaptation and Systems of Cultural Value." In *Adaptation, Awards Culture, and the Value of Prestige*, edited by Colleen Kennedy-Karpat and Eric Sandberg. Cham, Switzerland: Palgrave Macmillan.

Kermode, Mark. 2014. "*Heli* Is Harrowing and Often Unbearably Grim." *Guardian*, May 25. https://www.theguardian.com/film/2014/may/25/heli-review-mexican-drugs-drama-ultraviolent.

Klein, Naomi. 2017. *No Is Not Enough: Defeating the New Shock Politics: Resisting Trump's Shock Politics and Winning the World We Need*. London: Allen Lane.

Lavik, Erlend. 2012. "The Video Essay: The Future of Academic Film and Television Criticism?" *Frames Cinema Journal* 1 (July 2). http://framescinemajournal.com/article/the-video-essay-the-future/.

Leary, John Patrick. 2016. "Introduction: Latin America and the Meanings of 'Underdevelopment' in the United States." In *A Cultural History of Underdevelopment: Latin America in the U.S. Imagination*, 1–22. Charlottesville: University of Virginia Press.

Lebeau, Vicky. 2008. *Childhood and Cinema*. London: Reaktion Books.

Leitch, Thomas. 2007. *Film Adaptation and Its Discontents: From* Gone with the Wind *to* The Passion of the Christ. Baltimore: Johns Hopkins University Press.

León, Ariel. 2016. "Me da vergüenza decir que soy actriz en México: Maya Zapata." *El Universal*, March 31. https://www.eluniversal.com.mx/articulo/espectaculos/teatro/2016/03/31/me-da-verguenza-decir-que-soy-actriz-en-mexico-maya-zapata.

Leung, Wing-Fai W. 2009. "From Wah Dee to CEO: Andy Lau and Performing the Authentic Hong Kong Star." *Film International* 7, no. 40: 19–28.

Lie, Nadia, and Silvana Mandolessi. 2012. "Violencia y transnacionalidad en el cine latinoamericano contemporáneo: Sobre *Carancho* (P. Trapero, 2010) y *Los bastardos* (A. Escalante, 2008)." *Secuencias: Revista de historia del cine* 35: 103–19.

Loist, Skadi. 2016. "The Film Festival Circuit: Networks, Hierarchies, and Circulation." In *Film Festivals: History, Theory, Method, Practice*, edited by Marijke de Valck, Brendan Kredell, and Skadi Loist, 49–64. London: Routledge.

Lomnitz-Adler, Claudio. *Exit from the Labyrinth: Culture and Ideology in the Mexican National Space*. Berkeley: University of California Press, 1993.

López, Ana M. 1995. "Our Welcomed Guests: Telenovelas in Latin America." In *To Be Continued . . . Soap Operas around the World*, edited by R. C. Allen, 256–75. London: Routledge.

Luna, Diego. 2019. "Diego Luna Interviews 'Roma' Oscar Nominee Yalitza Aparicio—Exclusive." *Indiewire*, February 13. https://www.indiewire.com/2019/02/diego-luna-roma-interview-yalitza-aparicio-1202043684/.

Luna, Ilana Dann. 2018. *Adapting Gender: Mexican Feminisms from Literature to Film*. Albany: State University of New York Press.

Lury, Karen. 2010. *The Child in Film: Tears, Fears and Fairy Tales*. London: I.B. Tauris.

MacLaird, Misha. 2013. *Aesthetics and Politics in the Mexican Film Industry*. Basingstoke, UK: Palgrave Macmillan.

Madrazo Lajous, Alejandro, Jorge Javier Romero Vadillo, and Rebeca Calzada Olvera. 2017. "Los combates: La 'Guerra Contra las Drogas' de Felipe Calderon." *Nexos: Sociedad, Ciencia, Literatura* 39, no. 472. http://link.galegroup.com/apps/doc/A526871164/LitRC?u=livuni&sid=LitRC&xid=ef32d0ff.

Manovich, Lev. 2001. *The Language of New Media*. Cambridge: MIT Press.

Mantecón, Ana Rosas. 2013. *Ir al cine: Antropología de los públicos, la ciudad y las pantallas*. Mexico City: Universidad Autónoma Metropolitana; Barcelona: Gedisa.

Marketing Weekly News. 2011. "'La Reina Del Sur' Draws Best Audience Ever for Telemundo Entertainment Program, Averaging Nearly 4.2 Million Total Viewers." *Marketing Weekly News*, May 31. https://www.businesswire.com/news/home/20110531007102/en/%E2%80%9CLa-Reina-Del-Sur%E2%80%9D-Draws-Audience-Telemundo.

Marric, Linda. 2017. "Exclusive: Mexican Director Amat Escalante on Innovative Thriller *The Untamed*." *Hey You Guys*, August 18. https://www.heyuguys.com/amat-escalante-interview-the-untamed/.

Marten, James, ed. 2002. *Children and War: A Historical Anthology*. New York: New York University Press.

Martin, Adrian. 2014. *Mise en Scène and Film Style: From Classical Hollywood to New Media Art*. Basingstoke, UK: Palgrave Macmillan.

Martín-Barbero, Jesús. 1987. "Televisión, melodrama y vida cotidiana." *Signo y Pensamiento* 6, no. 11: 59–72. https://revistas.javeriana.edu.co/index.php/signoypensamiento/article/view/5741.

Marwick, Alice. 2013. *Status Update: Celebrity, Publicity, and Branding in the Social Media Age*. New Haven: Yale University Press.

Marwick, Alice, and danah boyd. 2011. "To See and Be Seen: Celebrity Practice on Twitter." *Convergence* 17, no. 2: 139–58. https://doi.org/10.1177/1354856510394539.

Matheson, Kristy. 2018. "'Somehow Images Are the Perfect Words': An Interview with Amat Escalante." *Senses of Cinema: An Online Film Journal Devoted to the Serious and Eclectic Discussion of Cinema*, March 1. http://sensesofcinema.com/2018/feature-articles/interview-amat-escalante/.

McCollum, Victoria. 2016. *Post-9/11 Heartland Horror: Rural Horror Films in an Era of Urban Terrorism*. New York: Routledge.

McCollum, Victoria. 2019. *Make America Hate Again: Trump-Era Horror and the Politics of Fear*. London: Routledge.

McKee Irwin, Robert, and Maricruz Castro Ricalde, eds. 2013. *Global Mexican Cinema: Its Golden Age*. London: BFI Palgrave.

Mendible, Myra. 2007. *From Bananas to Buttocks: The Latina Body in Popular Film and Culture*. Austin: University of Texas Press.

Mendieta Alatorre, Ángeles. 1961. *La mujer en la Revolución Mexicana*. México: Biblioteca del instituto nacional de estudios historicos de la revolución mexicana.

Mendoza, Enrique, and Adela Navarro. 2011. "Ya son 50 mil los muertos en la guerra antinarco: Zeta." *Proceso*, July 19. https://www.proceso.com.mx/276308/ya-son-50-mil-los-muertos-en-la-guerra-antinarco-zeta.

Mendoza, Vicente T. 1954. *El corrido mexicano: Antología, introducción y notas*. Mexico: Fondo de cultura económica.

Milenio. 2008. "Murió director mexicano Servando González a los 85 años." *Milenio*, October 7. Accessed June 10, 2015. http://www.milenio.com/node/91566.

Mistron, Deborah E. 1984. "A Hybrid Subgenre: The Revolutionary Melodrama in the Mexican Cinema." *Studies in Latin American Popular Culture* 3: 47–56.

Mittell, Jason. 2015. *Complex TV: The Poetics of Contemporary Television Storytelling*. New York: New York University Press.

Molina Guzmán, Isabel, and Angharad N. Valdivia. 2004. "Brain, Brow, and Booty: Latina Iconicity in U.S. Popular Culture." *Communication Review* 7: 205–21.
Molina Ramírez, Tania. 2007. "Ignoro dónde está lo que filmé el 2 de octubre del 68 en Tlatelolco." *La Jornada*, August 22. http://www.jornada.unam.mx/2007/08/22/index.php?section=espectaculos&article=a08n1esp.
Monsiváis, Carlos. 1989. "El difícil matrimonio entre cultura y medios masivos." *Chasqui* 6, no. 22. doi:10.16921/chasqui.v0i22.848.
Monsiváis, Carlos. 2000. *Aires de familia: Cultura y sociedad en América Latina*. Barcelona: Editorial Anagrama.
Monsiváis, Carlos. 2004. *Escenas de pudor y livianidad*. Mexico City: DeBolsillo.
Monsiváis, Carlos. 2009. *Apocalipstick*. Mexico City: Random House Mondadori.
Mora, Carl J. 2005. *Mexican Cinema: Reflections of a Society, 1896–1988*. Berkeley: University of California Press.
Moseley, Rachel. 2005. "Introduction." In *Fashioning Film Stars: Dress, Culture, Identity*, edited by Rachel Moseley. London: BFI Publishing.
Munich, Adrienne, ed. 2011. *Fashion in Film*. Bloomington: Indiana University Press.
Muñoz, Savannah. 2018. "Kim Kardashian and the Politics (and Privilege) of Being Racially Ambiguous." *Substance*, February 22. https://substance.media/kim-kardashian-and-the-politics-and-privilege-of-being-racially-ambiguous-bfa9cf1a2636.
Murch, Walter. 1995. *In the Blink of an Eye: A Perspective on Film Editing*. Los Angeles: Silman-James Press.
Netflix. 2018. "Netflix Establishes Its First European Production Hub in Madrid." Netflix Media Center, July 24. https://media.netflix.com/en/press-releases/netflix-establishes-its-first-european-production-hub-in-madrid.
Noble, Andrea. 2005. *Mexican National Cinema*. London: Routledge.
O'Malley, Irene V. 1986. *The Myth of the Revolution: Hero Cults and the Institutionalization of the Mexican State*. New York: Greenwood Press.
Ostrowska, Dorota. 2016. "Making Film History at the Cannes Film Festivals." In *Film Festivals: History, Theory, Method, Practice*, edited by Marijke de Valck, Brendan Kredell, and Skadi Loist, 18–33. London: Routledge.
Palacio, Manuel, and Rubén Romero Santos. 2017. "El espacio cultural transnacional en la post-transición: El caso de las series televisivas *Amores Difíciles* y *La Reina Del Sur* / The Transnational Cultural Space in the Post-Transition: The Case of the TV Series *Amores Difíciles* and *La Reina Del Sur*." *Secuencias*, nos. 43–44. doi:10.15366/secuencias2016.43-44.008.
Palmer, Lucia Mulherin. 2017. "Melancholia and Memory in Ciudad Juárez: Lourdes Portillo's *Señorita Extraviada/Missing Young Woman* (2001) and the Communal Mourning of Feminicide." *Studies in Spanish and Latin American Cinemas* 14, no. 3: 367–85. doi:10.1386/slac.14.3.367_1.

Parra, Max. 2005. *Writing Pancho Villa's Revolution: Rebels in the Literary Imagination of Mexico.* Austin: University of Texas Press.

Paz, Mariano. 2015. "Las leyes del deseo: Sexualidad, anomia y nación en el cine de Carlos Reygadas." *Bulletin of Spanish Studies: Hispanic Studies and Researches on Spain, Portugal, and Latin America* 92, no. 7: 1063–77.

Paz-Soldán, Edmundo, and Debra A. Castillo. 2001. "Introduction: Beyond the Lettered City." In *Latin American Literature and Mass Media*, edited by Edmundo Paz-Soldan and Debra A. Castillo. New York: Garland Publishing.

Penn, Sean. 2016. "El Chapo Speaks: A Secret Visit with the Most Wanted Man in the World." *Rolling Stone*, January 10. https://www.rollingstone.com/politics/politics-news/el-chapo-speaks-40784/.

Pérez-Anzaldo, Guadalupe. 2014. *El espectáculo de la violencia en el cine mexicano del siglo XXI.* Mexico City: Ediciones Eón.

Pick, Zuzana M. 2010. *Constructing the Image of the Mexican Revolution: Cinema and the Archive.* Austin: University of Texas Press.

Pineda Franco, Adela. 2019. *The Mexican Revolution on the World Stage: Intellectuals and Film in the Twentieth Century.* Albany: State University of New York Press.

Pisters, Patricia. 2017. "Imperfect Creative Criticism." *Cinema Journal* 56, no. 4: 145–46. doi:10.1353/cj.2017.0051.

Pitcan, Mikaela, Alice E. Marwick, and danah boyd. 2018. "Performing a Vanilla Self: Respectability Politics, Social Class, and the Digital World." *Journal of Computer-Mediated Communication* 23, no. 3 (May): 163–79. https://doi.org/10.1093/jcmc/zmy008.

Podalsky, Laura. 2011. *The Politics of Affect and Emotion in Contemporary Latin American Cinema: Argentina, Brazil, Cuba, and Mexico.* Basingstoke, UK: Palgrave Macmillan.

Porrúa, Israel Cervantes. 2017. "El Drama de Felipe Calderón en la guerra contra del Narcotráfico." *Andamios* 14, no. 34: 305–28.

Portal, Marta. 1997. "Introducción." In Mariano Azuela, *Los de abajo*. Madrid: Catedra.

Prince, Stephen. 1998. *Savage Cinema: Sam Peckinpah and the Rise of the Ultraviolent Movies.* Austin: University of Texas Press.

Prince, Stephen. 2003. *Classical Film Violence: Designing and Regulating Brutality in Hollywood Cinema, 1930–1968.* New Brunswick, NJ: Rutgers University Press.

Projansky, Sarah. 2001. *Watching Rape: Film and Television in Postfeminist Culture.* New York: New York University Press.

Qiong Yu, Sabrina, and Guy Austin, eds. 2017. *Revisiting Star Studies.* Edinburgh: Edinburgh University Press.

Ramírez Berg, Charles. 1992. *Cinema of Solitude: A Critical Study of Mexican Film, 1967–1983.* Austin: University of Texas Press.

Ramirez Berg, Charles. 1994. "The Invention of Mexico: The Poetics and Politics of the Fernández-Figueroa Style." In *The Mexican Cinema Project*, edited by Chon A. Noriega and Steven Ricci. Los Angeles: UCLA Film and Television Archive.

Ramirez Berg, Charles. 2015. *The Classical Mexican Cinema: The Poetics of the Exceptional Golden Age Films*. Austin: University of Texas Press.

Rancière, Jacques. 2016. "Béla Tarr: The Poetics and Politics of Fiction." In *Slow Cinema*, edited by Tiago de Luca and Nuno Barradas Jorge, 245–60. Edinburgh: Edinburgh University Press.

Rastegar, Roya. 2016. "Seeing Differently: The Curatorial Potential of Film Festival Programming." In *Film Festivals: History, Theory, Method, Practice*, edited by Marijke de Valck, Brendan Kredell, and Skadi Loist, 181–95. London: Routledge.

Reed, John. 2006. *Insurgent Mexico*. New York: International Publishers.

Rincón, Omar. 2009. "Narco.estética y narco.cultura en Narco.lombia." *Nueva Sociedad* (July–August). http://nuso.org/articulo/narcoestetica-y-narcocultura-en-narcolombia/.

Ross, Julian. 2016. "Ethics of the Landscape Shot: *AKA Serial Killer* and James Bennings Portraits of Criminals." In *Slow Cinema*, edited by Tiago de Luca and Jorge Nuno Barradas, 261–72. Edinburgh: Edinburgh University Press.

Ruétalo, Victoria, and Dolores Tierney, eds. 2011. *Latsploitation, Exploitation Cinemas, and Latin America*. London: Routledge.

Sadlier, Darlene J. 2009. "A Short History of Film Melodrama in Latin America." In *Latin American Melodrama: Passion, Pathos, and Entertainment*, edited by Darlene J. Sadlier, 1–18. Urbana: University of Illinois Press.

Sánchez Prado, Ignacio M. 2015. *Screening Neoliberalism: Transforming Mexican Cinema, 1988–2012*. Nashville: Vanderbilt University Press.

Sánchez Prado, Ignacio M. 2016. "Novel, War, and the Aporia of Totality: Lukács's Theory of the Novel and Azuela's *Los de abajo*." *Mediations* 29, no. 2 (Spring): 47–64. www.mediationsjournal.org/articles/novel-war-and-the-aporia-of-totality.

Sastre, Alexandra. 2014. "Hottentot in the Age of Reality TV: Sexuality, Race, and Kim Kardashian's Visible Body." *Celebrity Studies* 5, nos. 1–2: 123–37. doi: 10.1080/19392397.2013.810838.

Scherer García, Julio. 2008. *La reina del Pacífico: Es hora de contar*. Barcelona: Grijalbo Mondadori.

Scholz, Anne-Marie. 2013. *From Fidelity to History: Film Adaptations as Cultural Events in the Twentieth Century*. New York: Berghahn Books.

Sconce, Jeffrey. 1995. "'Trashing' the Academy: Taste, Excess, and an Emerging Politics of Cinematic Style." *Screen* 36, no. 4: 371–93.

Scott, A. O. 2014. "When Chaos Trumps Civility." *New York Times*, June 12. https://www.nytimes.com/2014/06/13/movies/heli-paints-a-harrowing-picture-of-mexico.html.
Serrano, Federico. 1978. "¡*Vámonos* con Pancho Villa!" *Cine* 1, no. 8: 57–64.
Shaw, Deborah. 2011. "(Trans) National Images and Cinematic Spaces: The Cases of Alfonso Cuarón's *Y tu mamá también* (2001) and Carlos Reygadas' *Japón* (2002)." *Iberoamericana* 11, no. 44: 117–31.
Shingler, Martin. 2012. *Star Studies: A Critical Guide*. London: BFI/Palgrave Macmillan.
Slaughter, Stephany. 2010. "Adelitas y coronelas: Un panorama de las representaciones clásicas de la soldadera en el cine de la Revolución mexicana." In *La luz y la guerra: El cine de la Revolución Mexicana*, edited by Fernando Fabio Sánchez and Gerardo García Muñoz. Mexico City: CONACULTA.
Slow Food. 2019. "Slow Food Manifesto for Quality." Accessed May 21, 2019. https://n4v5s9s7.stackpathcdn.com/wp-content/uploads/2015/07/Manifesto_Quality_ENG.pdf.
Smith, Paul Julian. 2013. "Cineteca Nacional, Mexico." *Film Quarterly* 66, no. 3: 64–65. doi:10.1525/fq.2013.66.3.64.
Smith, Paul Julian. 2014. *Mexican Screen Fiction: Between Cinema and Television*. Cambridge: Polity.
Smith Nehme, Farran. 2014. "'Heli' Lacks Compassion in Drug-War Plot." *New York Post*, June 11. https://nypost.com/2014/06/11/heli-lacks-compassion-in-drug-war-plot/.
Sobchack, Vivian. 1984. "Inscribing Ethical Space: Ten Propositions on Death, Representation, and Documentary." *Quarterly Review of Film Studies* 9, no. 4: 283–300. doi:10.1080/10509208409361220.
Solórzano, Fernanda. 2017. "Entrevista a Amat Escalante: 'La provocación es parte fundamental de cualquier tipo de arte.' Retratos de un país en llamas." *Letras Libres*, July 16. https://www.letraslibres.com/mexico/revista/entrevista-amat-escalante-la-provocacion-es-parte-fundamental-cualquier-tipo-arte-retratos-un-pais-en-llamas.
Sontag, Susan. 1967. *Against Interpretation, and Other Essays*. London: Eyre and Spottiswoode.
Sontag, Susan. 2003. *Regarding the Pain of Others*. London: Penguin.
Soto, Shirlene Ann. 1979. *The Mexican Woman: A Study of Her Participation in the Revolution, 1910–1940*. Palo Alto: R and E. Research Associates.
Spiegel. 2007. "'Bordertown' Booed at Berlinale." *Spiegel*, February 16. http://www.spiegel.de/international/j-lo-point-bordertown-booed-at-berlinale-a-466779.html.
Spivak, Gayatri. 2000. "The Politics of Translation." In *The Translation Studies Reader*, edited by Lawrence Venuti. London: Routledge.

Stam, Robert. 2000. "Beyond Fidelity: The Dialogics of Adaptation." In *Film Adaptation*, edited by James Naremore. New Brunswick, NJ: Rutgers University Press.
Stam, Robert. 2007. "Introduction: The Theory and Practice of Adaptation." In *Literature and Film: A Guide to the Theory and Practice of Film Adaptation*, edited by Robert Stam and Alessandra Raengo, 1–52. Malden: Blackwell.
Stutesman, Drake. 2011. "Costume Design, or What Is Fashion in Film?" In *Fashion in Film*, edited by Adrienne Munich, 17–39. Bloomington: Indiana University Press.
Telemundo Internacional. 2019. Accessed June 17, 2019. http://www.youtube.com/watch?v=bZCKHC_RPBQ.
Thornton, Niamh. 2011. Unpublished Interview with Nelson Carro. July 3. Available from the author.
Thornton, Niamh. 2012. "'It Just Looks Like More of Texas': Journeys and Travel Narratives in the Western." In *(Re)Discovering 'America' Road Movies and Other Travel Narratives in North America / (Re)Descubriendo 'América' Road movie y otras narrativas de viaje en América del Norte*, edited by Wilfried Raussert and Graciela Martínez-Zalce. Trier: Wissenschaftlicher Verlag Trier; Tempe, AZ: Bilingual Press/Editorial Bilingüe.
Thornton, Niamh. 2013a. *Revolution and Rebellion in Mexican Cinema*. New York: Bloomsbury.
Thornton, Niamh. 2013b. "Zapata on Film: Dreams, Nightmares, Realities." In *Imagining the Mexican Revolution: Versions and Visions in Literature and Visual Culture*, edited by Tilman Altenberg. Newcastle-Upon-Tyne, UK: Cambridge Scholars Publishing.
Thornton, Niamh. 2016. "Writing Cinema: The Communicating Vessels of Literature and Film." In *A History of Mexican Literature*, edited by Anna Nogar, José Ramón Ruisánchez Serra, and Ignacio Sánchez Prado. New York: Cambridge University Press.
Thornton, Niamh. 2017a. "Re-Framing Mexican Women's Filmmaking: The Case of Marcela Fernandez Violante." In *Latin American Filmmakers: Production, Politics, Poetics*, edited by Debbie Martin and Deborah Shaw. London: I.B. Tauris.
Thornton, Niamh. 2017b. "Where Cabaret Meets Revolution: The Prostitute at War in Mexico." In *Prostitution and Sex Work in Global Visual Media: New Takes on Fallen Women*, edited by Danielle Hipkins and Kate Taylor-Jones. London: Palgrave Macmillan.
Thornton, Niamh. 2020a. "The Cinematic Adaptations of *Los de abajo*." https://vimeo.com/manage/170219995/general.
Thornton, Niamh. 2020b. "Repeating Terror: Contemplating Death in Amat Escalante's *Heli* (2013)." *Tecmerin: Journal of Audiovisual Essays* 4, no. 1. https://tecmerin.uc3m.es/en/journal/.

Thornton, Niamh. 2020c. "Bodily Excess and Containment." https://vimeo.com/manage/409713506/general.
Tierney, Dolores. 2007. *Emilio Fernández: Pictures in the Margins*. Manchester: Manchester University Press.
Tierney, Dolores. 2018. *New Transnationalisms in Contemporary Latin American Cinemas*. Edinburgh: Edinburgh University Press.
Torchin, Leshu. 2012. *Creating the Witness: Documenting Genocide on Film, Video, and the Internet*. Minneapolis: University of Minnesota Press.
Tornero, Angélica. 2013. "Discursos híbridos y perspectiva en *2666* de Roberto Bolaño y en *Backyard/El Traspatio* de Carlos Carrera." *CIEHL: Cuaderno Internacional de Estudios Humanisticos y Literatura* 20: 25–37.
Treviño, Jesús Salívar. 1979. "The New Mexican Cinema." *Film Quarterly* 32, no. 3 (Spring): 26–37.
Triana Toribio, Nuria. 2013. "Building Latin American Cinema in Europe: Cine en Construcción/Cinéma en construction." In *Contemporary Hispanic Cinema: Interrogating the Transnational in Spanish and Latin American Film*, edited by Stephanie Dennison, 89–112. London: Tamesis Books.
Tuñón, Julia. 2011. "La literatura de la Revolución mexicana en el cine: *Los de abajo* de Mariano Azuela (1916, 1938) de Chano Urueta (1939) y de Servando González (1976). Cuando Ouroboros se muerde la cola." *Historias* 80: 63–75.
Valencia, Sayak. 2018. *Gore Capitalism*. Translated by John Pluecker. South Pasadena, CA: Semiotext(e); Cambridge, MA: MIT Press.
van Krieken, Robert. 2012. *Celebrity Society*. New York: Routledge.
Vásquez Mejías, Ainhoa. 2016. "De muñecas a dueñas: La aparente inversión de roles de género en las narcoseries de telemundo." *Culturales* 4, no. 2 (July): 209–30.
Vega Zaragosa, Guillermo. 2011. "El problema de adaptar una novela, generalmente es la extension." *Toma* 14 (January–February): 8–11.
Velasco Márquez, Jesús. 2006. "El punto de vista mexicano acerca de la guerra contra Estados Unidos." *PBS*, March 14. Accessed June 17, 2019. http://www.pbs.org/kera/usmexicanwar/prelude/md_a_mexican_viewpoint_esp.html.
Velazco, Salvador. 2005. "*Rojo amanecer* y *La ley de Herodes*: Cine político de la transición mexicana." *Hispanic Research Journal* 6, no. 1 (February): 67–80.
Velázquez-Zvierkova, Valentina. 2018. "Frankencine o la estética de la abyección: Chano Urueta y el cine mexicano de terror de los años 50." *El ojo que piensa: Revista de cine iberoamericano* 16 (January). http://www.elojoquepiensa.cucsh.udg.mx/index.php/elojoquepiensa/article/view/279.
Velez-Serna, Maria A. 2017. "Critics and Makers." *Cinema Journal* 56, no. 4: 143–44.
Venuti, Lawrence. 2007. "Adaptation, Tradition, Critique." *Journal of Visual Culture* 6, no. 1: 25–43.
Vertiz De La Fuente, Columba. 2018. "La Verdadera Kate Del Castillo." *Proceso* 2196, no. 2 (December): 70–73.

Villamil, Jenaro. 2011. "Fábrica de muertas . . ." In "La tragedia de Juárez," special issue, *Proceso* 34 (August): 8–13.
Virilio, Paul. 1989. *War and Cinema: The Logistics of Perception*. Translated by Patrick Camiller. London: Verso.
Virilio, Paul. 2002. *Desert Screen: War at the Speed of Light*. Translated by Michael Degener. London: Continuum.
Virilio, Paul. 2005. *City of Panic*. Translated by Julie Rose. Oxford: Berg.
Vulliamy, Ed. 2011. *Amexica: War along the Borderline*. London: Vintage.
Watt, Peter, and Roberto Zepeda. 2012. *Drug War Mexico: Politics, Violence and Neoliberalism in the New Narcoeconomy*. London: Zed Books.
Westerståhl Stenport, Anna, and Garrett Traylor. 2015. "The Eradication of Memory: Film Adaptations and Algorithms of the Digital." *Cinema Journal* 55, no. 1 (Fall): 74–94.
Whitehead, Neil L. 2004. *Violence*. Santa Fe, NM: School of American Research Press.
Williams, Linda. 1991. "Film Bodies: Gender, Genre, and Excess." *Film Quarterly* 44, no. 4: 2–13. doi:10.2307/1212758.
Wilson, Tamar Diana. 2003. "Forms of Male Domination and Female Subordination: Homeworker versus Maquiladora Workers in Mexico." *Review of Radical Politial Economics* 35, no. 1 (Winter): 56–72.
Women and Hollywood. 2018. "Cannes Film Festival Campaign." Accessed June 17, 2019. https://womenandhollywood.com/activities/campaigns/cannes-film-festival/.
Wong, Cindy Hing-Yuk. 2011. *Film Festivals: Culture, People, and Power on the Global Screen*. New Brunswick, NJ: Rutgers University Press.
Wood, Robin, et al. 2018. *Robin Wood on the Horror Film: Collected Essays and Reviews*. Detroit: Wayne State University Press.
Wright, Melissa W. 2004. "From Protests to Politics: Sex Work, Women's Worth, and Ciudad Juárez Modernity." *Annals of the Association of American Geographers* 94, no. 2: 369–86.
Yau, Wai-Ping. 2016. "Revisiting the Systematic Approach to the Study of Film Adaptation as Intersemiotic Translation." *Translation Studies* 9, no. 3: 256–67.
Zavala, Oswaldo. 2018. *Los cárteles no existen: Narcotráfico y cultura en México*. Barcelona: Malpaso.
Zavala Scherer, Diego. 2010. "El memorial del 68 (Nicolás Echevarra, 2008): Recuerdo vivo, forma expandida." *El ojo que piensa*, no. 1. http://www.elojoquepiensa.cucsh.udg.mx/index.php/elojoquepiensa/article/view/6.
Zielinski, Ger. 2016. "On Studying Film Festival Ephemera: The Case of Queer Film Festivals and Archives of Feeling." In *Film Festivals: History, Theory, Method, Practice*, edited by Marijke de Valck, Brendan Kredell, and Skadi Loist. London: Routledge.
Žižek, Slavoj. 2008. *Violence: Six Sideways Reflections*. New York: Picador.

Index

acousmêtre, 140. *See also* body
activism, 12, 13, 96, 118, 119, 120, 122, 130, 144; activist-journalist, 176; film star–activist, 178; #metoo activist movements, 189
adaptations: authorship and fidelity, 93; faithfulness, 92; fidelity, 92–94, 106, 112 of narratives of the Revolution, 16; neglected adaptations, 16; (pro-) fidelity criticism, 93; fidelity as a paradigm, 93; spacy emptiness, 94. *See also* *Los de abajo*; language; *novela de la Revolución*; translation; *The Underdogs*
aesthetic: aesthetic patterns, 18; aesthetics of prestige cinema, 65; aesthetic sensibility, 52; aesthetics of violence, 24; classical aesthetics, 134; European aesthetics, 33, 134; of filmmaking, 49; national and transnational aesthetics, 20; realist aesthetics, 33, 59; of slow cinema, 72, 190. *See also* arthouse; *Nuevo cine*; slow cinema
African Film Festival, 36. *See also* film festival
Age of Innocence, The, 40
AKA, Serial Killer, 73

Allá en el rancho grande/Out on the Big Ranch, 47
American Curious, 126
Amnesty International, 122
antihero, 154, 159, 160. *See also* telenovela
archive, 22, 23, 30, 34, 35, 41, 43, 44, 49, 72, 107, 187. *See also* Nelson Carro; Cineteca
Arráncame la vida/Tear This Heart Out, 126
Arthouse, 20, 30, 33, 59, 61, 85; aesthetics of the European arthouse, 33, 36, 66; arthouse aesthetics, 84, 190; arthouse auteur, 33; arthouse taste, 59; contemporary arthouse cinema, 85; global arthouse, 35, 41, 61, 85; prestige arthouse, 61, 66; transnational arthouse, 112, 125. *See also* genre
audience, 20, 33, 34, 42, 53, 57, 62, 67, 73–80, 84–85, 91, 100, 105, 107, 110, 124, 143, 146, 147, 148, 149, 157, 158, 168, 171, 179, 190; Anglophone audiences, 127; educated audience, 30, 119; female audiences, 18, 189; global audiences, 171; mobile audience, 56; non-Mexican audience,

audience *(continued)*
  130, 147; reader/audience, 93; telenovelas audience, 159–63, 169; US audiences, 127; white audience, 132. *See also* arthouse; body; Cineteca; slow cinema; telenovelas
auteur, 20, 33, 59, 61, 62, 64, 87, 98, 99, 106, 107, 111, 112; arthouse auteur, 33; auteurist, 33; low-budget auteur cinema, 112; ownership, 106; prestige auteurist, 85; self-presentation as an auteur, 61; transnational male auteurs, 6; authenticity, 62, 70, 89, 156, 176, 177, 178, 179. See also *Bordertown*; celebrity/stardom; *Los de abajo*; telenovelas; *The Virgin of Juarez*.
automóvil gris, El/The Gray Car, 5
Aventurera/The Adventuress, 45
Aves sin nido/Birds without a Nest, 95
Azuela, Mariano, 21, 88, 89, 91, 100, 103, 104, 106, 108

Back-Up Plan, The, 125
Bajo Juárez: La ciudad devorando a sus hijas/Bajo Juarez: The City Devouring Its Daughters, 117, 118, 120, 123
Bajo la misma luna, 173
Ballad of Cable Hogue, The, 40
bastardos, Los: aesthetics of prestige, 62, 65; editing, 20, 59, 62, 64, 70, 71, 73, 74–79, 85; good taste, 67, 85, 71; high-value filmmaking, 67; hyperrealism, 60, 62, 64, 71, 74, 85 190; prestige filmmaking techniques, 62; slowness, 74, 79, 86; soundtrack, 80, 81, 83; videographic criticism, 20. *See also* Amat Escalante; realism; slow cinema
Batalla en el cielo, 61
bella del Alhambra, La/The Beauty of the Alhambra, 39

Berlin, Film Festival, 33, 55, 116. *See also* film festival
Berman, Sabina, 55
body: black body, 127; body experiencing death, 5; body language, 101; body as mere propaganda, 77; body in pain, 6; body as victim, 116; clothed body, 131; contained body, 128; excessive body, 116, 144; femininity of body, 128; gendered body, 19, 148; Hispanic body, 27; Latina body, 132, 133; male body, 74, 128; non-whiteness, 128, 134; as objects, 125, 168; othered body, 131; racialized bodies, 116, 123–24, 128, 133, 148, 146, 184; sound of the body, 81; white body, 116; woman dichotomy, 135. *See also* acousmêtre; clothing/wardrobe; Kate del Castillo; Minnie Driver; Jennifer Lopez; Claudia Talancón; Maya Zapata
Bolaños, José, 48, 49, 53
border, 11, 12, 115, 120, 130, 133, 138, 151, 163, 164, 165, 185; border crossing narratives, 124, 126, 150; hard borders, 163; Mexican migrants, 167, 126, 180; Mexico-US border, 76, 82, 119, 120, 138, 141, 146, 165, 216; slow cinema, 190; successful border crosser, 129, 150. See also *Bordertown*; documentary
Bordertown, 21, 115–19, 121–25, 129–48, 190; clothing, 130, 131, 134; crime genre, 137; good victim, 133; hyperrealist violence, 190; Juniors, 122; Mexicanness, 124; rebirth, 140, 141; social trauma, 118; victim-blaming culture, 123; victim-survivors, 121: videographic criticism, 142; violence against women, 137; working conditions of the women, 122, 133. *See also*

body; border; Jennifer Lopez;
Gregory Nava; Maya Zapata
Bracho, Julio, 46, 48, 54, 173
Breaking Bad, 159–60, 180, 185. See also *La reina del sur*
Bronenosets Potemkin/Battleship Potempkin, 39

cabareteras, 45. *See also* genre
Calderón, Felipe, 30, 41, 50
Camelia la texana, 153, 154
camp, 14–15. *See also* kitsch
Cananea, 52, 53
Cannes Film Festival, 32, 33, 36, 55, 61, 69. *See also* film festival
capitalism, 8, 9, 10, 12, 84, 165; capitalist dictator, 29; critique capitalism, 72; global capitalism, 8; gore capitalism, 8–10, 76, 151; neoliberal capitalism, 8, 82; transnational capitalism, 137. *See also* global south
Carancho, 66
Cárdenas, Lázaro, 38
Carrie, 141, 143–44
Carro, Nelson, 20, 25, 27, 28, 31, 35, 40–46, 49–55, 57, 59, 88, 184, 185, 187; caretaker bureaucrat, 28, 41, 56; male-centered narratives, 53; male stories, 46; Mexican women filmmakers, 52; storyteller-curator, 28, 35. *See also* archive; Cineteca; curator; cycles
cartel 9, 10–11, 13, 161; cartel as a semiotics of terror 77; transnational cartels, 157. *See also* drugs; language; narcos
celebrity/stardom, 21, 23, 117, 146, 148, 172–75, 177, 178, 179; microcelebrity, 177–78; star-celebrity, 22, 149, 150, 158, 173, 176, 179, 189, 191. *See also* Kate del Castillo

Cell K-11, 172
Certain Regard, Un, 33, 61. *See also* Cannes; curator
Chapo, El, 149, 173, 174–79, 188
Choferos, Los (The Drivers), 122
Cinemundi, 36
Cineteca, 20, 23, 27, 28, 30–37, 41–44, 47, 53–57, 102, 187. *See also* Nelson Carro; cycles; Mexican Revolution
Cineteca Nacional de México. *See* Cineteca
clothing/wardrobe: celebrity image, 172; class and race, 130; guerrilla gang clothing, 135; Latina body, 132; low-value clothing, 134; sexuality, 130; as uniform, 132, 133, 135. *See also* body; *Bordertown*; Kate del Castillo; Minnie Driver; Jennifer Lopez; *La reina del sur*; Ana Claudia Talancón; *The Virgin of Juarez*; Maya Zapata
Club de Cuervos, 153
colonialism, 9, 18, 30
compadre Mendoza, El/Godfather Mendoza, 34, 46, 47, 54
conde de Montecristo, El/The Count of Monte Cristo, 95
Consejo Nacional para la Cultural y las Artes (National Council for Culture and Art), 98, 99
Contrabando y Traición (Contraband and Betrayal) (narcocorrido), 154
Contrabando y Traición (film), 154
corridos, 98, 109, 110, 154; Revolutionary *corridos*, 97. *See also* melodrama; narcocorrido
counter cinema, 83
crimen del padre Amaro, El/The Crime of Father Amaro, 126
Cristero rebellion, 38, 54. *See also* Mexican Revolution
Cuates de Sinaloa, Los, 156

Cucaracha, La/The Soldiers of Pancho Villa, 53
curator, 1, 20, 22, 27, 28, 31–33, 37, 41–43, 50–57, 185, 187, 191; curatorial agency, 1; curatorial storytelling, 27, 28, 42; transnational star curator, 41. *See also* Nelson Carros; cycles
cycles, 16, 20, 22, 27–55, 88, 96, 102, 111, 184; cycle booklets, 35, 42. *See also* archive; Cineteca; Carlos Monsiváis

Daens, 39
Day I Met El Chapo: The Kate del Castillo Story, The, 173, 178, 188. *See also* celebrity-star
de abajo, Los (film 1939), 21, 26, 97, 103, 105, 111, 113, 152, 187, 188. *See also* adaptations; translation; Chano Urueta
de abajo, Los (film 1976), 21, 26, 95, 96, 97, 103, 106, 107, 111, 113, 152, 173, 187, 188. *See also* adaptations, authenticity; Servando González
de abajo, Los (novel 1915), 21, 26, 87, 88, 89, 90, 91, 92, 94, 102, 155. *See also* adaptations; Mariano Azuela; *novela de la Revolucion*; thick translation
death: anonymity of, 111; death on-screen, 5; death as viewer and the filmmaker, 5; death of women, 12, 118; de-narrativization of, 111; ethical approach of, 7, 8; hyperrealist, 64; individual death, 105; representation of, 4, 6, 86, 111; spectacle of death, 4; taboo, 5; traumatic death, 73; violence and deaths, 8, 10, 73, 170. *See also* drugs; ethics
de Fuentes, Fernando, 34, 46, 47, 54, 102

De la calle/Streeters, 125
del Castillo, Kate, 21, 26, 149–61, 166, 170–81, 184, 188–89; celebrity/star persona, 21, 150, 158, 174, 178, 179. *See also* El Chapo; drugs; *La reina del sur*; telenovela
del Rio, Dolores, 47, 53
De todos modos Juan te llamas/ General's Daughter/Whatever You Do It's No Good, 54
Díaz, Porfirio, 29, 38
Dirty War, 30, 49
Dobson, Kevin James, 21, 115. *See also The Virgin of Juarez*
Documentales de Gobierno (Government Department of Documentaries), 95
documentary: conventions of documentary, 156; prestige documentary, 117
Dos siglos de libertad vistos por el cine, 31, 34–37, 39, 41–46, 48, 52, 55, 57. *See also* cycles
Double vie de Véronique, La, 103
Driver, Minnie, 21, 26, 115–16, 119, 120, 123–29, 134, 142, 146, 147, 184. *See also* body; *The Virgin of Juarez*; whiteness
drugs: hyperspecialization, 82; drug trafficker, 51, 175; trading drugs, 3, 8, 9, 10, 50, 82, 86, 151–52, 154, 156, 159–81, 187; war on drugs, 11, 180
Dueños del paraíso, 153

Enamorada/A Woman in Love, 45, 46, 102
endriago, 9, 76. *See also* masculinity
Entre Pancho Villa y una mujer desnuda/Between Pancho Villa and a Naked Woman, 55
Escalante, Amat, 20, 25, 59–62, 65–86, 184, 185, 189, 190; minimal editing,

62, 71, 73, 79, 85; slow cinema, 59. See also *Los bastardos*; *Heli*; realism
Estrada, Luis, 49, 51, 52
ethics: ethical act of looking, 77; ethical representation of death, 6, 7; ethical perpetrator/victim point of view, 20, 73, 190; of filming violence, 5, 6, 17, 25 144, 185; in language, 11; of slow cinema, 73
Expo 59, 95

Fast Food Nation, 126
Fédération Internationale des Associations de Producteurs de Films (International Federation of Film Producer), 32
Félix, María, 45, 46, 47, 53
female: denigrate the female viewer, 161; female audiences, 189; female-centered narratives, 53, 54, 156, 161, 162, 179; female drug dealer, 149, 170, 181; female-led subgenre, 153; female victim-hero, 143; Revolutionary melodrama, 102. See also telenovela
femicide/feminicide, 10, 12, 13, 119, 120, 122; killing of women, 3, 11–12, 13, 21, 115, 116, 118–23, 133, 135, 136, 138, 143, 145, 146, 147, 148, 171, 187; objective tragedy, 110; violence against women, 3, 19, 21, 82, 88, 110, 116, 130, 137, 142, 170, 171, 172. See also drugs; language; rape; *The Virgin of Juarez*; women of Juarez
femininity: archetypal femininity, 172; codified femininity, 172; femininity as performative, 133; horror of femininity, 128; working-class femininity, 133. See also body
Fernández, Emilio, 40, 45, 46, 102
Fernández Violante, Marcela, 48, 49, 52, 54

Figueroa, Gabriel, 34, 46, 104, 105
film festival: act as curator of national commemorations, 55; A-list 32, 33, 36, 55, 60, 61; European Film Festival, 36; history of, 32; prestige festivals, 61, 190; Women and Hollywood, 55. See also Cineteca; cycles
Film Festival Research network, 32
Flor silvestre/Wild Flower, 102, 104
Funny Games, 64, 65

Gangs of New York, 40
gender: cisgender, 172; conservative gender values, 123; conventional gendered scripts, 170–72; gender awareness, 54; gendered assumption, 167; gendered consciousness, 189; gendered horror representations, 144; gendered identities, 12; gendered roles, 144; gendered violence, 3, 13, 150; gender nonconforming, 18; gender violence, 148, 150; hierarchies of value, 180; nonstandard gender, 151; representation of violence, 173; transgendered woman, 172. See also femicide/feminicide; maquiladoras
genre: body genre, 148; cabaretera genres, 45; comedia ranchera, 47; convention al crime genre, 131; female-led subgenre, 153; genre-based criticisms, 190; genre films, 7; genre texts, 21; horror genre, 48, 59, 121, 143; hybrid genre, 117; low-culture genre films, 16, 95; maligned subgenre, 156; narco genre 155; nonrealist genre cinema, 5; rape revenge genre conventions, 115, 144; rural-based musical comedy genre, 47; stardom and genre, 21, 116; women-centered genre, 162; zombie subgenre, 143

Global South, 13. See also capitalism
global trade, 164, 168, 170, 181
Golden Age, 5, 45, 47, 48, 54, 55, 89, 95, 112, 152
González, Servando, 21, 48, 49, 89, 94, 96, 99, 105, 106, 187–89. See also *Los de abajo*
goodness, 123, 133, 135
guerra santa, La/The Holy War, 48, 49
Guzmán Loera, Joaquín El Chapo, 149. See Chapo, El

Hauptlehrer Hofer/Schoolmaster Hofer, 39
Heli, 20, 59, 61, 62, 67–85, 190; editing, 62, 79, 63, 70, 71, 73, 75, 76, 78, 79, 80, 86; eye-trace, 75, 76, 79; hyperrealistic slowness, 62, 71; point of view, 70, 73; unwatchableness of the violence, 80. See also drugs; Amat Escalante; slow cinema; videographic criticism
heteronormative, 19. See also masculinity
Hispanic-ness, 124. See also body
Hustlers, 125

imprescindibles de Monsiváis, Las (Monsiváis's indispensables), 45
Ingobernable, 153
Inland Empire, 103
Instituto Méxicano de Cinematografía, 99
Insurgent Mexico, 40, 49
Isaac, Alberto, 48, 49

Jeanne Dielman 23, Quai du Commerce, 1080 Bruxelles, 78

kitsch, 14–15, 16, 18. See also aesthetics; camp

Landeta, Matilde, 34, 54
landscape: cultural landscape, 3; fragmented media landscape, 176; landscape films, 73; media landscapes, 154–56, 158; political and social landscape, 29; tastemaking landscape, 21; television landscape as a telenovela, 179
Landscape Suicide, 72, 73
language, 10–13, 44; 132, 151, 155; as a curator, 43; encoded language, 154; historical languages, 94; language of adaptation, 92; language of fidelity, 92; local inflections in language, 170; marginalisation, 65; spacy emptiness, 94. See also cartel; feminicide/femicide; narcos; translation
Latinness, 127–28. See also body; Jennifer Lopez
Latsploitation, 15
Leduc, Paul, 40, 49, 50–52
Leñero, Vicente, 106, 107
Loong Boonmee raleuk chat/Uncle Boonmee Who Can Recall His Past Lives, 36
Lopez, Jennifer, 21, 26, 115–19, 123, 124–35, 142, 144, 146, 147, 172, 184; acting white and Hispanic, 124; good victim, 133; otherness of Lopez, 128; redefinition of women's bodies, 146; wardrobe/clothing, 130, 133, 134. See also body; *Bordertown*; celebrity/stardom; Mexican-ness
Los, 61, 62. See also *bastardos, Los*

Maid in Manhattan, 124
maquiladoras, 12, 13, 119, 133

Mar de Plata, 33. *See also* film festival
Martínez Ortega, Gonzalo, 46, 48, 49
masculinity: fantasies of masculinity, 117; heteronormative male privilege, 19, 31; male auteur, 61; male-centered narratives, 19, 41, 52, 53, 54, 153, 161; male cycle, 53; male film critics, 31; male film makers, 34, 48, 52, 53, 54, 57, 61, 184, 189; male high-value work, 42; male network, 96; male privilege, 86; male protector, 144; male Revolution, 102; male white body, 128, 177; Mexican masculinity, 9; privileged male stories, 46, 57. *See also* body; drugs; gender
mass culture, 134
melodrama: Golden Age melodramas, 5, 45; omission of melodrama, 55; Revolutionary melodramas, 29, 49, 53, 102, 110. *See also* telenovelas; genre
Memorias de un mexicano/Memories of a Mexican, 42
Mexican film criticism, 31, 112
Mexicanness, 70, 124. *See also* Jennifer Lopez
Mexican-ness, 130, 167. *See also* Ana Claudia Talancón; Maya Zapata
Mexican Revolution, 5, 3, 8, 16, 20, 27–31, 37, 38–57, 87–91, 97, 98, 100, 102–13, 188; mid-Revolution, 91; narratives of the Revolution, 16, 28, 30, 50, 53, 164; post-Revolutionary period, 49; Revolutionary melodramas, 29, 49, 53, 102, 110. *See also* Cineteca; Cristero rebellion; *novela de la Revolución*
micro-celebrity, 177–78
mise-en-scène, 24, 71, 76, 79, 105, 106

Monsiváis, Carlos, 16, 41, 45, 46, 47. *See also* cycles
Mujeres asesinas/Female Assassins, 153
multinodal, 25, 158
muñecas de la mafia, Las/The Mafia Girls, 153
My Family, 124

narco, 10, 11, 151, 152, 153, 176; narco culture, 15; narco-dramas, 164, 176; narco-genre, 155; narco-narrative, 176; Narco-state, 9; narco (tele) novela, 153; narco-violence, 13; narco-world, 154. *See also* language; narcocorridos; *La reina del sur*
narcocorridos, 10, 154, 156–58, 181
Narcos, 169
Narcos: Mexico, 152, 169
narrative: alternative narrative of the Revolution, 28, 31, 50, 56; antihero narrative, 159; audiovisual narrative, 16; border narratives, 124, 126, 150; counternarrative, 143; drug narratives, 150, 155, 164, 173, 179; female-centered narrative, 53, 54, 156, 179; linear narrative, 109; male-centered narrative, 19, 52, 53, 54, 153, 161; Mexican narrative, 61, 181; multigenerational narrative, 124; narco-narrative, 176; narrative of the cycle, 35; national narrative, 29, 30; rape-revenge narratives, 121; telenovela narrative, 158, 159, 161, 162, 165; women's bodies narrative, 123, 124; women-centered narratives, 55, 47; women's ethnicities narratives, 116. *See also* adaptations; otherness
National Film Institute. *See* Cineteca
nationalism, 17; cultural nationalism, 55

Nava, Gregory, 21, 115, 124, 137
negra angustias, La/Black Angustias, 54
Netflix, 149, 153, 169, 176
1968 massacre, 105
Nosotros los pobres/We, the Poor, 45
novela de la Revolución (novel of the Revolution), 21, 89. *See also* adaptations
Nuevo cine, 31, 46–49, 54, 96, 99
Nuyorican Films, 125

Oktyabar/October, 39
olvidados, Los/The Young and the Damned, 36, 72
One Man's Hero, 39
other/otherness, 7, 116, 124, 128, 134, 135, 156, 179, 186; Hispanic otherness, 127; Mexican bodies, 143; Mexican protagonist as other, 164; racially other, 129
Out of Sight, 125

PAN, 29, 30
Partido Acción Nacional (National Action Party). *See* PAN
Partido Revolucionario Institucional (the Institutional Revolutionary Party). *See* PRI
paso del norte, El, 88
Pérez-Reverte, Arturo, 155, 156, 158
perpetrator, 12, 18, 20, 63, 64, 70, 76, 77, 79, 82, 83, 95, 136; perpetrator's point of view, 70, 73, 137–38, 145, 190; rape on-screen, 190. *See also Heli*, victim
pícara, 166
Pinal, Silvia, 53, 153
PRI, 20

queer, 15, 172

radical mediation, 149–52, 154, 156, 158, 160, 170, 179
rape: as a form of torture, 119, 120, 136, 142; gang rape, 136; perpetrators point of view, 24, 138, 190; rape-murder, 136, 137; rape on-screen, 190; rape-revenge, 115, 121, 123, 142, 144, 145, 148. *See also* femicide/feminicide; videographic criticism; *La Virgin of Juarez*
recluso, El, 126
Reds, 39, 40, 51
Reed, John, 40, 51
Reed, México insurgente/Reed, Insurgent Mexico, 49–50
región salvaje, La/The Untamed, 61
Reina del Pacífico, 171
reina del sur, La (book), 150, 151, 157, 155, 160
reina del sur, La (television series), 21, 149, 150, 151, 153–71, 174, 176, 179, 180, 181; exotic and attractive other, 156, 179; female-centered, 161; female-led subgenre, 153; drug narratives, 150, 162, 164; high-value telenovela, 165; myth, 170; self-identification, 171; transnationalism, 149, 150, 157, 165, 168, 169, 180, 181. *See also* celebrity/stardom; Kate del Castillo; narcocorridos; telenovelas
Reina del Sur, La (narcocorrido), 150, 154, 156
Reygadas, Carlos, 61
Room with a View, A, 39, 40
Russian Revolution, 37, 51

Sangre, 61, 62
secreto de Selena, El, 125
Selena, 124

Señorita extraviada/*Missing Young Woman*, 117–18, 123
Si Adelita se fuera con otro (film), 109
Si Adelita se fuera con otro (If Adelita Went with Another) (song), 109, 110. *See also* corridos
Sicario, 76–77
Sicario: Soldado, 76
Sin tetas no hay paraíso/*Without Tits There's No Heaven*, 153
slow cinema, 20, 59, 62, 63, 64, 68, 70–74, 83, 85; ethics of, 73; diegetic sound, 80; hyperrealistic violence, 62; slow aesthetics, 71, 79, 86, 190; slowness, 69, 72–74, 79; slow rhythm, 78; sound of, 79, 81, 83, 85. *See also Los bastardos*; Amat Escalante; *Heli*
soldadera, La/*The Female Soldier*, 53
sombra del caudillo, La/*The Shadow of the Strongman*, 48, 49, 52, 54
Somewhere, 36
Soy tu fan, 126
split screen, 96, 98, 103, 136

Taboada, Carlos Enrique, 48
Talancón, Ana Claudia, 21, 26, 115, 116, 120, 124, 126, 127, 129, 134, 135, 142, 143, 184. *See also* body; Mexicanness; rape; *The Virgin of Juarez*
taxonomy, 92
Telemundo, 125, 126, 153, 157, 165, 176
telenovela, 21, 125, 126, 129, 152–73, 176, 179, 180, 181, 184, 189; adaptations, 160; authenticity of the telenovela, 156; female-centered telenovelas, 161; popular culture, 156; quality telenovela, 21, 153, 156, 158, 165, 179; sexism, 172,

173, 189. *See also* Kate del Castillo; melodrama; narcocorrido; *La reina del sur*
Televisa, 54, 188
Tigres del Norte, Los, 154, 156
Toronto, 33, 55. *See also* film festival
translation: creative mis-translation, 90; as derivative, 94; feminist translation theorists, 93; literal translation 30; thick translation, 90, 113. *See also* adaptations; *Los de abajo*; language
Traspatio, El/*Backyard*, 117–19
33, Los, 173

últimos zapatistas, héroes olvidados, Los/*The Last Zapatistas, Forgotten Heroes*, 42
UnderdogsUnder, The, 21, 87. *See also Los de abajo*
Urueta, Chano, 21, 89, 94, 96, 102, 109

¡Vámonos con Pancho Villa!/*Let's Go with Pancho Villa*, 46, 54, 102, 105
Venice Film Festival, 32, 36, 47, 55, 61. *See also* film festival
victim: body as victim, 116; female victim-hero, 143; good/bad victim, 62, 142; good victim, 133; good victimhood, 123; humanize the victims, 79, 83; normative perceptions of the victims, 132; perpetrator/victim point of view, 20, 63, 64, 73, 82 137; victim-blaming culture, 123, 138; victim-characters, 145; victim denied a point of view, 137; victim dichotomy, 123; victimhood, 146; victim-survivors, 121; victims of violence agency, 18, 59, 62; women's goodness, 123

Víctimas del pecado/Victims of Sin, 45
videographic criticism, 20, 21, 23, 24, 25, 71, 88, 90, 96, 97, 103, 111, 113, 116, 141, 142, 145, 190; controlled editing, 78; digital material thinking of, 24, 113; of hyperrealist violence, 60; point of view, 70
Villa, Pancho, 53, 88, 97, 105
Virgin of Juarez, The, 21, 115–21, 123–27, 129, 134, 138–48, 190; flashback, 121, 138, 139, 140, 141, 143. *See also* Kevin James Dobson; Minnie Driver; Mexicanness; rape; realism; Maya Zapata
virgen que forjó una patria, La/The Saint That Forged a Country, 54
¡Viva Zapata!, 39, 40

What to Expect When You're Expecting, 125
whiteness, 124, 125, 126, 127, 129, 134, 146; non-whiteness, 128, 134
Wild Bunch, The, 39, 40
Without Men, 172
women filmmakers, 52–55, 57
women of Juarez, 20, 115, 116, 119, 121, 122, 136, 146

Yo soy Betty, la fea/Ugly Betty, 157

Zacatecas, Battle of, 88, 109
Zapata, Emiliano, 39, 40
Zapata, Maya, 21, 26, 115, 119, 123–26, 129, 132–35, 142, 143, 146, 184. *See also* body; rape; *The Virgin of Juarez*
Ziema obiecana/The Promised Land, 39

www.ingramcontent.com/pod-product-compliance
Lightning Source LLC
Chambersburg PA
CBHW020651230426
43665CB00008B/393